CW01661865

Edward J. Epstein is [illegible] including *Legend: Th*[illegible] *Harvey Oswald; News From Nowhere: Television and the News* and *Inquest.*

The Death of the Diamond

EDWARD JAY EPSTEIN

SPHERE BOOKS LIMITED
30–32 Gray's Inn Road, London WC1X 8JL

First published in Great Britain by
Hutchinson & Co (Publishers) Ltd 1982 under the title *The Diamond Invention*

Copyright © Edward Jay Epstein 1982

Published by Sphere Books Ltd 1983

For Laurie Frank

Acknowledgement
I am greatly indebted to Rebecca Fraser and Marjorie Kaplin for their help in researching this book.

TRADE
MARK

This book is sold subject to the condition that it shall not, by way of trade or otherwise, be lent, re-sold, hired out or otherwise circulated without the publisher's prior consent in any form of binding or cover other than that in which it is published and without a similar condition including this condition being imposed on the subsequent purchaser

Printed and bound in Great Britain by
Cox & Wyman Ltd, Reading

Contents

Prologue

In Japan, the matrimonial custom had survived feudal revolutions, world wars, industrialization and even the American occupation. Up until the mid-1960s, Japanese parents arranged proper marriages for their children through trusted intermediaries. The ceremony was then consummated, according to Shinto law, by the bride and groom both drinking rice wine from the same wooden bowl. This simple arrangement had persisted for more than a millennium. There was no tradition for romance, courtship, seduction and prenuptial love in Japan; and no tradition that required the gift of a diamond engagement ring.

Then, in 1967, halfway round the world, a South African diamond company decided to change the Japanese courtship ritual. It retained J. Walter Thompson, the largest advertising agency in the world, to embark on a campaign to popularize diamond engagement rings in Japan. It was not an easy task. Even the quartering of millions of American soldiers in Japan for a decade had not resulted in any substantial Japanese interest in giving diamonds as a token of love.

The advertising agency began its campaign by subtly suggesting that diamonds were a visible sign of modern Western values. It created a series of color advertisements in Japanese magazines showing very beautiful women displaying their diamond rings. The women all had Western facial features and wore European clothes. Moreover, in most of the advertisements, the women were involved in some activity that defied Japanese traditions, such as bicycling, camping, yachting, ocean-swimming and mountain-climbing. In the background, there usually stood a Japanese man, also attired in fashionable European clothes. In addition, almost all of the automobiles, sporting equipment and other artifacts in the picture were conspicuous foreign imports.

The message in these ads was clear: diamonds represent a sharp break with the Oriental past and an entry point into modern life.

The campaign was remarkably successful. Until 1959 the importation of diamonds had not even been permitted by the postwar Japanese government. When the campaign began in 1968, less than 5 per cent of Japanese women getting married received a diamond engagement ring. By 1972 the proportion had risen to 27 per cent. By 1978, half of all Japanese women who were married wore a diamond on her ring finger. And, by 1981, some 60 per cent of Japanese brides wore diamonds. In a mere thirteen years, the fifteen-hundred-year Japanese tradition was radically revised. Diamonds became a staple of the Japanese marriage. And Japan became, after the United States, the second largest market for the sale of diamond engagement rings. It was all part of the diamond invention.

The diamond invention was an ingenious scheme for sustaining the value of diamonds in an uncertain world. To begin with, it involved gaining control over the production of all the important diamond mines in the world. Next, a system was devised for allocating this controlled supply of gems to a select number of diamond cutters who all agreed to abide by certain rules intended to ensure that the quantity of finished diamonds available at any given time exceeded the public's demand for them. Finally, a set of subtle, but effective, incentives were devised for regulating the behavior of all the people who served and ultimately profited from the system. The invention had a wide array of diverse parts: these included a huge stockpile of uncut diamonds in a vault in London; a billion-dollar cash hoard deposited in banks in Europe; a private intelligence network operating out of Antwerp, Tel Aviv, Johannesburg and London; a global network of advertising agencies, brokers and distributors; corporate fronts in Africa for concealing massive diamond purchases; and private treaties with nations establishing quotas for annual production. The invention is far more than merely a monopoly for fixing diamond prices; it is a mechanism for converting tiny crystals of carbon into universally recognized tokens of wealth, power and romance. For it to ultimately succeed, it must endow these stones with the sort of sentiment that would inhibit the public from ever reselling them onto the market. The illusion had to be inculcated into the mass mind that diamonds were forever – 'forever' in the sense that they should never be resold.

The invention itself was a relatively recent development in the history of the diamond trade. Up until the late nineteenth century, diamonds were a genuinely rare stone that were found only in a few riverbeds in India and the jungles of Brazil. The entire world production of gem diamonds amounted to only a few pounds a year. In 1870, however, there was a radical change in this situation. Huge diamond mines were discovered near the Orange River in South Africa. These were the first diamond mines ever discovered. Rather than finding by chance an occasional diamond in a river, diamonds could now be scooped out of these mines by the ton with steam shovels. Suddenly, the market was deluged by a growing flood of diamonds. The British financiers who had organized the South African mines quickly came to realize that their investment was endangered: diamonds had little intrinsic value, and their price depended almost entirely on their scarcity. They feared that when new mines were developed in South Africa, diamonds would become at best only a semi-precious gem.

As it turned out, financial acumen proved the mother of invention. The major investors in the diamond mines realized that they had no alternative but to merge their interests into a single entity that would be powerful enough to control production and, in every other way that was necessary, perpetuate the scarcity and illusion of diamonds. The instrument that they created for this purpose was called De Beers Consolidated Mines Ltd, a company incorporated in South Africa. As De Beers penetrated and took control of all aspects of the world diamond trade, it also assumed many protean forms. In London, it operated under the innocuous name of the Diamond Trading Company. In Israel, it was known under the all-embracing mantle of 'the Syndicate.' In Antwerp, it was just called the CSO – initials referring to the Central Selling Organization (which was an arm of the Diamond Trading Company). And in Black Africa, it disguised its South African origins under subsidiaries with such names as the Diamond Development Corporation or Mining Services, Inc. At its height, it not only either directly owned or controlled all the diamond mines in southern Africa, it also owned diamond trading companies in England, Portugal, Israel, Belgium, Holland and Switzerland. It was De Beers of course that organized the Japanese campaign as part of its worldwide promotion of diamonds.

By 1981, De Beers had proved to be the most successful cartel arrangement in the annals of modern commerce. For more than a half century, while other commodities, such as gold, silver, copper, rubber and grains, fluctuated wildly in response to economic conditions, diamonds continued to advance upward in price each year. Indeed, the mechanism of the diamond invention seemed so superbly in control of prices – and unassailable – that even speculators began buying diamonds as a guard against the vagaries of inflation and recession. Like the romantic subjects of the advertising campaigns, they also assumed diamonds would increase in value forever.

My interest in the diamond invention was sparked originally by a chance meeting that I had with an English diamond broker in St Tropez in the summer of 1977. The broker was Benjamin Bonas, and he represented De Beers' Diamond Trading Company. He was visiting some friends of mine for the weekend, and during the course of a leisurely lunch the subject of diamonds was broached. Bonas explained that despite revolutions, hostile governments and general turmoil in Africa, De Beers still firmly controlled the production of diamonds. He pointed out that this arrangement had proved so successful that even the Soviet Union sold the diamonds from its Siberian mines to De Beers. He did not elaborate at this point on the actual mechanisms used by De Beers to lock up the flow of diamonds from diverse quarters of the world. Nevertheless, I was intrigued by the possibility that a South African company, aided and abetted by Black African and Communist nations who were pledged to a total embargo of South African business, had succeeded in putting together a truly global alliance to protect the value and illusion of diamonds. As the former Portuguese colonies of Angola and Mozambique got their full independence, the pressures throughout Africa, and most of the world, to isolate South Africa would drastically escalate. Could the diamond invention survive the twentieth century under these circumstances?

In Washington, later that year, I filed a request under the Freedom of Information Act for all the reports and investigations of the Justice Department concerning the diamond cartel. The resulting archive of documents provided a fragmentary picture of De Beers' near collision with the antitrust laws of the United States, but it yielded few clues as to how this system had been organized on a truly global scale to sustain billions of dollars' worth of value in tiny crystals of carbon. Indeed, whatever traces existed in the file of the operation of the diamond invention all pointed to the mining companies in South Africa and the distribution arm in London. I therefore began my inquiry into the nature and likely future of the diamond invention in Johannesburg, South Africa.

Part One

The Diamond Investigation

A Reluctant Tycoon | 1

South Africa: 4 December 1978

If one man can be said to control the world's diamonds it is Harry Frederick Oppenheimer.

Sitting across the desk from Oppenheimer, however, it was hard to imagine that this small, shy man dominated a multibillion-dollar empire. He spoke quietly, but with great precision. He had a distinct Oxford accent, and as he explained an issue he tended to punctuate his answers with a self-effacing smile. He was far more candid in discussing his business than I would have expected someone in this position to be, and I assumed that this disarming openness proceeded from his confidence in his control over his immediate universe. His interlocking businesses did after all account for over half of the industrial exports of southern Africa. The heart of this complex is located at 44 Main Street in the center of Johannesburg. The block-long building, with its imposing neocolonial façade and marble entranceway, looked much more like a government institution than the headquarters of the mining company. As it turned out, it housed in its offices far more power than most government buildings. Indeed, Oppenheimer even had a private treaty with the Soviet Union, though the terms have never been publicly revealed.

Oppenheimer explained that it was no secret that De Beers acquired through subsidiaries all the uncut diamonds that the Soviet Union wanted to sell on the open market. 'We have of course no reason for concealing this arrangement other than that the Russians prefer not to receive any public attention for obvious reasons,' he said almost apologetically. The 'obvious reasons' for obscuring the arrangement with De Beers was that the Soviet Union had for some fifteen years called for a total boycott of South Africa and

South African businesses, and its dealings with De Beers, if made public, might prove embarrassing.

But how long could such an unholy alliance last? The Soviet Union apparently had ambitions of its own in southern Africa, and at some point geopolitical considerations might take precedence over business considerations. I asked how he could be sure that the Soviets would renew the deal.

'We paid the Soviet Union more than half a billion dollars last year,' he answered. 'This is not a sum it can easily replace, and I can see no conceivable reason why it would want to abandon such a profitable arrangement.' His logic was brutally direct: De Beers provided the Soviet Union with its single largest source of hard currency (only petroleum was a more important export for Soviet trade in 1977). If the Soviet Union withdrew its diamonds from De Beers, it would have to find other outlets to sell its uncut diamonds. And if it precariously dumped these diamonds on the market, the price would collapse, and the Soviet Union would lose an important source of foreign exchange. 'What could the Russians possibly gain by competing with us?' he asked rhetorically.

He further pointed out that De Beers provided the Soviets with certain types of industrial diamonds that were important for drilling and producing electronic wiring. Its Siberian mines apparently did not produce these strategically important diamonds. By selling gem stones to De Beers, the Soviet Union received the credits for importing the industrial diamonds it needed.

The Soviet Union also had considerable influence in other diamond-producing areas in Black Africa, such as Angola. I wondered if the logic of the arrangement between De Beers and the Soviets required the Soviets to use their power in these countries to help De Beers retain its control over diamond mines there.

'You will have to address that question to the Africans concerned,' he replied abruptly. The tone in his voice made it clear that there were aspects to the Soviet arrangement that he decidedly did not want to discuss.

African revolutionary movements had also been perceived as a threat to the stability of the diamond cartel. There had been particular concern expressed about the safety of De Beers' mines in Namibia, which were the world's single largest source of gem diamonds. Technically, Namibia was a United Nations trusteeship, and the responsibility of the United Nations. In fact, however, South Africa administered this diamond-producing territory as if it were a province of that country. This had led to a potentially explosive situation. The United Nations had demanded that South Africa recognize SWAPO, whose Soviet-backed guerrillas were battling for independence, as the legitimate nationalist group in Namibia, and then hold elections under the auspices of the UN. If South Africa failed to comply with this ultimatum, the United Nations threatened to impose economic sanctions, including possibly an oil embargo. To buy time, South Africa decided to stage its own election in Namibia – an election in which SWAPO would not participate. Since the election would not lead to a change in the status of Namibia, or in fact elect anyone to public office, it was being staged mainly for the benefit of the world press. Condemned by SWAPO as a 'charade,' it was scheduled to begin later in the week I saw Oppenheimer.

'What the South African government hopes to accomplish by this exercise is beyond me,' he commented. He suggested that even if the South African government turned out a massive vote, it would only delay the movement toward independence in Namibia.

If independence was inevitable, De Beers might eventually find that its diamond mines there would be controlled not by a friendly government in South Africa but by a SWAPO revolutionary government. Would this pose a threat to De Beers' diamond monopoly?

'We are prepared to deal with any legitimate government that comes to power there,' he replied unemotionally. The fact that SWAPO had announced that it planned to nationalize De Beers' diamond concessions in Namibia did not faze him. 'We now pay about eighty million dollars a year in taxes on those diamonds, and that provides the territory with most of its revenues,' he explained, and then added, 'whatever government eventually comes to power they will need this revenue to survive.' His point was clear: Namibia needed De Beers' money as much as De Beers needed Namibia's diamonds. He was confident that SWAPO, or any other group in Namibia, would accept this bargain.

Oppenheimer was concerned with the possibility of the

United Nations imposing economic sanctions against South Africa, since his empire exported billions of dollars' worth of South African commodities. He did not believe, however, that they could affect the diamond trade. 'I can think of no commodity less susceptible to dangers from UN sanctions than diamonds,' he said. He was stating the obvious: diamonds were after all one of the most convenient commodities to transport across borders. For example, an entire month's production of diamonds from the Namibian mines, worth $40 million, could be smuggled out of Namibia in an attaché case.

Oppenheimer also gave little credence to the fear that De Beers might be running out of quality diamonds. He pointed out that De Beers was developing vast new mines in the Botswanan desert, which he planned to visit the next day. These Botswanan mines would provide the world with an ample supply of diamonds well into the 1990s.

I asked Oppenheimer whether this move into the independent country of Botswana was meant to make De Beers less dependent on South Africa for its diamonds. According to the development plan that he had outlined, Botswana would soon be producing more diamonds than South Africa.

He scoffed at the idea that the mining of diamonds in Botswana would have 'any significant effect in divorcing De Beers from political and social problems in South Africa.' He emphasized, 'We are, and will remain, a South African company.'

It was clear, however, that in the 1980s De Beers would become increasingly dependent for its diamonds on African countries. In the light of the continuing – and intensifying – confrontation between South Africa and Black Africa, it seemed questionable how effectively De Beers could operate its mines in these independent countries with hostile regimes.

Oppenheimer insisted that the black–white confrontation in Africa would not present a problem for De Beers. He termed the arrangement between De Beers and Black African nations 'mutually advantageous.' He further suggested that it might be useful for me to inspect at first hand some of De Beers' mining operations in independent nations to understand more fully how the 'arrangement' works. He offered to provide air transportation and access to the mines in Botswana, Lesotho and other independent nations.

I had never been down a diamond mine. I accepted his offer.

2 The Desert Venture

Botswana: 5 December 1978

The small Cessna Air King took off from Jan Smuts airport in Johannesburg promptly at 7 a.m. for the two-hour flight to the Orapa mine in Botswana. On board the plane with me were four De Beers engineers who called themselves 'the flying circus.' Their job was to periodically inspect and evaluate the operations at all of De Beers' diamond mines, and then report back to Oppenheimer's headquarters in Johannesburg.

We flew directly over the eastern edge of the Kalahari Desert, which cut through Botswana in a swathe of brown barren earth. There were few signs of life anywhere below except for scattered clumps of twisted thorn trees and an occasional herd of oryx. By 9 a.m. the sun was baking down on the parched earth which was partially concealed by a nimbus of dust. Suddenly, appearing like some desert mirage out of this haze, was a modern city. 'Orapa,' the pilot announced, as he began circling for a landing.

Except for the fact that Orapa is in the middle of nowhere, it might have been any suburban city. I could see ranch houses with green lawns and rectangular swimming pools laid out along a cross-grid of paved streets. There were also a shopping center, football fields, parks and a number of high-rise apartment houses.

The De Beers engineer sitting next to me explained that most of the city of Orapa had in fact been prefabricated in Johannesburg in 1971, and then, piece by piece, reassembled on this stretch of desert. It had been an enormous undertaking. A road had to be bulldozed through the trackless wasteland so that trucks could move the mining equipment to make an artificial lake, a pipeline had to be constructed to bring water into Orapa, power lines had to be strung some 160 miles to the South African border, and an airstrip had to be built so that diamonds could be flown out. 'This was the first mine De Beers ever developed outside of South Africa,' he continued. (Like most South Africans, he considered Namibia to be part and parcel of South Africa.)

At the Orapa airstrip, it took only a moment to go through Botswana customs. Oppenheimer's headquarters had telexed ahead that I was arriving, and I was immediately issued with a red badge. Without such a badge, not even a citizen of Botswana is allowed into Orapa. I remarked to the engineer about how quickly we were admitted into Botswana, considering that we did not have visas and that he was a South African citizen.

'No problem,' he laughed, 'Harry Oppenheimer owns Botswana lock, stock and barrel.' I later found out that he wasn't far wrong. Botswana, a republic with some 6 million citizens, most nomadic tribesmen, derives more than 50 per cent of its national income from diamond, manganese and copper mines controlled by Harry Oppenheimer. The Botswanan government is dependent on these mines for almost all its revenues and foreign exchange.

Jim Gibson, a lanky Scotsman in his early forties, met me at the airport. He was De Beers' chief geologist at Orapa, and he had been asked to show me around the mine. He explained as we drove back to Orapa that he had been at the mine since it went into production in 1971.

When we arrived at the mine, he handed me a steel helmet. As a safety regulation, De Beers requires that everyone wear one at all its mines.

'You're looking at the second largest diamond mine in the world,' Gibson said, pointing to a long, oval-shaped depression in front of us. (The largest was the De Beers mine in Tanzania.)

I had imagined a mine deep underground honeycombed with labyrinthine tunnels. Instead I saw an open pit that looked like an excavation site for a skyscraper. A number of dirt roads wound their way down to the bottom of the pit, which was no more than 690 feet below the surface of the earth at its deepest point. On the floor of the mine I could see about fifty Botswanan workers. They were dressed in khaki jumpsuits and yellow helmets, and most of them were operating steam shovels and other mechanized equipment.

Every few minutes, a large yellow truck driven by a Botswanan would drive down the winding road to the bottom of the mine. A power shovel would then load it with a pile of bluish earth. When the truck returned to the surface, it would dump the bluish earth on a moving conveyor belt. The entire process was highly mechanized and required few workers.

'It is simply an earth-moving operation,' Gibson explained. 'Every afternoon at 4 p.m. a number of dynamite charges are detonated to loosen up the ground, then the power shovels simply scoop up the kimberlite.'

Kimberlite is the blue ore in the mine. 'What you are looking down into is a kimberlite pipe. If all the kimberlite was scooped out of that pit, it would look something like this.' He drew a sketch in the ground of something that looked like a funnel with an extremely long stem. 'Millions of years ago there were underground explosions that sent lava shooting up to the surface. When the lava cooled, it hardened into these pipelike formations.' The kimberlite, containing the diamonds, had come gushing up with the lava.

I picked up a handful of the kimberlite ore and crumbled it into a loose mixture of stones and bluish dust. 'Where are the diamonds?' I asked.

'Finding a diamond in kimberlite is like finding a very small needle in a haystack,' he responded. It is necessary to sift through more than two tons of kimberlite to find just one carat of diamonds.

A carat is a very minute measure. It is based on the remarkably uniform weight of the ancient carob seed, and weighs only 1/2000th of a pound. Separating the diamonds from this mass of bluish ore seemed a herculean task. I asked Gibson who separated out the diamonds.

'The diamonds are never touched by a human hand,' he explained, as we walked along a path parallel to the conveyor belt toward a glimmering structure about a quarter of a mile away. 'That's the separation plant,' he said, pointing to the building ahead.

It towered about twenty stories above the desert and looked like some medieval fortress. As we approached it, I could see that it was constructed of giant slabs of metal and surrounded by a barbwire fence.

I had heard a number of stories about natives stealing diamonds from mines by concealing them on their bodies. I wondered whether this fortress-like building was part of some draconian security system. I inquired whether they conducted body searches.

Gibson smiled and replied that there was no need for anything like that. He explained that the fully automated sorting machines kept the diamonds from tempting anyone.

The conveyor belt carries about one thousand tons of ore an hour into a plant. Inside the separation plant, the conveyor belt dumps the ore between two giant wheels – the 'crushers' – which are large enough to pulverize automobiles. The kimberlite must be broken into small fragments in order to be automatically processed. The tiny particles, mainly sand, are screened out by a series of sieves.

The kimberlite then moves on a conveyor belt into huge vats of swirling liquid that resemble enormous whirlpool baths. These 'cyclone baths' were designed by De Beers to take advantage of the heavy density of diamonds in separating them out from lighter-density materials. Gibson explained, 'They work on the same centrifugal principle as dairy creamers: at high speeds, ligher materials rise and are skimmed off.' More than 99 per cent of the ore is removed in the vats; what remains is a concentrate of diamonds and other heavy minerals.

Back on the conveyor belt, the concentrate is channeled into a battery of large, five-foot-high black boxes called 'sortexes.' These machines take advantage of one of the natural characteristics of diamonds: the fact that they, unlike most minerals, phosphoresce under X-rays. As the concentrate passes, the machines bombard it with X-rays. Whenever a diamond passes through, it glimmers, activating a photoelectric cell inside the sortex. The photoelectric cell triggers a jet of air that blows the diamond, and the stones on either side of it, off the conveyor belt, and down a chute that leads to the sorting room.

We went next to the sorting room, which is the most heavily guarded inner sanctum in the entire diamond mining complex. Three different guards were required to put their keys into separate locks before the door could be opened.

The windowless room had in its center a row of large glass boxes, which were all connected by pipes to the ceiling. 'Not even the sorters have the opportunity to lay a hand on the diamonds in this system,' Gibson explained.

On closer inspection, I could see that each box had a pair of rubber gloves, called 'evening gloves,' fastened to the glass wall of the box. Inside the box was a set of tweezers.

Suddenly, a stream of small stones came clattering through the pipe in the ceiling and spilled into the glass sorting box I was watching. A Botswanan sorter immediately went to work. He thrust his hands inside the evening gloves, which protruded into the sealed glass container, and through these gloves, he picked up the tweezers. He quickly separated the stones into two piles – diamonds and non-diamonds. The chief sorter then came over to double-check the sorting. The sorter then pushed the non-diamonds down a hole in one side of the box, where they clanked through a pipe. 'Those stones will be fed back onto the conveyor belt just in case the sorter missed any diamonds,' Gibson explained.

The diamonds left in the glass box were then released through a trap door in the bottom into a steel container. This container is continually guarded by two Botswanan soldiers with shotguns.

The chief sorter allowed me to examine the day's catch of diamonds through a window in the steel container. The vast preponderance of the diamonds were black chips resembling tiny fragments of coal. 'What are black diamonds used for?' I asked.

'They're industrial diamonds,' Gibson answered. 'Most of them are ground down into abrasive grit and used to grind tools and precision parts.

'They will probably bring about $2 a carat, which is only a hundredth of what good gem diamonds will fetch in today's market,' he added. It still is financially rewarding since the mine produces about 1.7 million carats of industrial grade diamonds in a year. The mix is roughly 80 per cent industrial diamonds and 20 per cent gems. The income from the industrial diamonds – even at a mere $2 a carat – is sufficient to pay the day-to-day operating costs of the mine.

I peered again into the box and saw that the whitish diamonds, which looked like tiny pieces of broken glass, had a wide variety of shapes. Some were flat chips, others were twisted triangles, and many were no larger than a grain of sand. It seemed difficult to see how this batch of uncut diamonds could ever be converted into fine jewels.

According to the chief sorter, there were between 1000 and 1500 carats of gems in the day's take. He explained that the exact determination of the number of gem stones, and their value, was made by an official appraiser in the Botswanan capital Gabarone. The diamonds were then flown to London.

'How many of those diamonds are large enough to cut into a one-carat engagement stone?' I asked recalling the concern about dwindling supplies of the large diamonds.

'You might find only two or three of that size here,' he said. In light of this low ratio in Botswana, it seemed that the concern was well founded.

When we left the separation plant, I looked at the huge mountain of kimberlite waste behind it. Each day the plant processed and spewed out some 20,000 tons of ore. It seemed to be an incredible undertaking for a mere handful of gem diamonds.

'Gem diamonds can be worth anywhere between $100 and $5000 a carat depending on their quality,' said Gibson, adding, 'and quality is, for all practical purposes, what the official appraisers say it is.' He explained that appraisers had to take into account such nebulous factors as the shade of color, shape, and the cutability of the uncut diamond in making their evaluation. This evaluation was of considerable importance to the Botswanan government, for it derived most of its revenue from the 50 per cent share of the profits it received on the diamonds.

Diamond mines, unlike most other kinds of mining operations, could not measure, or even reasonably estimate the value of their own product. Gold mines can calculate how many ounces they produce each day, and copper mines can estimate their tonnage, but the Orapa mine could not immediately determine whether its production of gem diamonds that day was worth $100,000 or a million dollars. Both the diamond mine and the Botswanan government had to await the outcome of the official evaluation by the De Beers-trained appraisers.

We had lunch that afternoon at the Orapa Club. During the meal, Gibson told the story of how he and another De

Beers geologist named Gavin Lamont discovered the Botswanan diamonds.

It began in 1962 when Harry Oppenheimer decided to acquire the prospecting rights in Botswana (which was then the British protectorate of Bechuanaland). Prospectors had already discovered three diamonds on the banks of the Moutlouse River but unable to find the source of the diamonds they had abandoned the search. For nearly four years, Gibson and Lamont scoured the headwaters of the Moutlouse without finding a trace of diamonds – or any of the minerals associated with them. At this point, Lamont came up with a highly speculative geological theory. Since there had been enormous upheavals of the earth's crust in southern Africa in prehistoric times, he suggested that the Moutlouse river may have been truncated by the rising earth; its previous source might have been on the other side of the mountains. Even though there was no corroborative evidence for this theory, Lamont and Gibson believed it was worth a gamble to explore it. They moved their prospecting team north to the edge of the Kalahari Desert.

Sand proved to be an immediate problem for the prospectors. If there was a rich kimberlite pipe in the desert, it would be buried under hundreds of feet of sand and gravel. How could they sample the minerals under the desert?

White ants, who had built towering mounds on the desert, provided the solution. Gibson and Lamont realized that these ants had tunneled hundreds of feet below the surface of the desert in searching for humid earth for their nest, and with the mud they retrieved they also brought up traces of minerals from below the surface. By analyzing samples from these ant colonies, Gibson and Lamont found traces of two other minerals – garnets and ilmenites. Since both these minerals frequently occur in kimberlite, they had reason to hope they were on the right track.

Finally, in March 1967, Gibson narrowed the search to a spot located a few miles away from a cattle trading camp called 'Orapa' by the natives. Here he began drilling for core samples with equipment that De Beers had flown up from its Kimberley headquarters. 'Those diamonds literally poured out of the small rotary pan,' Gibson recalled. 'We realized that we were on to something very big indeed.' Gibson next ordered a series of aerial photographs to be taken of the area. Examining them, he delineated a depression more than a half mile in diameter. It was, in fact, the mouth of the Orapa pipe. 'It was quite unbelievable that the whole area should in fact be kimberlite,' he remembered thinking then.

From that moment on, De Beers moved quickly to bring the mine into production. It cost some $33 million. Four years later, it went into production, and it was officially opened on 26 May 1971, by President Seretse Khama. Oppenheimer, indeed, had the entire Botswanan government flown in for the ceremony. 'It was, after all, the first diamond mine that De Beers had ever found,' Gibson added.

According to Gibson, De Beers had completely missed the 44-acre Finsch pipe in South Africa, and the 360-acre Mwadui pipe in Tanzania, the largest pipe mine ever found, even though both sites had been explored by its geologists several years before the respective discoveries. In every instance, up to Botswana, De Beers simply bought out the discoveries of others. De Beers presumably had been purposely avoiding unnecessarily expanding the supply of diamonds by uncovering new mines.

The scarcity of diamonds one carat or larger in Botswana raised the question of how De Beers intended to meet the demand for these stones. The answer suggested to me was a mine on a mountaintop in the kingdom of Lesotho, which was my next stop.

3 Shangri-la

Lesotho: 6 December 1978

Diamonds can be profitably mined in some of the most inaccessible locations in the world precisely because the operation does not require the construction of a vast transportation infrastructure to remove the final product. Almost all other mining enterprises, such as iron, copper, lead, zinc and potash, need to build railroad, pipelines or ports to bulk ship thousands of tons of ore a day. Most precious metals, such as gold, silver and platinum, must be chemically separated from the surrounding matrix of ore in a smelter that in turn usually requires massive daily shipments of coal and other materials. A diamond, however, requires only a primitive landing strip and a light plane to transport its final product which, though it may be worth tens of millions of dollars, seldom amounts to more than a few pounds of stones a day. Perhaps the best example of this phenomenon is the Letseng-La-Terai mine in the kingdom of Lesotho.

The twin engine Otter, which De Beers had bought from the US Air Force in Vietnam – and which still carried bullet scars from that war – flew low over the 10,000-foot-high Lesothan mountains. The kingdom, a landlocked enclave roughly the size of Belgium, was, until 1966, the British protectorate of Basutoland. Below, I could see the ruins of fortresses used centuries before by the Basutos to defend themselves against the invasions of Zulus and other tribes. The land in the valleys looked green and rich, and trails through the mountain passes led to clusters of huts with conically shaped roofs.

Suddenly, the plane headed directly into a mountain wall shrouded by dense clouds. Everyone aboard, even the South African engineers who made this trip each week, gripped the edge of the seats. There was dead silence in the cabin. The wings of the plane looked as if they were about to touch the rocks they were flying through. Only then did I see the landing strip. It had literally been carved out of the mountainside. The wheels touched with a dull but reassuring thump. The Otter then slowly taxied up a rocky hill, screeched to a stop on the edge of a cliff and in a moment a dozen Basuto workers had tied it down with ropes firmly lashed around its wings and tail.

Through the morning mist, I could discern the rectangular shape of a corrugated iron tower built against the side of the mountain, which, oddly enough, resembled some of the ancient citadels that the plane had passed over. It was, I realized, the separation plant for the diamonds. 'Welcome to Letseng-La-Terai,' the pilot said over the intercom. 'It's the highest mine in the world.' We were 10,000 feet above sea level on what is called 'the roof of Africa.' The pilot explained to me, as I sat for a moment recuperating from the landing, that this Otter was the only means of getting in or out of the mine in winter weather.

When I finally disembarked, I found standing on this mountaintop a tall, slender man impeccably dressed in a three-piece pin-striped suit and wearing a school tie. He seemed completely unruffled and impervious to the icy wind that blew across the mountain. He looked, in fact, as if he had just got out of a cab in the center of London.

'Rodney MacLean,' he said, introducing himself. He explained that he worked at the Diamond Trading Company in London, and he had been sent to Lesotho to evaluate the diamonds coming out of its mine. He said that he was in charge of evaluating 'large stones,' which De Beers defined as any uncut gem diamond weighing over 14.8 carats.

'How many large stones are found every year?' I asked.

'Very few. I'd say well under 200. This mine is one of the two places in the world we regularly get them from. The other place is Sierra Leone, but the fields there are just about exhausted.' MacLean explained, as we waited for a landrover to pick us up, that this mine had only been opened for some thirteen months, and it had already produced nearly 100 large stones. Most of these Lesothan diamonds had a brownish tint to them but aside from that, according to MacLean, they were of first-rate quality.

'How much are these diamonds worth?' I inquired.

MacLean explained that the value of diamonds increases

practically geometrically with their size. He estimated that whereas a one-carat diamond in good condition would be sold by the Diamond Trading Company for $300, a two-carat diamond of comparable quality might bring $2000 (or $1000 a carat), and a similar three-carat diamond would fetch $5400 (or $1800 a carat). 'When you come to my little specialties, a forty-carat diamond might bring a half million dollars,' he added.

Just then a bell began furiously ringing. Something extraordinary had apparently happened at the mine. A moment later, the landrover arrived, and the driver talked with great excitement to MacLean.

As we roared off in the landrover, MacLean explained to me that they were ringing a bell because a large diamond had just been found – the first in nearly two weeks.

When we pulled up in front of the sorting house, we were met by a youthful man with a craggy face and blue eyes. He introduced himself as Keith Whitelock, and said he was the manager of the mine. He seemed visibly elated about this diamond. 'Thought we might never find another big stone,' he said, as he led us past armed guards into the sorting house.

'Now you don't have to worry about closing the mine,' MacLean said, with a broad smile.

Whitelock winced at this joke, as if it contained a grain of truth. He told me that he had lived and prospected in Lesotho for over ten years. It was his personal Shangri-la. 'This mine depends on big stones – we need to produce two or three a month just to stay in business,' he explained.

When we got to the sorting room, Whitelock instructed the chief sorter to show MacLean the big stone that had just been found. A Basuto guard with a shotgun looked on as the sorter handed the diamond to MacLean.

The diamond itself looked like a large piece of broken glass, except that its edges were smooth. MacLean placed it on the scale. It weighed exactly fifty-eight carats. He nodded approvingly and pulled out his jeweler's loupe from his pocket. Looking through it, he examined the diamond for about a minute.

'It's a pity it has this crack in it,' he said, 'otherwise it could have been cut into a marquise shape.' He explained that because of this almost invisible crack, the diamond would have to be cut into two separate jewels. 'The most you could get out of this is two twelve-carat round diamonds.' MacLean concluded that more than half the weight would be lost in cutting and polishing – depending on the shape of the diamond, somewhere between one-third and one-half of the weight is lost in cutting.

'What about the color?' Whitelock asked.

'The color is superb,' MacLean answered, pronouncing 'superb' as if it were two distinct words. He pointed out that it was extremely fortunate that the diamond was pure white. If it had had a brownish tinge to it, as had the last large diamond he had examined from Lesotho, it would be worth only a tenth as much.

Whitelock perked up and asked MacLean how much money this diamond would fetch in London. This in turn would determine how much money De Beers would credit to the mine's account.

'I'd say it should bring between six and seven thousand dollars a carat,' MacLean responded, without hesitating. At minimum, then, this single diamond would be sold to a dealer for $342,000.

'Well, that's enough to keep the mine going for another two weeks,' Whitelock said, smiling.

It seemed extraordinary that a single stone, weighing a fraction of an ounce, could support for a half month a mining enterprise that employed 800 workers. It turned out, however, that Whitelock was not exaggerating. The Basuto workers earned on average $25 a week – the highest wages for labor paid in Lesotho. From this amount, De Beers deducts the cost of each worker's food and lodgings. The South African engineers and supervisors, most of whom commute to South Africa weekly in the Otter, earn about $250 a week. With other operating expenses, such as fuel for the trucks and electricity for the machinery, the mountaintop mine cost about $150,000 a week to operate.

Whitelock drove us from the sorting house to the mine itself. Like the desert mine at Orapa, it was a kimberlite pipe. It was, however, only one-thirtieth the size of the pit I had seen the day before in Botswana. 'This is the smallest diamond mine that De Beers operates,' Whitelock said, as we stood on the edge of the shallow pit. Below, about a dozen Basuto workers were loading a truck with a power shovel. 'We also have the dubious distinction of mining the lowest-grade ore of any De Beers mine.' He explained that they had to sift through three to four tons of kimberlite at the separation to find a single carat of diamonds. And most of the diamonds found are not of gem quality. In all, this mine had produced only 17,000 carats of gem diamonds in its first year of production.

Oppenheimer had told me that De Beers had invested more money in this mountain venture than in any other diamond mine outside of South Africa. It had cost some $45 million to develop. Why had such a huge investment been made in a mine that could yield, compared to other mines, only a trickle of diamonds?

'There is only one reason for this mine to exist: large stones,' Whitelock answered. 'Nearly 10 per cent of the total caratage taken out of this mine is in the form of large stones. The world is running out of large diamonds.'

MacLean wholeheartedly agreed. 'They are the romance of the diamond business. Movie stars won't want diamonds if you need a magnifying glass to see them.' MacLean explained that an important part of his mission to Africa was to determine why the supply of large stones was so rapidly diminishing. He said that part of the problem was that most of the older mines fed the ore directly into the giant crushers which, though they speeded the automated separation of the diamonds, also tended to smash larger diamonds into smaller ones. He had just visited Premier mine in South Africa, which had, seventy-three years ago, yielded the world's largest diamond – the 3106-carat Cullinan diamond. 'Today, the crushers at the Premier would break a diamond that size into a thousand fragments.' He argued that mines capable of yielding such large stones should install a bypass system in which the ore, before it goes through the crushers, is screened by X-ray machines to detect any larger diamonds.

'We have the bypass system,' Whitelock interrupted, 'but it has never turned up any colossal diamonds for us.'

'It will,' MacLean answered confidently. 'You'll save the cost of it with a single diamond some day.' He recounted how at the Premier mine he had reconstructed a million-dollar diamond from fragments he found at its sorting house. 'A bypass system would have saved that diamond, and that alone would have paid for the entire cost of the system twice over.'

'We could certainly use a million-dollar diamond here,' Whitelock said, as we continued walking around the site. 'Have you ever been to any place this beautiful?' he asked, turning to me.

I looked down the mountain to where he was pointing. A stream cut through the emerald green hill below, and then cascaded down over white rocks. Surrounding the hill were snow-covered mountain peaks. The roof of Africa was indeed extraordinary. I asked the mine manager how he had found this Shangri-la of his.

'I came here with Colonel Jack Scott twenty years ago – and I never left.' He explained that Scott was a South African adventurer looking for diamonds, and he had heard of kimberlite pipe in Lesotho. Even before diamonds had been discovered in South Africa, he continued, Basuto tribesmen mined these kimberlites. They had been looking not for diamonds but for ilmenite, a mineral used as a bright cosmetic by the Basuto women. Scott managed to persuade the paramount chieftainess of Lesotho to give him a concession to sift through the kimberlite pipe for diamonds. 'We came up on horseback then, and to hack a jeep trail up the mountain,' Whitelock recalled with some nostalgia. 'We were stranded for a week in a blizzard, but Scott got about 1800 carats of diamonds out. Shortly thereafter Scott gave up the concession.'

Whitelock continued to prospect on his own in Lesotho, enjoying the trout-filled streams and endless game. Then, in 1967, a Basuto woman found a mountain diamond weighing 601 carats. It was the eleventh largest diamond ever found in the world. Rio Tinto Zinc, a London mining conglomerate, then rushed in to buy the mining concession from the newly independent government of Lesotho. At this point, Whitelock joined Rio Tinto Zinc as a field geologist.

'They built the airstrip that you landed on this morning and they began digging out the mine,' he continued. Even though Rio Tinto Zinc excavated large amounts of kimberlite, it soon found that the ore yielded too low a percentage of diamonds to be economically profitable. In 1972, it abruptly abandoned the concession.

Chief Jonathan, the prime minister of Lesotho, then went to the 'logical candidate,' as Whitelock put it, Harry Oppenheimer. Oppenheimer's gold mines in South Africa were already the chief employer of Basuto labor, and Oppenheimer's companies had invested in timber and land in Lesotho as part of their diversification strategy. Chief Jonathan now proposed that Oppenheimer go into partnership in mining diamonds with his kingdom.

Oppenheimer, according to Whitelock, found the idea of discovering magnificent diamonds in this mountain wilderness to be an 'especially romantic' undertaking. He likened it to salvaging great works of art. He decided to take the gamble of finding large stones in Lesotho, even though economics remained at least problematical. 'And he hired me to manage the mine,' Whitelock concluded his story.

I looked around at the 100-foot-high separation plant erected on the side of the mountain, the Swiss-chalet style dormitories for the workers, and all the mechanized equipment in the mine. It seemed that an enormous amount of capital had been invested in this Shangri-la. Could this all be merely a romantic conceit of Oppenheimer's?

Oppenheimer had opened the Orapa mine less than a year before he negotiated the venture in Lesotho. He had also during this period acquired prospecting rights to other countries adjacent to South Africa – Swaziland and Rhodesia. This sudden expansion by De Beers into four neighboring countries – Botswana, Lesotho, Swaziland and Rhodesia – seemed to me to have been more than a coincidence. It was a time, after all, of increasing racial unrest in South Africa, and these neighboring countries could provide safe havens for De Beers.

We dined with the supervisory staff in a wood-paneled room that overlooked the spectacular mining site. They had a visitor from the Soviet Union, a geologist named George Smernoff. Smernoff, it turned out, had been stationed in Lesotho for nearly a year to observe De Beers' mining techniques. This arrangement with Smernoff was part of an 'exchange' between De Beers and the Soviets.

This remote kingdom seemed an odd place for an 'exchange.' On the other hand, since the Soviet Union was supposedly boycotting South Africa because of its racial policies, Lesotho provided a convenient official residence for a Soviet mining expert whose unofficial business was in South Africa. 'Does Smernoff have access to other De Beers' mines?' I asked. No one at the table answered.

4 Holding Back the Ocean

Namibia: 7 December 1978

The geopolitics of diamonds forges unlikely alliances in Africa. Only some seventy years earlier, German troops had nearly wiped out the Hereros as a race in Namibia. Now I watched the descendants of the original German settlers urging the Herero tribesmen to vote for their Democratic Trunsthale Alliance. It was a gay, festive atmosphere, with a crowd of Herero women, wearing red turbans and long Victorian dresses, lined up to vote at a polling booth in Namibia's capital city of Windhoek.

Namibia was still under the firm control of South Africa, which had administered it since 1915, and the election was clearly sponsored by South Africa. Nevertheless, it was the first election in Namibia's history, and considerable efforts had been made to win the support of chiefs of the Herero and Ovambo tribes, who constituted the vast majority of the population. There had been massive rallies, torchlight parades and tribal festivals staged by the South Africans to encourage the black population to vote. The South African army even provided trucks to take the Ovambos from their rural kraals to the polling booths. During the week-long election there had also been scattered assassinations and acts of sabotage attributed to the SWAPO guerrillas. SWAPO had demanded that blacks in Namibia boycott the election.

South Africa, in turn, had invited journalists from all over the world to witness this extravaganza. The purpose was to demonstrate to the United Nations, and the media, that SWAPO could not effectively speak for or control the black population of Namibia. It was, in short, a contest of terror, and the measure of success was the percentage of eligible voters who participated in the election. Those who abstained voted in effect for SWAPO.

I was told, according to the latest tally, that nearly 80 per cent of the eligible voters in all of Namibia had cast their vote, which was a resounding victory for South Africa. Returns coming in from the rural Ovambo villages close to the Angola border, where SWAPO guerrillas had their bases, showed that 90 per cent or more of the Ovambos were voting, despite SWAPO threats of assassination.

After making the rounds of polling places in Windhoek, I flew across the Namib Desert to Oranjemund, which is located, as its name implies, at the mouth of the Orange River. Even though the election was in its final day, this immaculately clean city was strangely silent. Unlike Windhoek, there were no boisterous rallies or blaring soundtracks in the palm-tree lined streets. The polling booths were nearly deserted. Although this was the second largest city in Namibia, with more than 7000 eligible Ovambo tribesmen, all the blacks seemed to be abstaining from the plebiscite. As it turned out, Oranjemund was the only city in all of Namibia that had, through its massive abstention, 'voted' in effect for SWAPO.

The difference between Oranjemund and the rest of Namibia was that it was not under the control of the South African army. It was, and had been since its inception in 1936, the private preserve of De Beers and its wholly owned subsidiary, Consolidated Diamond Mines. Oppenheimer's father had built the entire city from scratch, after he had obtained exclusive rights to the adjacent 200 miles of Namibian desert called the *Sperrgebeit*, or forbidden zone. Cordoned off from the rest of Namibia by two barbwire fences, it has continued to live up to its ominous name. No one, not even army or government officials, is allowed into the forbidden zone without the express permission of Oppenheimer's diamond company.

I was not surprised to find that De Beers had not cajoled, pressured or even encouraged its black workers in Namibia to vote. Since Namibian diamonds constituted the single largest source of profits for De Beers, Oppenheimer had to carefully weigh any intervention in Namibian politics. Not only the United Nations but western powers – including the United States, Britain, France and Germany – were demanding that South Africa relinquish its control over Namibia. The alternatives that were threatened were United

Nations' sanctions, which could include the severing of all telephone, mail, and air services to South Africa, and conceivably an oil embargo. Under these circumstances, there was a distinct possibility that South Africa would yield and SWAPO would come to power in Namibia. Oppenheimer would have then to renegotiate his subsidiary's concession to mine the diamonds of the forbidden zone with SWAPO.

I recalled Oppenheimer's confidence about Namibia. Whether or not he had already established contacts with alternative governments there, it was understandable that he should not want to offend gratuitously the leaders of SWAPO by pressing the diamond workers to vote in this election. He might have to deal with them in the foreseeable future for Namibia's diamonds.

The forbidden zone was a world unto itself. The only means of entering it was the Ernest Oppenheimer Bridge, which spanned the Orange River frontier between South Africa and Namibia. Armed guards manned barricades at both the South African and Namibian ends of the bridge. Before I was permitted to pass into the forbidden zone, I had to be met by an escort from the diamond company and issued with a plastic security badge.

Inside the forbidden zone is the city of Oranjemund, with its own food-producing farms and reservoirs, and the vast mining area alongside of the Atlantic Ocean. To enter into the mining area, one has to insert the plastic security badge into a slot in the wall and wait for a door to slide open automatically. The central computer, which opens and closes these passageways, tracks the comings and goings of everyone in the mining area. De Beers' helicopters constantly patrol overhead, and closely monitor the activities of the fishing craft that pass by in the ocean (even though the enormous waves would make landing a boat on the beach all but impossible). Behind the beach, a pack of Alsatian guard dogs patrol the no-man's-land between the two barbwire fences. And behind the barbwire fences is the Namib Desert, one of the most inhospitable areas on earth. It is made impenetrable by 1000-foot-high sand dunes and 120 degree temperatures.

The extraordinary security procedures are necessary in Namibia because what is recovered from the 200-mile-long beach is not kimberlite ore but pure gem diamonds, which can be easily pocketed by anyone. In one small crevice in a rock outcropping, some 15,000 carats of sparkling diamonds were found on this beach some years ago.

The mine, if it can be called a mine, is actually the continental shelf of the Atlantic Ocean. To get at the richest lodes of diamonds, the ocean must be literally pushed back – and held back long enough to dig out the diamonds. The mechanism for holding back the pounding surf is a ten-story-high mound, which, 600 feet out in the ocean, runs parallel to the beach.

Standing on this sandy mound, I looked down into the 'mine,' which was actually the exposed floor of the ocean. It was an incredible sight; a full-scale battle between man and nature.

'You are looking at the largest construction project in the Southern Hemisphere,' observed Clive Cowley. Cowley had been the editor of Namibia's leading newspaper, the *Windhoek Advertiser*; now he was the chief public affairs officer of De Beers in Namibia. He pointed to the thousands of workers and machines below. Giant bulldozers were belching smoke and scraping the ground with their blades like some sort of prehistoric animal. Powerful pumps were sucking the water out of the mining area through hoses as fast as it sprayed in over the barrier. Ovambo tribesmen, knee-deep in pools of water, were frantically sweeping the gravel off outcroppings of rock on the ocean's floor as if they feared that at any moment the barrier might give way, like a sand-castle on a beach, and the ocean would come flooding in.

In the center of all this activity was an enormous piece of machinery, more than a football field in length and two stories high, mounted on caterpillar tracks. A continuous belt of steel buckets traveled around it, like cars on a ferris wheel, scooping up sand at one end and depositing it at the other end. It was the largest machine I had ever seen.

'That's the bucket wheel excavator,' Cowley explained. 'It cost $3.5 million to build, and it can move 1800 tons of sand an hour.' The sand must be stripped away before the workers, called lashers, can get at the diamond-rich gravel.

The Ovambo tribesmen worked with their primitive brooms in the shadow of this colossal machine. The contrast between tribal and modern technology was striking. Ironically, as Cowley pointed out, it was the tribesmen, not the multimillion-dollar machine, who recovered most of the diamonds.

These Ovambos had been recruited to work in the ocean mine from the jungles of Ovambaland, a thousand miles to the north. According to Cowley, they usually received eight-month contracts from the diamond company. They would then board a Hercules cargo plane, leaving their families behind on the kraal, and fly to Oranjemund.

'They have to be literally fought off the plane,' Cowley said. For just sweeping the gravel from the rocks, they received $200 a month. For driving trucks and other more skilled jobs, they earned up to $450 a month. This salary is completely exempt from taxes. Their own expense for their eight-month stay at the mines is $22 a month for their dormitory room and food. 'By the time they return to Ovambaland, they have enough money to buy cattle, land or even a wife,' Cowley concluded.

Suddenly, a tractor the size of a locomotive came racing towards us. As it passed, an Ovambo waved from the cab. He then maneuvered the vehicle precariously on the edge of the mound, which was only about sixty feet wide, and dumped a load of dirt on top of it. Cowley explained that these tractors wage an around-the-clock battle with the Atlantic Ocean. Waves constantly rip away the sand, and these tractors, each of which carries a thirty-five-ton load of sand, constantly fill the breaches in the barrier. If an opening were not immediately filled, the ocean would break through and submerge the entire mine under fifty feet of sea water.

Every day, more than 190 million pounds of sand and gravel are dug out of the mine. From the massive moving of the earth, and holding back of the ocean, about two and a half to three pounds of diamonds are recovered each day. 'All this effort, and more, purely for the vanity of women,' Cowley added, with an edge of irony in his voice. That irony was only compounded by the fact that De Beers had millions of dollars invested in advertising to take advantage of this so-called vanity.

When I viewed the day's catch in the sorting house, which was that day about 6000 carats, I saw that unlike in Botswana and Lesotho there were no black or discolored diamonds in the tray. These were clearly not industrial-grade diamonds, but white, well-formed gem diamonds.

'These aren't the same sort of diamonds that come out of a pipe mine,' Cowley said. 'They have been pounded by ocean waves for millions of years. The inferior diamonds have been smashed to bits eons ago. Only the fittest survive, and these are pure gems.'

Pointing to the container of diamonds that had been recovered from the ocean floor that day, he continued, 'There are probably more pure gems in that dish than have been recovered today in all the pipe mines in South Africa combined.'

Cowley estimated that this single day's production would bring in over $1.5 million when they were sold by De Beers in London.

The profits on these Namibian diamonds were enormous. It cost no more to mine and separate these gem diamonds than it did for the industrial-grade diamonds that constituted the bulk of the production of most other mines. Yet these gems sold for one hundred times the price of industrial diamonds. From the $400 million in revenues it took in the preceding year for these Namibian diamonds, De Beers realized a net profit of more than $200 million, making Namibia De Beers' moneyspinner.

After we left the sorting house, Cowley took me over to see an extraordinary scrapyard. It was enclosed by barbwire and filled with enough antique machines to stock a museum. 'Once a vehicle or piece of equipment enters the mining area, it is never allowed to leave,' Cowley said. He explained that this prohibition was necessary in order to prevent anyone from smuggling diamonds out concealed in a piece of equipment. Since it was not practical to attempt to search for an object as small as a diamond, De Beers simply consigned all the vehicles and machines, when they became outmoded, to this graveyard.

This tangle of relics encapsulated the history of the Namibian diamonds. There was, for example, a train of turn-of-the-century railroad cars with German markings.

'Namibia was a German colony when diamonds were first found here at the turn of the century,' Cowley said.

He explained that the diamond fields were then about 100 miles north of Oranjemund. To mine the diamonds, the Germans had built Teutonic towns at Pomona and Kolmanskop, complete with beerhalls and skittle alleys. 'The Germans had the blacks sweep the streets every day to keep the sand out of their houses. When they could no longer find any diamonds on the beaches they abandoned these towns to the desert. It has become a ghost town; the beerhall is now filled with sand, sand comes halfway up the walls inside the houses, and the skittle alley is now in Oranjemund.'

There was also an ominous-looking Second World War battle tank with a British insignia on it. A huge steel blade had been welded in front of the gun turret.

'De Beers converted these tanks to bulldozers after the war,' Cowley continued, 'because there was no bridge across the Orange River then and it was next to impossible to float heavy equipment across on barges.' It took until the mid-1950s before the bridge was built.

Since De Beers' geologist found that most of the diamond lodes were on the ocean floor, a method had to be devised of holding the ocean back, Cowley explained. Assisted by oceanographers at the University of Capetown, engineers initially experimented with the idea of altering the ocean current so that it would rip up the beach and redeposit the sand further from the shoreline. This would create a natural barrier behind which the workers could sweep the diamonds out from the bedrock. To shift the direction of the ocean current, they dug a channel across the beach. Unfortunately, the ocean refused to follow the predicted course, and the engineers gave up on the attempt to harness the sea.

Next, the engineers attempted to erect an earthen dam in the ocean at low tide and cover it with a gigantic canvas tarpaulin before the tide returned. They postulated that the tarpaulin would prevent the ocean from dissolving the dam. Working in a rising tide, it took nearly two hours to lash down this cover. Less than an hour later, the waves ripped the tarpaulin to shreds.

The De Beers engineers had to return to their drawing boards. Finally, in the early 1960s they came up with a system for building a series of dams that would be replenished with sand from the mine as fast as the ocean could strip it away. 'After a good deal of trial and error, it worked,' Cowley concluded.

Leaving the mining area, we had to pass through a long narrow building. Along one wall were large mirrors, which,

Cowley explained, were two-way mirrors through which security guards observed everyone passing through. At the end of one maze-like corridor, there was a turnstile that led to two closed doors, side by side. We went through the turnstile, waited; then a buzzer sounded, and the door on the right opened. 'If the other door had opened, you would have had to undergo both an X-ray and body search,' Cowley said. He explained that the selection of who gets searched is completely at random. It would be medically dangerous to subject workers to constant dosages of X-rays, therefore only a small percentage of those who passed out of the mining area each day were actually searched. 'Everyone from Harry Oppenheimer to Ovambo workers have to pass through that turnstile, and they never know which door is going to open,' Cowley added, as he again inserted our security badges into a slot at the end of the passageway.

The last door buzzed opened, and a moment later we were walking down a suburban street in Oranjemund. The transition from the moonscape-like mine to the familiarity of the city was somewhat unsettling.

We dined that evening with a group of De Beers executives at the Hexen Kessel. The decor and cuisine were meant to evoke an 'Old World' European spirit, but, like everything else in Oranjemund, the restaurant had been designed and built by De Beers. As far as the De Beers executives were concerned, the Namibian diamond mining operation was a reality that had been created by De Beers. If a revolutionary government ever forced De Beers to relinquish the concession, the mines would be flooded by the ocean in a matter of months, and no more diamonds would be recovered. Confronted by this reality, the forces of nationalism in Namibia would have to come to terms with the diamond cartel.

5 | The Big Hole

Kimberley: 14 December 1978

In Kimberley I visited a mine that was completely different from all the others that I had seen in Africa. Instead of an open pit, the mine was entirely below the surface. In the entire world, there are only six such underground mines. All are in South Africa: five hemmed in in the mining city of Kimberley, and the sixth located 400 miles northeast in the Transvaal. The Wesselton, located only about a mile from downtown Kimberley, is the deepest of these diamond mines. The mine shaft extends 3300 feet below the surface, which is deep enough to accommodate both towers of the World Trade Center in New York, stacked one on top of the other.

Before I was allowed to descend into the Wesselton, I was taken to a spotlessly clean changing room and provided with the necessary mining gear. This included steel boots, a white jumpsuit, a steel helmet with a built-in lantern, and a portable battery, which I strapped around my waist. I then proceeded to the mine shaft where I was met by Edward Robinson, a soft-spoken South African, who had been born and raised in the mining area around Kimberley.

At the top of the mine shaft, we stepped into a steel cage, the size of a large freight elevator. The door clanged shut. Robinson pressed a button, and with a sudden jerk, we began hurtling down the mine shaft. We were falling at a rate of twenty feet per second, or twelve miles an hour. Even at that speed, it took slightly more than two minutes to reach the mining level, 2500 feet below the surface.

From all the films I had seen about coal mining, I expected to step out into a dark tunnel where men were hacking away at the rock with picks and shovels. Instead, I found myself standing in an enormous, well-lighted and air-conditioned chamber. The ceiling was at least fifteen feet high, and there was a road in it wide enough for a two-ton truck.

'We call this the block caving method,' Robinson said. 'It works on the same principle as punching a hole in the bottom of a bottle to drain the liquid out.' He explained that rather than scooping out the kimberlite ore from above, as is done in open-pit mining, a shaft is drilled in the bedrock that encases the volcanic pipe. Once underneath the main body of ore in the pipe, or 'the bottom of the bottle,' as Robinson put it, a series of tunnels that run parallel to the surface are dug under the pipe. This is the 'mining level.' The kimberlite above, loosened by dynamite, then simply pours into the tunnels.

Robinson's attention focused on something happening at the end of the tunnel we were entering. He held up his hand. Suddenly, everyone around us froze.

A voice counted in Afrikaans . . . *schwi* . . . *di* . . . *ein*. . . . Then there was a loud explosion, followed in rapid succession by four other blasts. I could feel the reverberations of the concussion and smell burnt sulphur in the air.

'They're dynamiting ahead,' Robinson calmly said. The dynamite came, he explained, from De Beers' own explosives factory, which was the largest in Africa.

Robinson motioned me to follow him into the tunnel. At one end, kimberlite ore was flooding in.

A black worker operated a powerful winch. It manipulated a bulldozer blade about thirty yards away. The blade scraped kimberlite ore through a hole in the floor of the tunnel.

The ore poured into a train of hopper cars on the level below.

It was fully automated. The train arrives under the opening just before the scraper forces the ore through it. When full, it then shuttles over to the mine shaft where it dumps its ore. A belt of continuous buckets then brings the ore to the surface and deposits it on the conveyor belt. In all, this highly mechanized form of mining required about 165 men, including supervisors, below ground.

Most of the workers were black, and the supervisors white.

Robinson said that it was the white labor unions which insisted that the whites be given supervisory positions, rather than the blacks. He explained that some 40 per cent of the black workers were tribesmen from Lesotho on seasonal contracts (while in South Africa, they lived in De Beers-owned dormitories, called 'hostels,' and received about $40 a week in salary).

Before Robinson became manager of the Wesselton mine he had worked at one of the Anglo-owned gold mines. The mining level there was more than one mile below the surface of the earth, and the temperature of the walls in the cramped tunnels reached 120 degrees Fahrenheit. Unlike kimberlite, which when loosened flows by gravity into the mining tunnels, gold ore must be chiseled out of bedrocks with picks and drills. 'The seam at times was no wider than a pencil line, and there were literally thousands of men chipping away at it,' he said. 'There are more workers in a single gold mine than in all the De Beers diamond mines in South Africa.'

When we returned to the surface, I was momentarily blinded by the glare of the sun. It was also at least thirty degrees warmer above ground than below. We then took another elevator to the top of the tower of the mine shaft, which was about ten stories high. From this vantage point, the entire history of the mine could be clearly seen.

Robinson pointed to a yawning pit, almost 500 feet deep, across the parched earth. It was the original mine. Like all pipe mines, the Wesselton had begun as an open-pit mine. At some point it became too deep to haul out the kimberlite ore profitably. 'The only way it could be mined,' Robinson said, 'was to get the ore out from below.'

The half-mile-deep mine I had just visited was below that open pit. The continous belt of buckets dumped the ore from the shaft onto the conveyor belt.

At Wesselton, according to Robinson, more than 6000 tons of kimberlite ore is brought up the mine shaft every day by this automated equipment. Yet there are only some 1400 carats of diamonds recovered from this mass of ore. Of these, only about 150 carats are of gem quality. 'More diamonds are recovered per ton from the waste dumps than from the mines,' he said, pointing to the mountains of kimberlite ore that had been spewed out of the separation plants over the years.

Some of this waste was more than a hundred years old.

Diamonds smaller than a tenth of a carat were difficult to sell then, and De Beers had not invested until recently in sophisticated technology for recovering a high proportion of the minute diamonds. Now, however, with factories in India polishing diamonds as small as 1/25th of a carat, there was a ready market for these 'small goods.'

Even with the 'mining' of the old dumps, Robinson admitted that the Wesselton and the other mines around Kimberley were rapidly reaching the point of diminishing returns. He estimated that the De Beers mines in Kimberley would begin to run out of gem diamonds some time in the 1980s. Kimberley might then become a ghost town.

It was here that the diamond invention was devised, and the inseparable connection between Kimberley and De Beers is still evident when one walks through the town. The zig-zagging streets follow the pattern of the original mining claims. They then end abruptly in an enormous crater above which the city is precariously perched. It is about one-quarter of a mile deep and partly filled with rain water, which reflects the buildings on the edge of the city. This abyss is called the 'Big Hole,' and it is what remains of the Kimberley Central Mine. This was the deepest open-pit mine ever dug. The ore was lifted out by a system of ropes and pulleys that looked like a giant spider web. Before it was finally abandoned in 1914, it produced over three and a half tons of diamonds. This flood of diamonds not only transformed Kimberley into a city, but it necessitated the creation of a global system for distributing and controlling the sale of diamonds.

The Harry Oppenheimer House is a darkly tinted glass skyscraper that stands in a private park in the center of Kimberley. Built in 1974, the entire building was designed and dedicated to a single purpose: the evaluation of uncut diamonds. The total output of all the diamond mines and diggings in South Africa and Namibia are shipped here to be sorted, classified and valued. The diamond consignments generally arrive early in the morning in armored trucks, which drive into a concrete bunker in the sub-basement of the building. The sealed containers of diamonds are then sent in a special elevator, which makes no intermediary stops, to the top floor. The seal is broken in front of witnesses, and the diamonds immersed in an acid bath to clean off any particles of dirt. After the diamonds are dried by hot-air jets, they are weighed on a highly precise electronic scale. This weight is then entered into a central computer, which will track the shipment as it moves through each stage in the sorting process.

If at any point the weight of the categories it has been divided into adds up to less than the original weight of the consignment, the computer sets off an alarm. This automatically locks the doors of the Harry Oppenheimer House. Only when the missing weight of diamonds is found will the computer permit anyone to leave the building.

Unlike gold or other precious metals, diamonds cannot be assigned a value merely by weighing them. An ounce of diamonds can be worth $100 or $100,000 depending on the quality of the diamonds. Before either a mine – or the South African tax authorities – can determine the value of the diamonds, they have to be sorted into categories according to size, shape, color and clarity. 'By the time we finish, a shipment is broken down into some two thousand different categories.'

The preliminary sorting is done by a series of ingenious machines that De Beers engineers invented specifically for this purpose. First, the diamonds are passed through a series of sieves. Diamonds too small to be cut into jewels are screened out as industrial diamonds. The remaining diamonds are then divided into sixteen different groups according to sizes that range from under .2 carat to over 1 carat.

Next, within each group, the diamonds are sorted for shape by a series of machines, which by vibrating and twisting are able to separate flat and triangular shapes from the more valuable tetrahedral-shaped diamonds. At each stage in the separation process, the resulting groups are weighed and registered into the computer.

Finally, in this rough sorting, the diamonds are fed into a series of X-ray machines, which by employing different filters are able to automatically sort the diamonds into different colors. The opaque and black diamonds, called bort, as well as the smaller brown and golden diamonds, are separated out to be crushed into industrial abrasives. The diamonds are then again reweighed and sent to the floor below for hand-sorting.

Here the gem-grade diamonds are laid out by colors on

separate tables, which have been perfectly positioned in respect to the light. A team of sorters – women in uniformly colored dresses and men in suits – then examine each diamond with a six-power jewelers' loupe to make sure that it is correctly classified. If any of the five sorters disagree in their opinion, the chief sorter, John Gie, is called in to arbitrate and make a final decision on that particular diamond.

'These are all highly skilled and trained quality controllers,' Gie explained to me. 'All are given periodic eye examinations by De Beers and are tested on their ability to match unsorted diamonds to the De Beers "sample." ' The sample contains some 240 different shades of colors and shapes which serve as a De Beers standard for sorting operations in both Kimberley and London.

After every gem diamond is checked for microscopic imperfections – which generally stem from the inclusion of a foreign mineral – representatives of the Diamond Producers Association, which represents individual producers as well as the De Beers-owned mines, are allowed to question any classification they disagree with. In fact this generally is nothing more than a formality.

'A single diamond can be examined as many as ten times,' observed Gie. When everyone has agreed on the proper classification of each diamond, the data is fed into the computer. As each diamond is finally weighed, the computer assigns a dollar value to it according to a complex formula. The computer then instantly tallies up the total value of the shipment and credits that amount to the account of the individual mine.

A small percentage of these sorted diamonds are retained at Harry Oppenheimer House and distributed to a select number of local South African dealers. All the rest of the diamonds of South Africa and Namibia are shipped in sealed containers by air to the Diamond Trading Company's headquarters in London. These consignments from Kimberley amounted to some 5,400,000 carats and accounted for about half of all the gem diamonds shipped to London.

I next followed the trail of diamonds from the sorting house in Kimberley to the Diamond Trading Company in London. The trip to the African mines had explained how diamonds were extracted from the earth but this was only a rudimentary part of the diamond invention. The crucial element in the invention was controlling the supply available to the major diamond cutters and manufacturers, and this allocation took place in London.

Part Two

The Elements of the Invention

The Rules of the Game | 6

On the special calendar that De Beers sends to some 250 chosen clients, there are ten circled days on which diamonds are distributed. On these designated dates, the clients, who own diamond-cutting factories in New York, Tel Aviv, Bombay, Antwerp and Hong Kong, come to Number Two Charterhouse Street in London to attend what is called in the trade a 'sight.' These occasions, which occur every five weeks, involve the transfer of a preselected number of diamonds from the De Beers stockpile to the diamond-cutting industry around the world.

The block-long building at Number Two Charterhouse Street is the headquarters of the Diamond Trading Company. Its four-story-deep vault holds virtually the entire world supply of uncut diamonds. As clients arrive at the fortresslike entrance, they are met by uniformed commissionaires and are escorted to a reception room on the second floor. One by one, the clients are shown to private viewing rooms. These rooms, which all face the northern light, are equipped with an electronic scale for weighing diamonds, a magnifying glass for evaluating the quality of the uncut stones, and a telephone for consulting associates.

After a brief wait, a guard delivers a small cardboard box to each room, weighs the contents on the scale, and then leaves. Inside the box are a number of paper envelopes containing uncut diamonds that look like bits of broken glass. The type, quality, and exact weight of each diamond is marked on the outside of the envelope. On a sheet of paper accompanying the box is the price of the diamonds. The price of a diamond is heavily dependent on its quality. A discolored flat diamond weighing one carat may be worth no more than $50; but a flawless, colorless, octahedron diamond of the same weight may be worth $10,000. The price tag for the entire box may vary between $1 million and $25 million.

In these 200-odd shoeboxes are almost all the diamonds that will eventually be sold in engagement rings and other jewelry throughout the world. The determination of who gets which diamonds in their shoeboxes completely shapes and orders the multibillion-dollar diamond business. The man who makes this decision at Number Two Charterhouse Street is E. M. Charles, a tall, gray-haired man who everyone in the trade calls Monty.

Monty Charles has been close to the Oppenheimer family since he was a child. In the 1930s, his father owned an inn at Brae that was a favorite weekend retreat of Otto Oppenheimer, an uncle of Harry's, who was then the director of the Diamond Trading Company in London. Oppenheimer took a liking to young Monty Charles and persuaded him to come to London to work for him as a sorter of diamonds. When the Second World War began, Monty Charles enlisted in the British Army. Soon afterward he was captured by the Japanese and forced to take part in the infamous death march. He was one of the few British officers who survived the ordeal.

In 1945, he was released from a Japanese prisoner-of-war camp. When he returned to England, he was again employed by the Oppenheimers at the Diamond Trading Company. A hard, determined man, he rose within years to the position of managing director. Nominally, he worked under Sir Philip Oppenheimer – Otto's cousin – but as far as most of the clients were concerned, Monty Charles was their court of last appeal.

Before each sight takes place, Monty Charles has to decide how many diamonds of each quality will be distributed in all, and then how this supply will be divided up among the different clients. To begin with, before each sight is held, Monty Charles must himself have a dependable picture of the world demand for diamonds. A full-time staff of economists and researchers are employed by the Diamond Trading Company to track such crucial indicators as the rate of family formation in the United States and Japan, economic conditions in each country, and the amount of income after taxes that might be available to diamond markets. From this data, the demand for diamonds is determined. Next, market analysts calculate the number of diamonds that jewelry stores, wholesalers and diamond cutters already have in inventory in the 'pipeline,' as the route all diamonds between De Beers and retailers take is called. N. W. Ayer, the cartel's advertising agency, assists here by surveying retail stores and asking in telephone interviews about the quantities of diamonds that they have on hand. A group of Diamond Trading Company executives are responsible for making regional assessments. In putting together these regional assessments, the executives also receive continuous data from De Beers' partially owned subsidiaries in Israel, Belgium, India and Portugal.

Through this private intelligence system, the Diamond Trading Company is able to ascertain the categories of diamonds that are either in short supply or are a glut on the market. In 1978, for example, small yellow diamonds were found to be in excess supply. They were omitted from the boxes for the sights in 1979.

About ten days before the scheduled sight, the staff makes a final determination of the total number of diamonds that should be distributed in each category. The sorters then take this quantity of diamonds out of the vault and lay them out on tables, according to size, shape and color, in the sorting room on the third floor of the Diamond Trading Company. The massive display of glittering diamonds is truly extraordinary: when, for example, I was shown around the sorting room in January 1979, there were more than a quarter-billion dollars' worth of gem diamonds heaped onto the tables.

Moving among these tables strewn with diamonds, Monty Charles and his staff decide which clients are to receive which diamonds. About a month before a sight takes place, clients submit requests for the number and types of diamonds they want. Most clients receive, however, not what they asked for but what Monty Charles decides to give them. There are, after all, only a limited number of really lucrative diamonds distributed at each sight, and those clients who receive a large share of them will prosper – and be able to expand their businesses. For the major diamond dealers, the objective is to increase the allocation of diamonds that they receive in their shoebox at each sight. It is, as one dealer put it, 'the name of the game.' But it is Monty Charles who spells out the rules of the game.

The first rule: *No one may question the authority of the Diamond Trading Company to decide who gets which diamonds.* Monty Charles, as director of the operation, must be accepted as the sole arbiter of both the number and quality of the diamonds placed in each box. Since the number of uncut diamonds a manufacturer receives roughly determines his volume of business, and the quality of diamonds determines his profitability, the allocation of diamonds is a crucial factor in surviving in the diamond business. Yet no client may request a larger – or smaller – consignment of diamonds than he receives. Nor may he seek redress from the Oppenheimers or any higher executive of De Beers. Monty Charles's decision is final.

The second rule: *There shall be no haggling over price.* The price for each of the 2000 classifications of diamonds is fixed by De Beers, and determines how much money the mines in Africa and Siberia will be credited for the diamonds they shipped to the Diamond Trading Company. De Beers can change the price at will, without any advance notice, or add a 'surcharge,' as it did in 1977 and 1978. Since the price that De Beers charges its clients at sights is usually at least 25 per cent below the wholesale price for uncut diamonds, the privilege of being invited to a sight is worth about one-quarter of the value of the box. Even when wholesale diamond prices are depressed, clients are still expected to pay the fixed price, which may be above prevailing market prices. This is the price for admittance to future sights. If a client refuses to pay this price, he may not receive an invitation to future sights. For example, when wholesale prices fell in the 1974 recession, Baumgold Brothers, which was then one of the three largest distributors of diamonds in the United States, refused to pay more than the market price for its box of diamonds. Joseph Baumgold, the president of the firm, believed that because of the size of his company and because his family had always dealt loyally with De Beers, his firm would not be cut off from its source of supply. He explained to Monty Charles that he could not afford to cut these diamonds and sell them without suffering a huge loss. Nor could his firm afford to tie up capital and keep these diamonds in inventory until the price rose. When

Charles refused to lower the price, Baumgold rejected the box of diamonds. For the next few years, Baumgold Brothers was not invited to another sight. They had to lay off workers, close factories and forgo profits. When Baumgold Brothers was finally allowed to attend another sight, it found that Monty Charles had filled its box with low-quality diamonds that were only marginally profitable to cut.

The third rule: *Take the entire box or none at all.* Diamond mines produce diamonds of all sizes, shapes, colors and clarities. Some diamonds, such as the octahedron-shaped clear stones, are relatively easy and profitable to cut and polish into jewels. Other diamonds, such as the twisted crystals called macles, require enormously skilled labor and yield low profits. If manufacturers were allowed to choose only the more profitable diamonds in their box, De Beers would be left with all the unprofitable diamonds. Monty Charles therefore arranges a 'series' of diamonds for each client in which the less profitable diamonds are mixed in with the more profitable gems. Under no circumstances may clients pick from this series the diamonds they want. They must accept all – or none.

The fourth rule: *No client may resell the diamonds in his box in their uncut form without a special dispensation from Monty Charles.* To maintain its international monopoly over the supply of diamonds, De Beers must control the world stockpile of uncut diamonds. If it permitted its clients to resell their boxes, some outside party could amass its own stockpile by bidding for the boxes. This actually occurred in 1977, when Israeli dealers paid a premium of up to 100 per cent to De Beers clients for their unopened boxes. Many clients, seeing the opportunity to double their money overnight, took advantage of this windfall. The result was that by 1978 the stockpile in Israel was rapidly approaching in size De Beers' own stockpile in London. If the Israelis suddenly panicked and threw their uncut diamonds on the market, the price would collapse. If the Israelis continued to amass diamonds, they would be in a position to offer their own 'sights,' and undercut the mechanism De Beers had invented for controlling the market. De Beers succeeded in gradually forcing the diamonds out of Israeli hands in 1979. To prevent a recurrence, Monty Charles insisted that clients must immediately cut and polish all the diamonds supplied to them in their boxes and then return the cardboard container to ensure that no one was selling their sealed box. He dramatically demonstrated that violators of this edict would be severely punished by purging some forty clients from the sights for reselling some of their uncut diamonds. This retribution was not lost on the other clients.

In some cases, a select number of clients are permitted to act as subdistributors for De Beers and resell their diamonds to small cutting factories. Clients with such a dispensation are given what is called a 'dealer's sight' (as opposed to a 'manufacturer's sight'). They are expected to sell uncut diamonds only to trustworthy manufacturers, and are held accountable for any leakage of their diamonds into private stockpiles.

The fifth rule: *Clients will supply De Beers with whatever information it needs to assess the diamond market.* Before attending a sight, a client must fill out a detailed questionnaire, specifying the number of uncut diamonds he has in inventory, the number of diamonds in the process of being cut, the number of diamonds previously sold, and all other relevant details of his business. He further estimates his future sales in each category. This data is processed through the computer at Charterhouse Street and helps provide a clear picture of the number of diamonds in the pipeline. The entire system requires that no more diamonds be released from the stockpile than the public can absorb.

Indeed, to make sure that its clients are not secretly disposing of or privately stockpiling diamonds, the Diamond Trading Company requires that they submit to a 'diamond audit.' In this procedure, a De Beers representative pays a surprise visit to a client's cutting factory to see the financial records, the actual inventory of diamonds, machinery, and employees at work. He then makes his own estimate of how many diamonds the client is cutting per month. If this tally does not square with the number of diamonds the client had received at the London sights, the discrepancy is reported back to Monty Charles.

Aside from the penalties that it can impose at will, De Beers also provides more positive incentives to clients who support the system by using the 'carat and schtick' approach, as one Israeli client joked. Not only can the assortment of diamonds be arbitrarily upgraded for a favored client but

Monty Charles can also add very lucrative 'large stones' to a box. These larger diamonds can usually be resold for a windfall profit.

The sights in London thus are not merely occasions for major gem manufacturers to select the uncut diamonds that they wish to purchase but an integral part of the mechanism through which De Beers establishes and maintains the value of diamonds. Through these ten events a year, De Beers extends its control from the diamond mines of Africa to the cutting factories of Belgium, Israel, India and the United States. And through its clients – whose fortunes depend heavily on the contents of the shoeboxes they receive – De Beers is able to monitor and regulate the flow of diamonds that pass through the world pipeline into the retail market. The stakes are indisputably high: at the ten sights in 1980, for example, De Beers distributed more than $2 billion worth of uncut diamonds that would eventually be resold in the retail market for more than $8 billion.

7 | The Empire Builders

In July 1980, a black crowd armed with whips and mallets toppled the bronze statue of Cecil John Rhodes from its pedestal in Salisbury, Zimbabwe. The caption of the Associated Press photograph of the event read, 'Symbol of Colonialism Toppled in Zimbabwe.' Rhodes was the only man in history to have two nations and a federation named after him – Rhodesia (now Zimbabwe), Northern Rhodesia (now Zambia) and the Rhodesian Federation (which had included Malawi, Zambia and Zimbabwe). In less than ten years, under the royal charter granted to him by the British government, he had colonized millions of square miles of the richest part of southern and eastern Africa. This territorial empire proved ephemeral – not even his bronze statue lasted out the century. He created another empire, De Beers, which endured far better than all the Rhodesias.

Rhodes arrived in the port of Durban in South Africa in September 1871. He was then a gangly boy of eighteen with a long face that made him appear taller than he was. He spoke with a squeaky voice that disconcerted other passengers on the boat.

He had left England and traveled to South Africa because of his failing health. He had a collapsed lung and a weak heart, and his doctor predicted that he would not live to the age of twenty-one. His father, a poor vicar in Hertfordshire, sent him on this voyage so that if he did not miraculously recover he would at least die peacefully in a warm climate. His total stake in the world, a gift from his aunt, was £2000.

Rhodes was possessed by a dream. He wanted to extend the British Empire throughout the world. In a will he drew up several years later, he directed that whatever money he had acquired be used to form a secret society that would attempt, among other things, to bring the United States back under British rule. He also envisioned building a railroad from Capetown, at the southern tip of Africa, to Cairo, at the other end of the continent. The railroad, like all his other economic schemes, was only a means to an end as he had no interest in wealth. The end was colonizing the entire eastern coast of Africa, from Capetown to Cairo, for the British Empire.

As he believed that his life was not destined to be a long or healthy one, he set out immediately to acquire the capital to realize his grandiose ambitions. A year earlier, diamonds had been discovered near the Orange River on the edge of the great Karoo Desert in South Africa. Never before had diamonds been found in Africa, and fortune hunters from all over the world were converging on this spot. His older brother Herbert, who was a prosperous cotton grower in Natal province, had already staked out a number of small claims. Rhodes decided to join his brother and the diamond rush.

He hired an oxcart for the rugged trip to the diamond fields, which took a month of traveling across open veldt. He bought a pick, shovel, and other prospecting gear in Durban, and as he was also preparing himself for the entrance examinations for Oxford, he took along with him a set of the Greek classics.

His brother's claims were on a farm owned by two brothers, D. A. and J. N. De Beer. The De Beer brothers were Boer settlers, interested in farming, not diamonds. They sold off their land to the swarm of prospectors and moved on, leaving behind only their name: De Beers.

When Rhodes arrived at the De Beers' farm, he found the diamond rush in full frenzy. After setting up his canvas tent, he wrote to this mother, 'I would like you to have a peep . . . from my tent door at the present moment. . . . Imagine a small round hill, at its highest point only 30 feet above the level of the surrounding country, about 180 yards broad and 120 feet long; all round it a mass of white tents.' He added, 'It is like an immense number of ant heaps covered with black ants as thick as can be; the latter represented by human beings.'

This encampment, which was occupied by some 50,000 fortune hunters, was the second most populous 'city' in the whole subcontinent of southern Africa. Within the next couple of years, the tents were replaced by corrugated iron shacks brought by oxcart from Capetown, and the city was named Kimberley in honor of Lord Kimberley, the British secretary of state for the colonies.

For Rhodes, however, Kimberley remained a human ant-hill. When his brother's claim yielded only meager results, he decided that immediate profits were not in mining but in servicing the needs of the multitude of 'ants' who were pouring into Kimberley by the thousand each week. He began his enterprise by importing ice cream, and then jugs of water, which he sold to the thirsty diggers.

He realized that water was a two-fold problem for the claim owners. On the one hand, they needed an ever increasing amount of fresh water for their black laborers as they dug deeper into the ground for diamonds. On the other hand, the seepage of ground water into the mines, as the diggers approached the water table, was threatening to collapse the dirt walls of the mines. There were thousands of adjacent mines surrounding Kimberley, and the owners needed a means of pumping the water out. Rhodes saw an opportunity for making a windfall fortune.

He reckoned that soon a steam-powered pump would be needed to suck the water out of the mine. No such machine existed in Kimberley. In fact, there was only one steam pump in all of South Africa. Seizing the opportunity, Rhodes invested all the money he had in buying it.

No sooner had Rhodes' steam pump arrived in Kimberley than a torrent of water flooded the Kimberley Big Hole mine. As the walls began to collapse, the thousands of black workers in the mine had to be pulled out with ropes. The individual claim owners, who each owned various sections of the floor of the mine, desperately needed Rhodes' pump – and they had no choice but to pay whatever he demanded.

Rhodes reinvested the money he made in ordering bigger and better steam pumps from England. He then ruthlessly drove whatever competition existed out of his business. His would-be competitors charged him with sabotaging their pumps; but he established a water-pumping monopoly in all the mines around Kimberley.

As he progressively raised the charges for his pumps, the

small owners, and even syndicates, could not afford to pay him in cash. Instead, he took from them a share of the mines. He gradually squeezed them for a larger and larger proportion until, at the age of twenty-seven, he was the largest mine owner in Kimberley.

Rhodes himself had no interest in using this wealth to increase his personal amenities. He shared a tiny one-room shack with a business associate. He wrote that the 'chief good in life' was not for him a happy marriage, great wealth, or interesting travel, but 'the absorption of the greatest portion of the world under [British] rule.' In between his sharp dealings in Kimberley, Rhodes managed to find time to take a degree at Oriel College, Oxford. Here John Ruskin's lectures on the virtues of imperialism renewed his ambition to colonize Africa.

Returning to Kimberley, he merged his interests with two large mining syndicates to form the De Beers Mining Company. He held the controlling block of stock in this new company and applied to the Colonial Office in London for a charter. It was granted in 1880, and was unlike any other charter ever given to a mining company. Under its terms, Rhodes' company was not confined to mining. It could build railroads, lay telegraph wires, annex territories, raise armies and install governments. Since the East India Company had been established in the seventeenth century, no company had ever been granted such unrestricted powers. It was all part of Rhodes' dream of empire.

As the Kimberley mines kept spewing out tons of diamonds, the price of diamonds fluctuated wildly, and then, as diamond merchants were unable to absorb these quantities, the price dropped to a few shillings a carat. Mines closed, and claims were abandoned. Rhodes wrote in a letter that diamonds were on the verge of becoming a 'frightful drug' on the market unless production was brought under control. To accomplish this, he proposed a new grand design for Kimberley: the amalgamation of all the other mining companies into his De Beers Company. Most of the other mine owners were willing to be bought out by Rhodes. One was not. His name was Barney Barnato.

Barnato, like Rhodes, was an English subject. He had been born on 5 July 1852, in the East End of London. By coincidence, it was the same day, but one year later, that

Rhodes was born; but here the similarity between the two men ended. Barnato came from a Jewish slum, and instead of attending school, he had to eke out a living on the street selling rags and performing magic tricks for children. His real name was Barney Isaacs, but he changed it to 'Barnato' so that he could join his brother in a music hall act. The name stuck.

Barnato arrived in Kimberley in 1873. He was twenty-one years old, and had in his possession £30 in English currency and forty boxes of defective cigars. He proceeded to sell the cigars to the diggers in the diamond fields. He also gave boxing exhibitions, performed in a cabaret and traded everything from feathers to garden vegetables. The most profitable trading commodity proved, however, to be diamonds.

Walking from digging to digging, Barnato bought diamonds for cash and quickly resold them. With his profits, he bought up a number of unproductive claims on the floor of the Big Hole. Then, to everyone's amazement, these claims began yielding extraordinary quantities of diamonds, even when rainstorms made working the adjacent claims impossible. Barnato was accused by other mine owners of having salted his claim with diamonds that he had illegally bought from smugglers and thieves. Barnato heatedly denied the charges, which in any case were impossible to prove.

Whatever the provenance of these diamonds, Barnato continued to expand his production. With the money he sold them for, he began buying up, piece by piece, the patchwork of claims on the floor of the Big Hole. When cave-ins made it impossible to dig any deeper in the Big Hole, mine owners rushed in panic to sell their claims. Barnato continued to buy these pieces of the jigsaw puzzle. Then, in 1883, he gambled on sinking an underground shaft – the first ever attempted for diamond mining. It worked, and the claims he had bought for a pittance became worth a fortune. Just as Rhodes had gained control of the De Beers mine, Barnato got control over most of the Kimberley Central mine.

Rhodes and Barnato – both in their mid-thirties – dominated, by 1887, the world's two giant diamond mines. A confrontation between these enormously ambitious men became inevitable. Rhodes, if he was ever to have his empire, had to buy out Barnato. He made the first move, attempting, with financial banking from the Rothschild bank in London, to buy one of the few pieces in the Kimberley mine that Barnato did not own. He offered the then staggering sum of £1,400,000 to the French financiers who owned it, not because the diamonds in it were worth that sum but because it would paralyze Barnato's effort to consolidate the Big Hole into a single mine.

When Barnato received word of Rhodes' bold offer, he himself offered £1,750,000 to the French financiers for this crucial section. He had no choice but to outbid his rival.

Rhodes, at this point, decided to offer Barnato a deal that would seem too lucrative for him to refuse. Instead of bidding up the price, which would only benefit the French investors, Rhodes suggested that Barnato withdraw his bid. In return, Rhodes agreed to buy this section of the mine at the lower price and then immediately resell it to Barnato for £300,000 and a one-fifth interest in Barnato's Kimberley Central mine.

Barnato immediately accepted the offer. It permitted him to acquire the section for £1,450,000 less than he had offered, and with it, he could operate the mine as a single entity. He realized that giving Rhodes a one-fifth interest in his mine would provide him with a bothersome wedge into his company, but he assumed that he and his close associates still owned a sufficient number of shares to make it impossible for Rhodes to attempt to gain control. Barnato made the fatal mistake of underestimating Rhodes' boundless ambitions.

To Rhodes, the deal was only the opening gambit in his war for control. You can never deal with obstinate people until you get the whip hand,' he explained to an associate at the time. The one-fifth interest was to be his whip.

Rhodes set about asking the most powerful bankers in Europe, including Rothschild, Jules Porges, and Rodolphe Khan, to help him buy enough stock in Barnato's company to allow him to merge it into his own. He argued that as long as there were competing diamond mines, the market would continually be flooded. Then prices would fall to pennies, and soon the public would realize that diamonds had no intrinsic value.

The bankers were quickly persuaded that Rhodes was

right: diamond mining would only remain profitable if it were done by a monopoly that could systematically restrict the supply. They not only agreed to use the stock that they and their clients held in Barnato's mine to bring about the merger but they also advanced Rhodes money to buy up shares of Barnato's stock on the open market.

The rest simply required an exercise in stock manipulation. Rhodes first drove the price of diamonds down by having De Beers dump its inventory of diamonds. The price of diamond stocks plummeted, and as soon as many of Barnato's associates unloaded their stock, Rhodes bought it. When no more stock was available, Rhodes and his backers began again bidding up the price, which tripled in three months. By the time Barnato realized that Rhodes was attempting to buy up his company, it was too late. By March 1888, Rhodes and his associates had acquired the additional 30 per cent they needed for control of the Kimberley Central mine.

Barnato had no choice but to acquiesce in the proposed merger. He met Rhodes at the Kimberley Club, and over an amicable lunch they worked out the terms of the consolidation. Barnato would exchange his stock in the Kimberley Central mine for stock in De Beers Consolidated Mines, as the new company would be called. This would make Barnato the largest single shareholder, though Rhodes, with his bankers and allies, would be firmly in control of the new company. Barnato would also be appointed one of four life governors of the monopoly – a position he would hold as long as he lived. The two men then shook hands on the deal. Barnato told him, Rhodes later noted, 'You evidently have a fancy for building an empire in the north and I suppose we must give you the means to do so.'

There were still, however, some dissident shareholders in the Kimberley Central Company who opposed the merger. They sued Barnato and Rhodes, claiming in court that the new company would no longer be a mining company but an adventure in imperialism. They argued that under the De Beers charter the company might 'undertake warlike operations' in central Africa.

To prevent further litigation, Rhodes and Barnato, who

between them controlled four-fifths of the stock in the Kimberley Central mine, simply liquidated the company and sold its assets to De Beers. The £5,338,650 check that De Beers paid for the assets was framed and hung on the wall of the De Beers boardroom, where it is still conspicuously displayed.

Rhodes then proceeded to buy up two other small pipe mines in the Kimberley area – the Duitspan and Bulfontain. By 1890, he controlled more than 95 per cent of the world's diamond production. The next order of business was restoring the balance between world supply and demand. Rhodes believed that the demand for diamonds was determined by the number of 'licit relationships,' as he termed engagements, between the sexes each year. By estimating the intended marriages each year in the United States, which was then the main market for diamonds, Rhodes believed it was possible to project the market for diamonds each year. In accordance with this 'licit relationship' calculus, he began to reduce production in Kimberley from three to two million carats a year.

Rhodes further held that there should be a single channel of distribution of diamonds. He therefore contracted to sell De Beers' entire production to a London syndicate of diamond merchants, who would then resell the diamonds to cutters in Antwerp.

Once the diamond business was rationally ordered into a monopoly, Rhodes moved on to the matter of restoring the British Empire. He was elected prime minister of the Cape Colony and organized a military putsch, aimed at taking over the Transvaal from the Boer settlers, that failed. Rhodes did, however, succeed in colonizing a large portion of central Africa.

Barnato, who by now was one of the richest men in the world, returned to the music hall and acted in a number of amateur productions in Kimberley. Then, in 1897, on an ocean liner back to England, he either jumped or fell overboard and disappeared beneath a wave.

Rhodes died four years later at the age of forty-nine. His body was buried on a remote mountaintop in Rhodesia. He had never married and he had no heirs. He left almost his entire fortune to Oxford to finance future Rhodes scholars.

At De Beers there was no immediate successor to Rhodes, but the vacuum would not remain unfilled for long. Within a year of Rhodes' death another young entrepreneur arrived in South Africa. His name was Ernest Oppenheimer.

The Jewish Connection | 8

The syndicate in London to which Rhodes contracted to sell De Beers' entire production of diamonds in 1893 was made up of ten firms. These were Wernher, Beit & Company, Barnato Brothers, Mosenthal Sons & Company, A. Dunkelsbuhler, Joseph Brothers, I. Cohen & Company, Martin Lilienfeld & Company, F. F. Gervers, S. Neumann and Feldheimer & Company. All these firms were interconnected by marriage and family ties, and all were owned by Jewish merchants. The fact that Jewish companies completely dominated the distribution of diamonds at the end of the nineteenth century was not particularly surprising. For a thousand years, diamonds had been almost entirely a Jewish business.

Until the early part of the eighteenth century, the entire world supply of diamonds came from India. The caravans that brought them across Arabia traded these rare stones to Jewish traders in Aden and Cairo for gold and silver. The traders then resold them to Jewish merchants in Venice, Lithuania and Frankfurt. It was a natural enterprise for the Jews scattered throughout central Europe. Since they were moneylenders, they had to concern themselves with assessing, repairing and selling gems that had been offered to them as collateral for loans. They also had close connections with the Jewish trading centers in the Ottoman Empire through which all the Indian diamonds passed.

The cutting and polishing of diamonds, moreover, was one of the few crafts that Jews were permitted to participate in by the medieval guilds in Europe. For most Jews, there was no choice in those days. If they wanted to have a vocation, it had to be either gem-polishing or moneylending. In either case they dealt with diamonds.

In the sixteenth century, when the Portuguese succeeded

in establishing an ocean route to India, the caravan routes were supplanted by ships. The Jews in Portugal, who were mainly Sephardic (i.e. non-European) Jews, quickly made arrangements in Lisbon for ships' officers to buy diamonds directly from the Indian miners in Goa. Lisbon became the main entry point in Europe for diamonds, and Jewish entrepreneurs set up cutting factories in both Lisbon and Antwerp. They employed the poorer Ashkenazi Jews from Eastern Europe as cutters and polishers in these factories. Until nearly the end of the sixteenth century, the diamond industry thrived in Portugal.

During the Inquisition, diamonds proved to be an invaluable asset for the Jews. Unlike almost any other asset, they were small enough to be concealed on the body; and they were also instantly redeemable for money in any country in Europe. For the Jewish people, who lived for centuries in constant fear of expulsion from their homes, diamonds became a logical means of storing and preserving wealth.

When the Jewish diamond merchants and workers were forced by the Inquisition to flee from Lisbon and Antwerp, they resettled in Amsterdam. Since cutting factories required no equipment except for tools, which were portable, and skilled labor, the Jews instantly transformed Amsterdam into the diamond center of Europe. By the middle of the seventeenth century, Jewish diamond merchants helped finance the Dutch East India Company, which organized its own trade route to India. Amsterdam then replaced Lisbon as the port of entry in Europe for India's diamonds.

Just as the fields in India began to cease yielding diamonds, more were discovered in 1725 in Brazil. The Dutch maneuvered to gain control of this traffic, but now they had to contend with the rise of British sea power. By the mid-eighteenth century, the British had almost completely taken over the trade in diamonds, both from India and Brazil. As the trading center for uncut diamonds shifted from Amsterdam to London, so did the Jewish diamond merchants. In England, they were granted licenses to import uncut diamonds, and they quickly organized a triangular trade in silver, coral, and diamonds. Silver was exported to Leghorn, Italy, where the proceeds from the sales were used to buy coral; the coral was then imported into England and the proceeds used to buy diamonds from Brazil and India. The

Jewish traders sent the diamonds to cutting factories that had been re-established in Antwerp, and from there the jewels were sold to all the royal courts of Europe. To select and evaluate these diamonds, the courts chose Jewish gem experts, who became known as 'Court Jews.' In Sweden, it was the Isaac family; in Hamburg, it was the Lippold family; in Vienna, it was the Oppenheimer family.

According to the records of the British East India Company, Jewish traders controlled virtually the entire world diamond traffic by the end of the eighteenth century. The Brazilian fields, however, were becoming rapidly depleted of diamonds, and no more diamonds were coming out of India. Just as it appeared that the world might run out of diamonds, the South African mines were discovered in the 1860s.

The ten leading Jewish merchants in London, fearing that the market would be flooded with South African diamonds, quickly formed a syndicate to buy up all the production from these new mines. A number of the merchants in this syndicate had also acquired large stock holdings in the De Beers monopoly itself. One of the merchants who took the lead in arranging the deal with Cecil Rhodes was A. Dunkelsbuhler. Dunkelsbuhler brought into his London company a young apprentice from Friedberg, Germany, named Ernest Oppenheimer who would complete the diamond invention.

When Ernest Oppenheimer joined Dunkelsbuhler, he was only sixteen years old. He came from a large German Jewish family and had two brothers and three cousins who worked in the diamond syndicate. Thus, even as he began as a junior clerk in Dunkelsbuhler's London office, Oppenheimer was well connected in the diamond world.

He began by sorting rough diamonds, under the supervision of his brother Louis. Louis Oppenheimer not only managed Dunkelsbuhler in London but also coordinated the pricing and classification of diamonds in all the other firms in the syndicate. During this period, Ernest Oppenheimer read and reread all the correspondence that came in from Dunkelsbuhler's representative in Kimberley. Almost from the beginning, he had his heart set on going to the diamond fields, according to a memoir by a diamond sorter who worked with him in 1900. 'Ernest had bought a sixpenny book, in which he carefully noted, meticulously ordered, everything that might be conceivably of some use to him,' the sorter, Etienne Fallek, later recalled.

Finally, in 1902, his brother dispatched Ernest to South Africa to run Dunkelsbuhler's small buying office in Kimberley. His salary was £500 a year. He was in many ways the prototype of the multinational businessman: German by birth, British by naturalization, Jewish by religion, and South African by residence.

He usually wore a white starched collar, a dark tie and a long frock coat. He rarely spoke to his fellow workers and he always kept his notebook at his side. Although some of the other sorters in the office simply assumed that he was a compulsive scribbler, Oppenheimer was in fact preparing a detailed analysis of the diamond-mining business. He had an excellent vantage point. Diamonds poured into the office from all the mines in Africa and were graded according to their size, shape, color and quality. By studying the records in the office, he was able to determine both the special characteristics and profitability of the production of each mine. He also traveled to the independent diggings around the Orange River to buy diamonds and evaluate claims for Dunkelsbuhler. It was all part of his education in the diamond business.

In 1908, his cousin Frederick Hirschhorn became the syndicate's chief representative in Kimberley. Oppenheimer, who was close to his cousin, spent considerable time in the syndicate's sorting room. Here he became familiar with the way in which the diamonds were divided among the members of the syndicate and the particular categories of diamonds that the various syndicate members preferred.

Oppenheimer's initial success in acquiring capital came, however, from gold rather than diamond mines. A group of German investors, who were clients of Dunkelsbuhler, wanted to invest in gold properties in the Transvaal, and Oppenheimer arranged for them to buy an interest in operating gold mines. In making these deals, he took for himself a small percentage of the venture, as well as an option to increase his participation at a future date.

By 1914, the Germans had sunk an enormous amount of capital into expanding these gold mines. The outbreak of the First World War made their investment increasingly precarious: Germany was, after all, now an enemy of the

British Commonwealth. Moreover, there were constant demands in the press for the expropriation of enemy assets in South Africa. As the pressure mounted on the South African government, Oppenheimer found a solution for the German investors. He personally created an international corporation in which the German interest could be subtly diffused with those of investors of other nationalities. He blended into this new corporation the percentages and options that he had obtained as a dealmaker and also a number of interests that had been acquired by his cousins and other relatives in South Africa.

To avoid drawing any unnecessary attention to the German investments, he proposed giving the corporation a name that would strongly suggest an 'American connection,' as Oppenheimer put it. In a letter to his associates, he wrote, 'Our aim should be for our company to make its debut as a "new" factor in South Africa finance.' After considering the name United South Africa Company, which would be purposely abbreviated to USA Company, and then Afro-American Company, they finally decided on the title Anglo-American Corporation, which sounded very much like the Anglo-American alliance that was then winning the war. The mask seemed to work – at least with the South African press: when the new corporation was announced in September 1917, the *Rand Daily Mail* proclaimed in a headline, 'American Millions for the Rand.'

After establishing his corporation, Oppenheimer quickly shifted his attention from gold back to diamonds. As early as 1910, he had concluded in a memorandum that 'the only way to increase the value of diamonds is to make them scarce, that is, to reduce production.' He believed that De Beers could bring about such scarcity but only if it expanded its reach beyond the borders of South Africa. He viewed control of the South African mines as a necessary, but not sufficient, condition for a completely effective diamond monopoly.

After Rhodes' death, the management of De Beers had predicated its monopoly on the proposition that there would be no major new discoveries of diamonds. When a bricklayer named Thomas M. Cullinan claimed to have discovered diamonds in a huge oval of yellow dirt some 600 miles north of Kimberley, De Beers geologists scoffed at the idea of diamond pipes existing outside the Kimberley area. Francis Oats, who had succeeded Rhodes as head of De Beers, went so far as to declare that 'the whole thing was a fake,' and suggested to De Beers' stockholders that the mine, which had been named the Premier mine, had been 'salted' with diamonds from the Kimberley area. It quickly turned out that Oats had been wrong: the Premier was a diamond pipe, larger than any other found in the world, and four times the size of Kimberley's Big Hole mine. When the news was conveyed to Alfred Beit, who along with Rhodes and Barnato had been a life governor of De Beers, he had a heart attack from which he never recovered. Cullinan himself was prepared to fight another diamond war rather than sell out to De Beers. To raise capital for this mine, he sold a majority interest to the Transvaal government. Fortunately for De Beers, the British had just triumphed over the Boer settlers in the Transvaal in the so-called Boer War, and they were able to pressure the Transvaal into coming to terms with De Beers.

Before Oppenheimer could achieve this world monopoly, he first, of course, had to get control of De Beers. The device he used to win a dominant position in De Beers was very similar to the one used by Rhodes a generation earlier. He acquired a diamond property for Anglo-American that De Beers desperately needed to maintain its monopoly. He then offered to exchange the property for a substantial number of shares in De Beers itself. This property was in the German colony of South-West Africa (now Namibia).

The first diamond was found there by a railroad worker in 1908 and identified as such by August Stauch, the railroad station master in Luderetz. Then it was discovered that the entire stretch of beach behind the Namibian desert was strewn with diamonds. Laborers who had been working on the railroad were quickly transferred to the Namibian beaches where they were lined up and forced to crawl on their hands and knees sifting through the sand for diamonds. The laborers were gagged by the Germans to prevent them from putting the diamonds in their mouths and stealing them. Whenever they found a diamond it was dropped in a tin that the German guards carried with them.

When the Germans realized that they had broken the British monopoly on diamonds, the colonial authorities immediately ordered the entire beach sealed off into a *Sperrgebiet,* or forbidden zone, and consigned all the diamonds found there to a German syndicate called the 'Diamond Regie.' As the extent of this discovery became clear to South African officials in Capetown, the prime minister termed the German discovery 'a hideous calamity for us all.' The De Beers monopoly would certainly have been broken by the Germans with their Namibian diamonds if it had not been for the outbreak of the First World War in 1914. South African troops immediately seized the diamond beach and shut down production.

With the German investors in a state of near panic, Oppenheimer saw the possibility of staging his coup. He had personally assessed the various German properties in the forbidden zone on behalf of the London syndicate, and working through his network of cousins in Germany, he offered each of the major German investors shares in the Anglo-American Corporation for their holdings in the Namibian diamond beach. It was a deal they found difficult to reject. Since most of these Germans fully expected their assets to be expropriated by the allies for the duration of the war, they had little hope of receiving any income from them. The Oppenheimer exchange provided them with a liquid asset. Those who preferred not to accept Anglo-American stock received a cash payment. In the end, Oppenheimer acquired almost all of the German properties, which he reorganized into a company called Consolidated Diamond Mines.

Before he could complete his coup, Oppenheimer needed the permission of the South African government to transfer the seized German assets to a South African Corporation. Here he relied on the close working relationship he had with Jan Smuts, the South African prime minister. By 1919, the transfer was complete, and he had the bargaining chip he needed for dealing with De Beers.

As Oppenheimer had perceived from the beginning, De Beers could not afford to wage a diamond war against his Consolidated Diamond Mines. The beaches of Namibia held far too many diamonds for competition to prove anything but ruinous. Nor did Oppenheimer have any intention of competing with De Beers.

Instead, Oppenheimer offered the Namibian diamond

mines to De Beers in return for a large block of stock. He was immediately given a place on the board of directors and at every opportunity bought more shares of De Beers. So did his cousins. By 1927, he had become the most powerful force in the diamond monopoly. When an English peer, Lord Bessborough, was made chairman, he objected: 'I cannot imagine anything worse for De Beers. . . . One can only have influence with the government if De Beers is looked upon as a South African company, and that feeling would be entirely destroyed by making a man in London chairman.' He appealed to Lord Rothschild, whose bank still owned a large block of stock in De Beers, to support his candidacy, and in 1929 Oppenheimer became chairman of the board of De Beers. He was then knighted by the king of England for his services to the British Empire.

Whereas Rhodes had seen the diamond monopoly as a means of extending the British Empire, Oppenheimer saw it as an end in itself. He wanted to create a truly international business that owed its allegiance to no single nation. His strategy, he explained to his brother Louis in a letter, was to make De Beers 'the absolute controlling factor in the diamond world.' By 'absolute,' he meant control of each and every link in the diamond chain that led from the mines to the distribution network for diamonds. He reasoned that 'the danger to the security of the diamond industry is not the discovery of a new rich diamond field, but the irrational exploitation of it.' If De Beers could choke off the 'irrational' sale of diamonds before they reached the retail market, it could contain any temporary oversupply of diamonds that developed from new mines. It was imperative to prevent at all costs the retail price of diamonds from falling.

Oppenheimer moved quickly to consolidate his position. He merged Consolidated Diamond Mines into De Beers, and strove through his banking connections to gain additional financial support for the company. When all the complicated exchanges of stock were completed, Oppenheimer's Anglo-American Corporation emerged as the controlling shareholder in De Beers.

In 1929, the onslaught of the worldwide Depression strained the ability of the syndicate in London to continue to absorb the world's diamond production. Since the public virtually stopped buying diamonds, the syndicate had to retain almost all the diamonds mined in the world. By 1931, it was on the verge of bankruptcy, and cabled its office in Kimberley: 'No sale possible. Best offer for small quantities were well below cost price. Market quite demoralized. Inform Sir Ernest Oppenheimer.'

Oppenheimer immediately understood the gravity of the situation. The syndicate could no longer afford to keep its stockpile intact, and if it placed even a small portion of the diamonds on the market, the price would totally collapse. He further realized that this could forever destroy the public's trust in diamonds as a store of value. He had only one alternative: to take over the syndicate.

Since Oppenheimer and his relatives owned shares in three of the leading members of the syndicate, there was little resistance to the takeover. The subsequent exchange of stock in fact enhanced, rather than diluted, Oppenheimer's control of the monopoly. He put his younger brother Otto in command of the distribution arm in London, which was now called the Diamond Corporation. He then created the Diamond Trading Company, which took over the responsibility from the syndicate for allocating diamonds to manufacturers and wholesalers.

World sales had fallen to practically nothing – a mere $100,000 worth in 1932 – and Oppenheimer next moved to curtail the supply of diamonds. One by one he closed all the major mines in South Africa. Production fell from 2,242,000 carats in 1930 to 14,000 carats in 1933. He also closed the beach mines in Namibia. A confidential market analysis commissioned by De Beers, noted, 'The diamond market is exceedingly sensitive to adverse conditions and rapidly dwindles when such conditions are in the ascendant.' Prices were plunging even after the cutback in supply. According to the same report, 'During the years 1930 to 1932 there was a pronounced and steady decline in prices of approximately 50 per cent.'

Oppenheimer was able to close down his own mines, but he could not prevent newly discovered diamond mines in the Belgian Congo and Portuguese Angola from continuing to produce diamonds. Even though there was no market for these diamonds, De Beers had to continue buying them up through its Diamond Corporation in London to prevent them from being dumped on the market. To finance these diamonds, De Beers issued bonds.

By 1937, De Beers' stockpile of diamonds had grown to some forty million carats – which was, even in pre-Depression times, nearly twenty years' supply. Oppenheimer's empire, which had invested millions of dollars in borrowed money in these diamonds that could not be sold, was now itself on the verge of bankruptcy. According to one United States government report, Oppenheimer was even considering dumping several tons of these diamonds into the North Sea to prevent them from reaching the market in the event of his company being forced into liquidation by his creditors.

Oppenheimer was saved from having to implement this radical solution to the oversupply problem by the invention of the diamond grinding wheel. In essence, the wheel was a metal-grinding surface impregnated with crushed diamond powder that permitted a quantum leap in the mass production of automobiles, airplanes and machinery. Steel dies and machine tools had always been used to cut precision parts for industry. As steel blades had to be constantly honed or changed, the production of standardized parts moved at a slow pace. In the early 1930s, the Krupp Company in Germany developed a tungsten carbide alloy that was far more resistant to wear than steel. Before tungsten carbide dies and blades could be adopted by industry, however, some means had to be found for shaping them. Diamonds proved to be the only material hard enough, and the diamond-grinding wheel thus became an indispensable tool for mass production.

Instead of jettisoning the small and poorly crystallized diamonds, called bort, into the sea, De Beers began crushing them into powder, and supplying them to the automotive, aircraft and machine tool industry. With Europe re-arming for war, millions of tons of this powder could be profitably sold each year. Oppenheimer immediately saw the potential for 'industrial diamonds.'

Oppenheimer realized that controlling this vital supply of industrial diamonds was necessary to protect the power of his cartel. He was especially concerned about the Forminière Mines in the Belgian Congo, where black, poorly crystallized diamonds could be mined by the ton rather than the carat. He wrote to his son Harry: 'There can only be one policy for De Beers . . . make sure of this Congo production even if the Forminière diamonds have to be bought in addition [to crushing bort]. . . . Forminière will dictate the post-war policies of the diamond trade. By controlling the Congo production De Beers will maintain its leading position in diamonds.'

To ensure that these crucial mines in the Congo did not slip out of De Beers' control, Sir Ernest negotiated what amounted to a private treaty with the Belgian government. In return for guaranteeing that the Forminière Mines would sell all its bort to a De Beers' subsidiary in London called the Industrial Diamond Corporation, Oppenheimer agreed to provide the Belgian cutting industry with the lion's share of gem diamonds from all of De Beers' mines. London would thus have a complete monopoly on the distribution of diamond powder, and Antwerp, which employed some 20,000 cutters, would remain the preeminent center for cutting gems. Working through the Belgian banks, Oppenheimer further insured his leverage in the Congo by buying a large block of stock in a Belgian holding company called Sibeka, which owned controlling shares in the mines in the Congo. Pierre Crokaert, a Belgian financier whose family's banking interests were closely allied with those of Oppenheimer's, became a board member of De Beers and a deputy to Oppenheimer. He undertook the responsibility for regulating the production of diamonds from the Congo in accordance with the quota set by De Beers. With the completion of this arrangement with the Belgians, De Beers truly became an international cartel.

9 | Diamonds at War

The strategic importance of diamonds became acutely clear to both the Allies and Axis powers with the approach of the Second World War in 1939. Only diamonds were hard enough to stamp out the millions of precision parts that were necessary for mass-producing airplane engines, torpedoes, tanks, artillery and the other weapons of war. Only diamonds could be used to draw the fine wire needed for radar and the electronics of war. Only diamonds could provide the jeweled bearings necessary for the stabilizers, gyroscopes and guidance systems for submarines and planes. Only diamonds could provide the abrasives necessary for rapidly converting civilian industries into a war machine. Without a continuing supply of diamonds, the war machine would rapidly slow to a halt. Yet nearly all the diamond mines remained closed, and De Beers controlled the world supply of diamonds. Obtaining these industrial diamonds thus became a paramount objective for both the United States and Hitler's Germany.

In Washington, DC, the administration of President Franklin D. Roosevelt began to hold emergency meetings about diamonds in 1940 when Hilter's armies swept across Europe in a blitzkrieg and threatened to invade England. The possibility had to be at least considered that England, like France, might be overrun – or surrender. In that event, the world diamond stockpile would fall into Hitler's hands. Since the United States had less than one year's supply of industrial diamonds, the loss of De Beers' stockpile would make it difficult, if not impossible, to continue the war. The economic planners for the war estimated that the United States needed at least 6.5 million carats of industrial diamonds to convert its factories to war production.

When apprised of this critical shortage in diamonds,

President Roosevelt ordered the War Production Board, which had the responsibility for mobilizing the American economy for war, to buy the necessary 6.5 million carats from De Beers. Since the United States was supposed to be the 'arsenal of democracy' for the Allies, Roosevelt expected De Beers to honor this request.

De Beers, however, had other interests to consider. Its entire system for monopolizing diamonds depended on its controlling the available stockpile. Transferring a large portion of the stockpile from London to New York City, where it would be out of its control, ran counter to the De Beers logic.

Even though the Americans persisted in the negotiations for the diamonds, they found that Sir Ernest Oppenheimer personally opposed any transfer of diamonds to the United States. He argued that if the United States had its own stockpile, and the war suddenly ended, it might release the diamonds and undercut the entire world system that he had so laboriously constructed. Moreover, he held that the United States had sufficient diamonds for present needs, and that De Beers would continue its delivery of diamonds to American manufacturers on a monthly basis. In one letter, he characterized the American demand for a stockpile as 'farcical.'

The Americans were dismayed by this intransigence. In an official Justice Department memorandum, the War Production Board expressed incredulity at the fact that 'the leaders of the syndicate are intentionally risking the war production of the Allies.' President Roosevelt, disturbed by this development, ordered the State Department to intervene directly with Winston Churchill's war cabinet in London.

The State Department found, however, that the British government was reluctant to press De Beers to part with the diamonds. An investigation by US intelligence indicated that the division of the British government responsible for acting on the request was entirely staffed by former executives of the De Beers 'syndicate.' In a secret memorandum, the War Production Board noted, 'The diamond section of the government and the syndicate seem to be the same.'

After the Roosevelt administration had made continuing efforts to persuade the British government that the diamonds were of critical importance to the United States war effort, it ordered the State Department to play its trump card and threaten that the United States would interrupt the supply of airplanes that was vitally needed by the British to defend themselves against the Luftwaffe bombing raids. According to a confidential report in this Justice Department archive, dated 16 April 1942, 'It was said unofficially that we would not give planes to England if the syndicate would not sell us the diamonds with which to make them.' This dramatic threat had the desired effect. The British government pressed De Beers to accommodate President Roosevelt, and De Beers yielded.

Oppenheimer agreed to supply the United States immediately with only one million carats – 14 per cent of the American request – and deposit an additional stockpile in Canada for the duration of the war. This Canadian stockpile, which would remain under De Beers' control, was meant to mitigate American concern over the possible capture of the London stockpile.

The Roosevelt administration was not entirely satisfied with this compromise. It continued to apply pressure to the British government, demanding that De Beers supply the additional 5.5 million carats. By this time, the air of crisis had passed, and De Beers was able to procrastinate successfully. At first, it claimed that it did not have enough diamonds in its vaults to supply this amount. Then, after US intelligence debunked this claim, De Beers advised that its 'vaults were bombed shut' in an air raid on London. A year passed, and then De Beers asserted that it needed time to prepare an inventory of the diamonds it had available.

By this time, it became sufficiently clear to American officials that De Beers, despite the pressure exerted on it, had no intention of allowing a diamond stockpile of any magnitude to be established, even in Canada. Moreover, manufacturers of diamond tools in the United States had begun complaining to the Office of Price Control that De Beers had effectively raised its prices as much as 60 per cent through the device of reducing the quality of the diamonds it delivered. Even though the official price per carat remained unchanged, manufacturers had to buy more of the lower quality diamonds to build the tools and dies for industry. Since it was exceedingly difficult for the price control officials to measure the relative quality of industrial diamonds, De Beers was able to persist in its claim that it had not raised prices. In any case, the Justice Department concluded that the De Beers monopoly, by manipulating supplies from the stockpile, was in a position to impede the war effort.

The Justice Department decided then to launch its own investigation into the diamond monopoly. It had the full cooperation of the War Production Board, which still wanted control of the diamond stockpile, and the OSS, the US wartime intelligence service. The investigators were not held back by postwar civil liberties inhibitions about intercepting mail, borrowing bank records or other such extra-legal measures.

They all shared a common objective: helping the war effort. In their roughshod manner, they soon began turning up bits and pieces of evidence indicating that De Beers had systematically stifled diamond mining in areas of the world over which it could not exert control. For example, intercepted letters from Oppenheimer's associates suggested that litigation had been initiated in Venezuela to prevent Nelson Rockefeller and other Americans from developing diamond resources in that country. One such letter detailed the possibility of competition in Venezuela, and asked an intermediary to suggest to Oppenheimer that he be 'ruthless in stamping it out.' Another intercepted letter from a Belgian diamond executive suggested that De Beers was intentionally exhausting the diamond mines in the Belgian Congo, while preserving its mines in South Africa, so that after the war was over De Beers 'will have complete control over the market.'

Justice Department investigators also looked into charges that De Beers had conspired to buy out and shut down potential diamond mining areas in British Guiana (now Guyana) and the state of Arkansas. In Arkansas, it was charged that after diamonds were found there, Oppenheimer bought control of the company that was to mine the diamonds. Then, when the separation plant built on the site failed to produce a sufficient quantity of diamonds per ton of ore to make the mine profitable, it was closed. Subsequently, it was charged that the separation plant had been designed by the engineer in such a manner that it could not possibly retrieve diamonds. It emerged that the engineer was in the employ of De Beers. The mine, which was bought out by associates of Ernest Oppenheimer, was ordered closed in 1921 after Oppenheimer met the mine officials in New York, and the mine's records were ordered destroyed. 'An inference could be drawn . . .' the Justice Department memorandum noted, 'that the property was sabotaged and then closed at the insistence of Sir Ernest Oppenheimer.' The evidence was admittedly highly circumstantial, and from the same evidence it could also be inferred that the Arkansas mine had been closed by Oppenheimer simply because it was unprofitable to operate.

Whatever the specific tactics of De Beers, the Justice Department investigators reached the conclusion that the singular effect of these efforts was to artificially restrain the production of diamonds. This, in turn, produced higher prices. A 1944 memorandum to the attorney general concluded, 'The United States is paying monopoly prices for an essential material needed in wartime production.' If De Beers were an American company, the memorandum continued, 'There would be no question as to [its] having violated the anti-trust laws.' Since De Beers was a South African corporation, the Justice Department had to demonstrate that it had some jurisdiction over its activities before it could consider prosecuting it.

The FBI was called in to interview the leading diamond dealers in New York to determine whether De Beers, which sold them diamonds, could be construed as transacting business in the United States. The FBI reported, 'The domestic trade operates in relative secrecy. . . . The syndicate will sell only to a small group of hand-picked dealers.' It further noted that De Beers officials avoided coming to the United States, and all transactions took place in London. Further inquiry showed that De Beers had closed all its bank accounts in the United States at the outset of the investigation.

The assistant attorney generals at the Justice Department who had superintended the investigation realized that the antitrust division had little chance of ever bringing De Beers to court in the United States. Despite all the prodigious investigative efforts, the case was abandoned in late 1945.

None of these documents cast any light on the question

of how Hitler continued to obtain diamonds for the duration of the war. There was, however, an intriguing investigation of this problem by the OSS, the forerunner of the CIA.

According to a summary of OSS documents, the OSS learned through its agents in Germany that in November 1943 Hitler had only an eight-month supply of industrial diamonds. When these diamonds ran out, Hitler's war machine would be crippled. It would no longer be possible to build V-2 rockets or other exotic weaponry. It was thus a crucial wartime goal to prevent Hitler from replenishing his supply.

As all the mines in South Africa were closed, there seemed only one place on earth from which the Germans could get industrial diamonds in sufficient quantity to maintain their military-industrial complex: the Belgian Congo. The Belgian Congo was, however, administered by the Belgian government in exile, which was in London and completely under British control. Moreover, the mines were supervised, and policed, by the De Beers syndicate. In fact, when the Justice Department began to move against De Beers, the War Department objected on the grounds that it might undercut the security system that De Beers had developed in the Belgian Congo. In an exchange of secret correspondence between the War and Justice departments (which was declassified under my Freedom of Information request), it was argued by an official responsible for maintaining the diamond blockade that 'almost the entire [diamond] production of Africa is policed through the operation of elaborate controls extending through every mining area of the continent.' Further, De Beers, which administered this program, sent 'this controlled production . . . in a closely guarded stream to London.'

As the OSS pursued the investigation, it found that the diamonds were reaching the Axis powers through Tangiers and Cairo. Its agents, posing as illegal buyers in these entrepots, found that industrial diamonds were being sold for $26 a carat, which was thirty times the official price. It became increasingly clear that enormous profits were being made on the millions of carats that were being smuggled into Germany. Tracing their way back through the chain of illegal sellers, an OSS agent code-named Teton reported back from Leopoldville that 'the major source of leakage was the Forminière Mines,' which had been under the control of the syndicate ever since they were developed. According to the OSS report, Teton, pretending to be an Amerian official who had come to the Congo to register 'all American males of draft age,' made highly productive 'contact' in Leopoldville and eventually turned up evidence 'that a full year's supply of diamonds had reached Germany from Forminière through Red Cross parcels.' The shipment of several million carats of diamonds through the parcels that were regularly sent from the Congo to Nazi-occupied Belgium required considerable organization and support in the intervening areas.

Teton suspected that a Belgian official in Leopoldville was involved in the massive smuggling operation, and to test his suspicions he gave money to a Belgian citizen to make illegal diamond purchases in Leopoldville. As Teton suspected, the diamonds were traced back directly to the official.

Before Teton could follow the trail any further, however, the Belgian citizen was arrested by the police. The Belgian identified Teton as his source for the funds, and Teton was declared persona non grata by the governor general of the Congo, and expelled.

In February 1944, British and American intelligence officials met in Accra to attempt to resolve the jurisdictional problem, but their meetings were inconclusive and, with the end of the war in 1945, the OSS was dissolved.

De Beers had managed to dispose of a large portion of its stockpile of diamonds during the war. With the proceeds, it paid the debt that it had accumulated during the Depression years. With the end of hostilities, American servicemen returned from overseas and purchased diamond rings for the engagements that they had deferred until peacetime. To meet this new demand, De Beers reopened its mines in South Africa. The diamond invention had survived the war intact.

The Arrangement | 10

To perpetuate the diamond invention, it was not sufficient for De Beers merely to own the large mines that produced most of the world's diamonds. It had to control the production from *all* significant sources, including the scattered diggings in Africa and the jungle streams of South America. It had to be able to assure the major diamond cutters and dealers that they had no alternative source for their diamonds other than at Charterhouse Street in London. If its clients believed that it would be possible to buy diamonds from diggers, tribesmen, smugglers and small mine owners, De Beers could no longer compel them to adhere to its rules for distributing diamonds and avoiding price competion. Ernest Oppenheimer therefore negotiated a series of secret arrangements to block the availability of diamonds from the sources that his company did not directly own or control. In South Africa and the Belgian Congo, he pressed the governments into passing laws that forced independent prospectors and diggers to sell their diamonds only to government-licensed diamond buyers, who in turn contracted to sell their diamonds to De Beers' subsidiary, the Diamond Trading Company. In British colonies, such as the Gold Coast (now Ghana) or Sierre Leone, he contracted to buy whatever diamonds were unearthed from British mining companies, such as the Selection Trust, which held the mining concessions there. In South America, where the alluvial diamond fields were scattered over vast areas, he arranged his deal with local buying agents. In all cases, Oppenheimer required that the total production of diamonds be turned over to De Beers or its subsidiaries at an agreed-upon price.

When diamonds were found in the British colony of Guiana in 1925, De Beers, acting through its diamond syndicate in London, made an arrangement to buy the entire production, which amounted to about 12,000 carats a year. The agreement, drawn up by Otto Oppenheimer, specified that the price paid by the syndicate for these diamonds would be established through a sorting procedure. Moreover, it was stipulated that Oppenheimer would be the 'technical advisor' to the Guianan diamond miners, and, as such, he would be solely responsible for defining the assortment. According to the contract, Oppenheimer's decision on the sorting could not in any way be questioned or redressed. This meant, in effect, that Oppenheimer could determine what price would be paid to the Guianans, and if they found the price too low, they were restricted by the contract from selling the diamonds to anyone else.

As De Beers found that its own mines were producing more diamonds than it could market, its interest in this arrangement was not to stimulate further production in South America but to prevent these diamonds from finding their way into the market at an inopportune time. Once the contract was signed, Oppenheimer began adjusting the sorting procedures by creating grades of 'finer' diamonds. This maneuver effectively reduced the average price paid by the syndicate for Guianan diamonds by over 50 per cent. At these low prices, the Guianan mining company, United Diamond Fields of British Guiana Ltd, could no longer afford to buy diamonds from the native diggers. Consequently, the company's production, which was based entirely on what these diggers found and turned in, fell from 12,000 carats to 3000 carats a year. Bound by its contract to accept the syndicate's price, the company went bankrupt in 1927, and Guianan diamonds ceased to be a threat to De Beers. The details of this arrangement emerged only in 1932 when a director of United Diamond Fields sued Otto Oppenheimer for fraud. After demonstrating that Oppenheimer had falsified an important certificate of valuation, the director's lawyer, Sir Patrick Hastings, forced the syndicate to pay his client a large cash settlement.

There was, however, one maverick geologist who refused to accept this crucial arrangement – Dr John Thornburn Williamson. Williamson was a rugged Canadian geologist who, after he had left the employ of De Beers in 1932, began prospecting on his own for diamonds in what was then the British colony of Tanganyika (now Tanzania).

In 1943, Dr Williamson intrepidly traced a mineral often found in association with diamonds back to its source in the Tanganyikan wilds. There, at Mwadui, Williamson uncovered the largest diamond mine that had ever been found. The oval-shaped volcanic pipe, which was filled with diamondiferous ore, covered some 361 acres on the surface; and it was four times larger than any of the diamond pipes found in South Africa.

A De Beers team of prospectors had explored the territory around Mwadui a decade earlier without reporting any trace of diamonds; now De Beers had to prevent Williamson from flooding the market with these Tanganyikan diamonds. When the extent of the diamond strike became clear in 1945, Ernest Oppenheimer offered Williamson £2 million for the mine. Even though this was an enormous sum of money then, and Williamson himself was penniless, he turned down the offer. After spending ten years in the jungles of Africa in solitary pursuit of diamonds, he was not about to sell out. He wanted to build his own empire. With the backing of a number of Indian merchants in Tanganyika and a task force of Italian prisoners of war, he began excavating the diamonds from the pipe. By 1946, he had some 6000 workers living with their families at Mwadui, and over 200 armed guards protecting his budding empire. The entire encampment was surrounded by two barbwire fences and protected by primitive gun fortifications.

As the diamonds began to pour out of Mwadui, De Beers became increasingly concerned about its ability to control world prices. The corporate minutes of De Beers on 20 June 1946 reflect this growing apprehension. 'The chairman [Sir Ernest Oppenheimer] said that he was sure that a satisfactory outcome would result [from negotiations with the British Colonial Office over a prospecting license for De Beers for Tanganyika], but he said that the position would not be secure until they were able to come to terms with Williamson. He mentioned that the Tanganyika production was now one and one-half million pounds per annum. . . . He very much doubted whether, at the moment, he had 65 per cent effective control of world production.' Oppenheimer pointed out that this uncontrolled production could prove 'embarrassing' if there was an economic recession, and he recommended, according to the notes of the meeting, 'that their efforts should be energetically directed towards obtaining effective control of all African production.'

The diamond sights in London proved to be one effective means of reasserting control of the Tanganyika diamonds. Dr Williamson had to sell the low- as well as high-quality diamonds he mined to diamond cutters in order for his mine to be profitable. Most of the major cutting factories, especially for the more difficult-shaped diamonds, were clients of De Beers. When these clients came to the London sights, they were told, according to reports reaching the US Department of Justice, that they should not buy any of Williamson's diamonds. The threat was implicitly made that they might find their consignment drastically reduced or even abruptly ended if they bought any diamonds from Williamson. Since few of the cutting factories in Antwerp were willing to risk their sight in London by violating this rule of the game, Williamson found that he could only sell the clear, octahedron crystals that were in demand by small independent cutters. He had to store most of the clear diamonds. This severely squeezed his cash reserves.

De Beers also applied pressure on Williamson through the British Colonial Office. When its representatives privately advised the British Exchequer of the stockpile of Tanganyika diamonds, De Beers quickly put pressure on the Colonial Office to remedy the situation. Diamonds, after all, earned at that time more foreign exçhange for Great Britain than almost any other export, and the British government was understandably concerned with preserving its value. At about this time, Colonial Secretary Arthur Creech Jones consulted the Tanganyika government about a proposal to nationalize the Williamson diamond mine. In an official white paper, Creech Jones suggested that the government, through nationalization, might better be able to control the exploitation of a mineral resource than a private company.

For Williamson, the message was clear: either he make his deal with De Beers or his mine might be nationalized. Finally, in August 1947, Williamson acquiesced to these pressures, and Creech Jones announced in the House of Commons that Williamson had agreed to sell his entire output through the Diamond Trading Company in London. Williamson was now part of the arrangement.

Oppenheimer went on to make similar arrangements with any other person, corporation or nation that discovered diamonds. He was in a position to either buy them out directly or to contract to buy all the diamonds their mines produced. It was a mutually profitable arrangement.

During Sir Ernest's lifetime, De Beers never discovered a diamond mine itself. Oppenheimer saw little point to investing profits in exploring for diamonds, since De Beers made its profits from a scarcity, not an abundance, of diamonds. As he established it, one of the cardinal principles behind the diamond invention was that demand for diamonds was fixed each year and varied only with the number of engagements.

Any sudden increases in the production of diamonds would therefore have to be added to De Beers' stockpile rather than its profit, and it made little sense for Oppenheimer to create new mines until the old ones were depleted. Instead, Oppenheimer reinvested the stream of profits into gold mines in the Orange Free State province of South Africa. The gold production would provide a reserve of capital for De Beers that would allow it to buy back diamonds if the retail market ever slackened.

By the time Sir Ernest died in 1957, he had turned the diamond invention into a powerful instrument for preserving the price of diamonds. By merging the mines in South Africa with the syndicate in London, he created a double-edged sword – production and distribution – for maintaining his control over the diamond industry. Through secret arrangements that he patiently and meticulously made with independent mine owners, he managed to channel almost all the world's uncut diamonds through this system.

11 Diamonds Cut Diamonds

In its rough form, a diamond is a lusterless, translucent crystal that resembles a chip of broken glass. For it to be transformed into a jewel, it must be cut into a particular gem shape and then polished facet by facet. When Sir Ernest Oppenheimer organized the diamond cartel, there were no machines that could cut and polish diamonds. The crucial transformation from rough stones to jewels had to be done by hand, and only a relatively few craftsmen, mainly in Antwerp and Amsterdam, possessed the necessary skills. Oppenheimer therefore set out to extend the control of the cartel to diamond cutting as well as to diamond mining. He realized that although outsiders might conceivably discover new sources of diamonds, they could not compete with De Beers unless they also had the means to cut diamonds. The art of diamond cutting was thus ingeniously incorporated into the diamond invention.

Until the late fifteenth century, diamond cutting had been a primitive business. Diamonds were first 'cleaved' by placing a chisel at the stone's weakest point of molecular cohesion and striking it with a mallet. If the precise point was located on the diamond's structure, the adhesion would be so weak that the diamond could be separated with a fingernail. If pressure was applied to the wrong point, or in the wrong direction, the diamond would shatter. After the medieval cutter had succeeded in cleaving the diamond into the basic shape of the desired jewel, he placed it in an egg-shaped tin cup, called a dop, and attempted to remove any imperfections in it by striking it with another diamond, since only diamonds were hard enough to cut diamonds. This process, which was extremely slow and painstaking, was called bruting. Even though the medieval cutter could eventually give the stone a jewel-like appearance through these methods, he was extremely limited by the natural shape of the diamond.

The situation suddenly changed at the end of the fifteenth century when a Jewish diamond cutter in Antwerp named Lodewyk van Berken invented the scaif. The scaif was simply a polishing wheel that was impregnated with a mixture of olive oil and diamond dust, but it completely revolutionized the art of diamond cutting. The rough diamond was clamped in a dop and held against this whirling disc, while the diamond dust on it ground away the diamond to the desired angle. With the scaif, it became possible to polish symmetrically all the facets of the diamond at angles that reflected the maximum amount of light. As disciples of Van Berken applied the laws of optics to these angles, they created sparkling gems that fascinated the princes and aristocrats of Europe. Charles the Bold, Duke of Burgundy, became the patron of Van Berken and commissioned him to recut a 137-carat diamond, which became known as the Florentine.

Diamond cutters from all over Europe came to Antwerp to study Van Berken's methods, and orders for these light-reflecting gems flowed in from all the royal courts, making Antwerp the preeminent diamond-cutting center in the world. At the head of the Pelikenstrasse, the street that winds through Antwerp's diamond district, is a bronze statue of Van Berken dressed in a jerkin and skull cap, with a holster full of diamond tools strapped across his waist. He holds in his right hand a diamond.

The next major innovation came in the twentieth century with the invention of the diamond saw. Cleaving diamonds, although an economic and efficient process, had limited cutters to shaping the stone according to its natural lines of cleavage. The diamond saw, a circular steel blade lubricated continually with oil and diamond powder, allowed the cutters to go against the grain of the diamond without shattering it. The diamond saw, moreover, allowed cutters to salvage jewels from badly misshapen and deformed diamonds. To be sure, sawing was a more expensive process than cleaving. It required about one-tenth of a carat of diamond dust for every carat of diamond sawn through. And it was also a much slower process than cleaving a diamond with a single stroke. Indeed, it took days to saw through a two-carat diamond. Despite such disadvantages, the diamond saw became the common method of shaping diamonds in the postwar years. Since it was far easier to train workers to saw than to cleave diamonds, it quickly transformed diamond cutting in Antwerp from an esoteric craft to a semi-mechanized industry.

The final refinement of the process for cutting diamonds came in 1919 when a twenty-one-year-old mathematician named Marcel Tolkowsky calculated the formula for the ideal proportions of a cut diamond. Master cutters had achieved an inner light in diamonds by choosing angles that sacrificed some reflected light in order to get refracted light. They did this by relying mainly on intuition, trial and error, and experience. Tolkowsky's formula gave the optimum ratio between the angles of facets opposing one another in a diamond. Following this formula, a cutter would achieve the maximum refracted (or inner) light with the least sacrifice of reflected (or outer) light. This formula led to the popularization of the so-called 'brilliant cut' diamond, which had fifty-eight facets polished exactly to the tolerances of the ideal proportions.

With the reduction of diamonds to a mathematical formula, it became possible to devise semi-automatic machines to polish diamonds. In the early 1960s, a De Beers subsidiary introduced the Pieromatic diamond-cutting machines in Antwerp. Although these machines still required trained workers to guide diamonds through the polishing operation, they greatly reduced the need for master craftsmen or even long apprenticeships. According to the literature accompanying the Pieromatic machines, men could be trained to operate them in a matter of months.

As the diamond business expanded in the postwar years, Sir Ernest Oppenheimer made every effort to keep the cutting industry anchored in Antwerp. Not only was Antwerp just across the channel from England, and highly convenient to De Beers, but Sir Ernest considered it essential to maintain a special relationship with the Belgian government, which controlled the huge diamond deposits in the Congo. Under his express orders, Monty Charles thus provided the Antwerp diamond cutters with ample supplies of diamonds at the London sights while cutting back on supplies to their competitors. Amsterdam, which had been a major diamond-cutting center in the nineteenth century, gradually lost almost all its gem cutters to Antwerp. (Strict working conditions imposed on the Dutch diamond-cutting factories by the labor unions greatly accelerated the exodus in the prewar years.) Despite all De Beers' efforts, Antwerp did not achieve a monopoly in diamond cutting. The larger and more expensive diamonds were sent to be cut directly to New York, in order to avoid paying the tax on finished jewels, while the smaller diamond chips were sent to India to be polished by cheap labor. The 'melees,' or medium-sized diamonds, generally under a half carat in weight, tended to flow to Israeli factories. Nevertheless, Antwerp's cutters continued to receive most of the valuable diamonds and virtually all the difficult-shaped diamonds that required special skills.

To see how these diamonds were cut, I visited the Trau Frères factory in Antwerp in January 1979. Founded over a century ago, Trau Frères specializes almost exclusively in cutting a triangular-shaped twisted crystal known in the trade as a 'macle.' As Trau Frères is invited to De Beers' sights in London on a regular basis, it receives all its macles from De Beers. The factory employs about a hundred workers – mostly men – who receive on average a salary and benefits of $400 a week, which makes them among the highest paid workers in Europe. Each worker was seated in front of a table cutting and polishing an individual macle.

The diamond I watched being shaped at Trau Frères started out looking like two triangles folded into one another. It took about ten hours for the craftsman to saw it into its basic shape which resembled a valentine heart. The heart-shaped stone was then placed in a cuplike dop and rubbed against a second diamond in order to wear away the sharp and irregular edges. Finally, the craftsman began polishing the individual facets of the diamond on his whirling scaif. By the time this arduous process was completed, the diamond would have lost at least 40 per cent of its original weight. This particular diamond had weighed 10 carats when Trau Frères received it in their box at the London sight, in mid-1978. It cost them $4000, or $400 per carat. The labor and interest costs on this individual diamond amounted to about a thousand dollars. The final heart-shaped diamond, once cut, weighed only 6 carats. To break even, Trau Frères would have to sell it to a wholesaler for at least $5000 or $837 per carat.

The thin margin of profit for specialty diamond cutters like Trau Frères depends almost entirely on the price they pay the Diamond Trading Company for the uncut diamonds in their box at the sights. If Monty Charles elects to raise the price even slightly – or to provide them with an inferior selection of diamonds – these specialty cutters would be forced out of business. And, according to at least one Antwerp specialty cutter, De Beers still uses its leverage over these cutters to prevent them from cutting diamonds from independent mines. By controlling the activities of these few cutters, De Beers makes it extremely difficult for any independent mine to sell the full range of its diamonds. Rather than forgo the profits from these poorly shaped diamonds, most potential competitors have been forced to sell their entire production to De Beers – or one of its many subsidiaries. De Beers has thus turned diamond cutting into an important fulcrum in the diamond invention.

The Corporate Underground | 12

Harry Oppenheimer was forty-nine years old when he succeeded his father as chairman of both De Beers and the Anglo-American Corporation. A shy, quiet man formerly in the background of the diamond cartel, he was now in sole command of it. It was a position that he had been prepared for all his life.

Oppenheimer was born on 28 October 1908 in Kimberley – a city literally built on diamond mines. When he was four years old, his father became the first mayor of Kimberley, and was rapidly amassing a major financial interest in the diamond mines. During his childhood, Harry dreamed of other careers. He explained to me, 'I first wanted to be an engine driver, then an admiral – nothing less! – in the Royal Navy and then an ambassador.' He added wistfully, 'However, all these ambitions had to be abandoned before the age of twelve in favor of a business career.' He went to Charterhouse School in England, and then was admitted to Christ Church college at Oxford. At Oxford, he took his degree in 'PPE' – politics, philosophy and economics. He was at that time, he subsequently explained, most interested in economics and least interested in politics. His tutor for economics was Sir Roy Harrod, the Keynesian economist; his tutor for politics was Sir John Masterman, who ten years later organized Britain's celebrated 'double-cross' espionage system against the Germans. Even with such impressive tutors, Oppenheimer enjoyed a carefree time in Oxford – perhaps the only truly carefree period in his life. It was still the roaring twenties, and he went on champagne picnics in the Oxfordshire countryside and spent weekends at the Spreadeagle Inn on the Thames (which Evelyn Waugh once termed 'Oxford's only civilizing influence').

He returned to South Africa in 1929 – the year the worldwide Depression began – and went to work at the De Beers sorting house in Kimberley. During this apprenticeship, he learned to separate and evaluate diamonds in their uncut form. He then moved to Johannesburg where he became his father's personal assistant in running the corporate empire. In 'devilling' for his father, as he called it, he did everything from ghostwriting speeches to going on secret missions to New York. Although his public role remained minimal during this period, his father had him appointed to the De Beers' board of directors in 1937 – when he was only twenty-nine.

When the Second World War began in 1940, Oppenheimer volunteered to be an officer in the South African Union Defence Force. He was commissioned as a second lieutenant in the Intelligence Section. After serving for several months on the General Staff in Pretoria, Oppenheimer was sent to Egypt as an intelligence officer with the Fourth South African Armoured Car Regiment.

Within weeks, his regiment was engaged in battles against German *Panzer* divisions led by General Rommel. Even during this bitter desert campaign, he found time to correspond regularly with his father about the prospects for the diamond business. 'Not the profits but the many problems of the diamond trade make the diamond business the most interesting I know,' his father wrote to him in 1941. In another letter, his father stressed the critical importance of maintaining the monopolistic system of distribution and added: 'Nothing I have said must be construed that I have lost my belief in limitation of output or sales through one channel.' The channel was, of course, De Beers. In this wartime correspondence, Sir Ernest had no time for sentiment about the diamond invention. Stripping away all illusions he wrote, 'No diamonds are cheap if they cannot be sold or if they must be kept for years. The interest charge which one should remember – and which one always forgets – eats up the profit.'

In July 1942, Lieutenant Oppenheimer was reassigned to the Coastal Command in South Africa, which had been set up to guard against Japanese infiltration and sabotage. He was stationed at Capetown Castle, a fortress on Robbins Island near the southern tip of Africa. Except for one attempt by four Japanese commandos to sabotage South

Africa's largest dynamite factory, in which De Beers owned a controlling interest, there were no wartime activities for the Coastal Command to concern itself with. During this relatively quiet tour of service on Robbins Island, Oppenheimer met Bridget McCall, a young officer in the Women's Auxiliary Army Service who had just returned from school in England. Within months he proposed to her, and they married in a military ceremony on 6 March 1943. Nine months later, on New Year's Eve, they had their first child – Mary Oppenheimer – and then, less than two years later, their second, Nicholas Oppenheimer.

When the war ended, Oppenheimer returned to the family business. He was managing director of De Beers, and second in command to his father. Even though he remained intimately involved with the strategic planning of the diamond cartel, he focused a great deal of his energies on South African politics. 'If you are involved in a large business enterprise, you've simply got to concern yourself with politics: it is not realistic not to do so,' he has explained. In the postwar period, South Africa was deeply divided by two political forces. On the one hand, there was the United party, headed by General Jan Smuts, and backed by the English-speaking and relatively liberal segments of the white population, which was committed to a policy of gradual accommodation with the nonwhite majority of the population and to keeping South Africa in the British Commonwealth. On the other hand, there was the Nationalist party, backed mainly by the Afrikaans-speaking settlers of Dutch origin, which insisted that South Africa maintain a policy of strict separation of the races, or apartheid. Since many of the leaders of the Nationalist party had been interned by the British in a De Beers-owned diamond mining camp for the duration of the war because of their suspected pro-German sympathies, they were eager to cut the ties with Great Britain and, if necessary, withdraw South Africa from the British Commonwealth. As the 1948 general election approached, white South Africans were confronted with a critical choice: they could vote for General Smuts's United party, and move toward gradual racial integration within the British Commonwealth, or they could vote for the Nationalist party, and proceed down the road of racial apartheid and international isolation.

For Harry Oppenheimer, there was only one conceivable course of action: to finance and support General Smuts. Smuts, who had been a poet, soldier, statesman and hero in South Africa since the Boer War, had been a close family friend of the Oppenheimers for forty years. He had even flown to England to attend Harry Oppenheimer's gala twenty-first birthday party at the Spreadeagle Inn. Aside from personal considerations, Oppenheimer realized that his family business operated throughout the British Empire – the sights were in London, small diamonds were cut in Israel (then a British mandate), and diamonds were mined in British colonies in West Africa – and that if Smuts was defeated in the election, relations with England would be strained, if not completely severed. Diamonds were an international business, and Oppenheimer did not want to see De Beers isolated from its distribution network in London. Moreover, Oppenheimer personally opposed apartheid as both impractical and immoral.

Not only did the Oppenheimer interest provide financing for most of the United party in 1948, but Harry Oppenheimer himself stood for Parliament in the district of Kimberley where he had the support of the diamond workers from the De Beers mines. When the votes were counted, however, the United party found itself decisively defeated. General Smuts, after serving as prime minister for sixteen years, lost his own seat in Parliament. The Nationalist party, led by Hendrik Verwoerd, won a resounding majority of the seats, and immediately moved to form a government that would begin implementing its policy of apartheid.

One of the handful of United party candidates to win a seat in 1948 was Harry Oppenheimer. He had, however, no opportunity to influence the government. As he sat in Parliament, he saw apartheid laws enacted over his protest, and the nonwhite population stripped of every right they had gained. He also saw South Africa gradually slipping from the British orbit. Since the United party had collapsed, Oppenheimer provided most of the funds for a new party called the Progressive party – but it was never able to elect more than a few members to Parliament. The Oppenheimer interest also bought an important share, through subsidiaries, of the English-language press in South Africa, which shrilly attacked the government's racial policies. It was, however, to no avail. The Nationalists kept winning elections – and Harry Oppenheimer retired from Parliament, although he continued, almost single-handedly, to finance the Progressive party.

When his father died in 1957, Oppenheimer withdrew entirely from South African politics and concentrated his energies on planning out a new future for the diamond cartel. He recognized that the geopolitical forces in Africa were rapidly changing, and that the problems he would confront in his efforts to preserve the diamond invention would be very different from the ones that his father had faced in colonial Africa. When Sir Ernest had brilliantly forged the elements in the diamond cartel, South Africa and most other diamond producing areas in the world were part of the British Empire, and he could count on the administrative powers of the British Colonial Office to help him protect one of the leading British exports – diamonds. The only diamond producers outside the British sphere of influence were the Belgian Congo and Portuguese Angola, both of which were colonies of countries allied with Great Britain. Sir Ernest did not have to concern himself with Marxist revolutions, nationalist movements and hostile regimes.

Whereas Sir Ernest had only to worry about economic changes, Harry Oppenheimer realized, even as early as 1958, that he would have to prepare himself for violent political changes. A decade of apartheid under the Nationalist government had served to alienate South Africa from the rest of the Commonwealth. In 1961, South Africa was formally expelled from the Commonwealth and became a 'republic.' As British colonies, such as Sierre Leone, Ghana and Tanzania, achieved their independence, they severed diplomatic relations with South Africa. Belgium also relinquished control of the Congo (which became Zaire), with its vast reserves of diamonds. As these newly independent nations grew increasingly hostile to South Africa, De Beers, which was, after all, a South African corporation, could no longer openly control their diamond fields. Then in 1963, the Soviet Union called for a world boycott of trade with South Africa, and almost every nation in Africa joined it (in theory, if not in fact). The United States even cut off military aid to South Africa. By the mid-1960s South Africa had become a pariah-nation.

To keep control over the world supply of diamonds, Harry Oppenheimer had to make covert arrangements with both the Russians and the African nations that produced diamonds. As early as 1964, Oppenheimer informed investors in his company that the 'political situation in Africa has created new problems for our group. . . . There are obvious political objections to the purchase of production from African states.' He further reported, 'This unfortunate state of affairs has necessitated a considerable reorganization of the group's activities . . . [diamond] buying operations in the newly independent African states are now, in every case, undertaken by companies registered and managed outside the Republic of South Africa, and which are not subsidiaries of De Beers.' In fact, however, these companies were created and controlled by Oppenheimer for the purpose of serving as intermediaries in the diamond arrangements. In other words, a complicated system of corporate fronts had been set up to obscure the movement of diamonds to De Beers from African states pledged to the destruction of South Africa.

The Oppenheimer strategy was not aimed at deceiving the African governments themselves, for they were fully aware that De Beers was the ultimate operator of their mines and marketer of their diamonds. It was intended merely to provide a necessary cloak of 'deniability' for African politicians. If any journalists or dissidents charged them with trading with the enemy, they could deny the charges and be at least technically truthful. The corporations with which they dealt were registered in Luxembourg, Liechtenstein, Switzerland, or England, and had innocuous names, such as the Diamond Development Corporation, or Mining and Technical Services Ltd. They could remain conveniently blind to the fact that these intermediaries were creatures of De Beers, or that they immediately transferred their diamonds to De Beers' Diamond Trading Company in London. The distinction was, however, a crucial one for many African governments because, at the very time they were earning a large portion of their hard currency from the Oppenheimer empire, they were demanding through the United Nations that other nations boycott South African business.

The ever-expanding number of diamonds coming out of the Soviet Union proved to be an even more vexing problem for Harry Oppenheimer. His father had only had to concern himself with restricting and allocating the production of the diamond mines in Africa; he had to find ways to prevent the Soviets from flooding the world market with their diamonds. According to the geological reports he received, Soviet mines in Siberia had a potential for producing more diamonds than all the mines in South Africa. He realized that if the Soviets ever attempted to market their diamonds in competition with De Beers, the price might collapse. He therefore moved to bring the Soviet Union into the cartel arrangement, since, as he eloquently put it, 'a single channel . . . is in the interest of all diamond producers whatever the political difference between them may be.' In return for not competing with De Beers, he offered to buy up the entire Soviet production, year after year, of uncut gem diamonds at prices higher than the Soviets could otherwise obtain on the free market.

The Soviets immediately saw the benefits of this monopolistic arrangement. Since, however, Soviet foreign policy was designed to isolate and undermine South Africa, the Soviets preferred to remain silent partners with De Beers in the diamond business. The Soviet Union had insisted from the outset that Oppenheimer publicly deny the existence of any deal, and, in 1963, in the annual report of De Beers, he noted: 'On account of Russian support for the boycotting of trade with South Africa, our contract to buy Russian diamonds has not been renewed.' What he did not put in the annual report was that Russian diamonds were arriving through a corporate front in ever-increasing numbers. Indeed, Oppenheimer had arranged to buy out the entire Russian production of uncut diamonds – an arrangement that persists to this day.

Oppenheimer needed a tight-knit staff that could discreetly direct all the operations of the mines, the diamond buyers, and the distribution network from South Africa. He located his headquarters, as had his father, in the Anglo-American Building at 44 Main Street in Johannesburg. In theory, Anglo-American and De Beers are two separate entities; in fact, the Oppenheimers, who own a controlling interest in both companies, treat them as a single empire – Anglo-De Beers. The Anglo-American Company provides De Beers with 'technical services' such as mine managers, engineers, architects, bookkeepers, lawyers, and public relations advisers. These technicians nominally remain on the payroll of Anglo-American and are only on 'loan' to De Beers. In fact, they operate the mines, supervise the logistics, make the financial arrangements and hire personnel for De Beers. They report directly through a global telex system to a suite of offices on the fourth floor of 44 Main Street, called simply 'Diamond Services.'

Diamond Services is in reality Oppenheimer's staff for running the diamond cartel. It is composed of only about a dozen men. The strategic objective of the staff is to preserve the delicate equilibrium between the world supply and world demand for diamonds. To achieve this balance, the staff uses its detailed knowledge of all diamond prospecting possibilities to determine when new diamond mines will be brought into production – or closed – and the level of production. It also formulates plans for dealing with possible competitors, either by making arrangements with them or buying them out directly. And it closely monitors all aspects of the far-flung diamond business.

In England, Oppenheimer controls the distribution of gem diamonds through the Diamond Trading Company, which is headed by his cousin, Sir Philip Oppenheimer, and operated by Monty Charles. Also, in England, Oppenheimer controls the Charter Company which, in turn, owns substantial interests in some of the supposedly independent mining companies with which the Diamond Trading Company has an arrangement to buy diamonds. For example, Charter owns 25 per cent of the Selection Trust Company, which holds diamond concessions in Ghana and other West African countries – and sells these diamonds to the Diamond Trading Company.

In Luxembourg, Oppenheimer has a subsidiary called Boart International that holds, in turn, controlling interest in some of the largest manufacturers of diamond drilling equipment in the world. Through this Luxembourg corporation, he is able to dominate the entire industrial diamond business. Moreover, through a subsidiary in Ireland called the Shannon B Corporation, he is able to control the distribution worldwide of diamond abrasive powders for industry.

With the enormous profits from the diamond cartel, Oppenheimer has built a $15 billion mining conglomerate that operates in five continents. His father had invested heavily in gold mines in the Orange Free State, even though the price of gold was then fixed at $35 an ounce, and gold mining was unprofitable. As the price of gold rose, Oppenheimer expanded the gold mining until, in 1980, his companies produced nearly one-third of all the gold produced in the world. As the gold mines in South Africa also yield uranium oxide as a by-product, Oppenheimer has also become one of the world's largest producers of uranium. Oppenheimer also expanded into platinum, copper, tin, manganese, oil, lead, zinc, titanium and other strategic minerals. By 1980, his congeries of companies accounted for more than half the value of South Africa's mineral and industrial exports. They also had international connections. For example, through the Anglo-American Corporation, he had become the second largest foreign investor in the United States in 1980.

Oppenheimer is personally able to control this vast corporate complex, though he has only a small percentage of the equity in it, through an ingeniously constructed pyramid of ownership.

At the top of the pyramid is a private firm called E. Oppenheimer and Son. The chief shareholder in it is Harry Oppenheimer, and the only other significant shareholders are his two children, Nicholas and Mary. (Sir Philip Oppenheimer, and the other English relatives, have only a token interest in the firm.) The principal asset of E. Oppenheimer and Son is somewhere around 10 per cent of the shares of the Anglo-American Corporation. This block of stock appears to be a relatively small fraction of the equity of the company, but it is sufficient to give Oppenheimer undisputed control of it, since another 41 per cent of the stock is held in the treasury of De Beers and is effectively controlled by Oppenheimer.

At the next level of this complex structure, Anglo-American holds a 52 per cent interest in an investment trust called Anamint. Anamint, in turn, holds 26 per cent of the shares of De Beers, which gives Anglo-American, together with the shares it and its subsidiaries hold, effective control of De Beers. Oppenheimer thus manages to control both Anglo-American and De Beers and to appoint the board of directors of both companies.

The pyramid then dramatically widens with De Beers and Anglo-American owning pieces which when combined are tantamount to a controlling interest in seven of the largest conglomerates in South Africa. These investments, which include the Anglo-American Gold Investment Company, Anglo-American Coal Corporation, and Johannesburg Consolidated Investment, encompass most of the mining and industrial economy of South Africa: the companies, which themselves are holding companies, own more than half of all the gold mines, the major insurance companies, the largest privately owned steel company in Africa, and virtually the entire petrochemical industry in South Africa. (In 1967, the Nationalist government in South Africa conducted a secret investigation into the holdings of the Oppenheimer empire and found that it exercised direct control over 900 major companies in South Africa.)

Finally, at the base of the pyramid, Anglo-American controls two international companies – Mineral and Resources Corporation in Bermuda and Charter Consolidated in Great Britain – which together dominate mining companies on all five continents.

Because public investors own stock in most of these corporations but do not exercise control, the pyramid structure has permitted Oppenheimer to expand the reach of his empire without diminishing his personal hold over it. Because of his enormous leverage over these interlocking companies, he can act with swiftness and, if necessary, stealth, in acquiring new properties. In 1980, for example, he stunned the entire financial world by secretly buying up through agents and front companies some 28 per cent of the stock in Consolidated Gold Fields Ltd, which produced then nearly 12 per cent of the world's gold. To expedite this coup, he used some $340 million from the treasury of De Beers.

The gigantic financial holdings of the Anglo-De Beers corporate pyramid provide the means for protecting the diamond invention in adverse times. When new diamond strikes are made – as, for example, in Australia in 1980 – Oppenheimer can quietly orchestrate their purchase, using corporate intermediaries. When there is a temporary decline in retail sales of diamonds in the United States and other important markets, Oppenheimer can use the multibillion dollar cash surplus to buy back diamonds in the pipeline to prevent any decline in price. When some measure of political influence is needed in countries important to the diamond industry, such as Zaire, Oppenheimer can arrange for subsidiaries he controls to invest in other resources, such as copper and cobalt mines, to ensure that the diamond concession will not be infringed. Like pawns on a chess board, the swirl of corporations in the complex are used to safeguard the all-important queen in the game: the diamond cartel.

13 | The Diamond Mind

Control of the world's diamond mines was a necessary but not sufficient condition for perpetuating the price of diamonds. If the public's appetite for diamonds decreased precipitously, as it had in the Depression, or women's fashions suddenly changed, as it had with coral and pearls, De Beers would not be able for long to keep prices from collapsing – no matter how ruthlessly it cut back on production from the mines. To complete the diamond invention, De Beers had to control demand as well as supply, and this required some manipulation of the psyche of the diamond buyer. What was necessary was the creation of a mass mentality in which women would perceive diamonds, not as precious stones that could be bought or sold according to economic conditions or fashions, but as an inseparable part of courtship and married life.

In September 1938, Harry Oppenheimer journeyed to New York City to investigate the possibilities of creating such a diamond mind. He was met by Gerold M. Lauck who was the president of one of the leading advertising agencies in the United States, N. W. Ayer. Lauck and N. W. Ayer had been recommended to Oppenheimer by the Morgan Bank, which had helped his father consolidate his financial empire. His bankers were clearly concerned by the worldwide decline in the price of diamonds.

In Europe, where diamond prices had collapsed during the Depression, there seemed little possibility of restoring public confidence. In Germany, Austria, Italy and Spain, the notion of giving diamond rings to commemorate an engagement had never taken hold. In England and France, diamonds were still presumed to be a jewel for aristocrats rather than the masses. And in any case, Europe was on the verge of war, and there seemed little possibility of expanding diamond sales. This left the United States as the only real market for De Beers' diamonds.

Even though the 'tradition' of giving diamond rings for engagements in America was barely fifty years old, it had survived the Depression. In fact, in 1938, some three-quarters of all the cartel's diamonds were sold for engagement rings in the United States. Up to this point, however, American men tended to buy the smaller and poorer quality diamonds – averaging under $80 apiece – for their loved ones. Oppenheimer and the bankers believed that Americans could be persuaded to buy more expensive diamonds through an advertising campaign.

During their initial meeting, Oppenheimer suggested to Lauck that his agency prepare a plan for creating a new image for diamonds among Americans. He assured him that De Beers had not contacted any other American advertising agency with this proposal, and if the N. W. Ayer plan met with his father's approval, it would be the exclusive agents for the placement of the newspaper and radio advertisements in the United States. Moreover, Oppenheimer offered to underwrite the costs of the research necessary for developing the scheme. Lauck, envisioning a new and potentially lucrative account, instantly accepted the offer.

In their subsequent investigation into the American diamond market, N. W. Ayer's staff found that ever since the end of the First World War in 1918, there had been a consistent decline in both the number and the quality of the diamonds sold in America. During this nineteen-year period, the total number of diamonds, measured in carats, had declined by 50 per cent; while the quality of the diamonds, measured in dollar value, had declined by nearly 100 per cent. This suggested that well before the Depression, Americans had begun buying poorer quality and cheaper diamonds. They concluded, according to an Ayer memo, that the present depressed state of the market for diamonds was 'the result of the economy, changes in social attitudes and the promotion of competitive luxuries.'

Although it could do little about the state of the economy, N. W. Ayer suggested that through a well-orchestrated advertising and public relations campaign, it could significantly alter the 'social attitudes' of the public at large and thereby channel American spending toward larger and more expensive diamonds instead of 'competitive luxuries.' Specifically, the Ayer study stressed the need to vitalize the association in the public's mind between diamonds and romance. Since 'young men buy over 90% of all engagement rings,' it would be crucial to inculcate in them the idea that diamonds were a gift of love: the larger and finer the diamond, the greater the expression of love. Similarly, young women had to be encouraged to view diamonds as an integral part of any romantic courtship. The study found that there was already an increasing number of marriages among middle-income wage-earners who were 'the backbone of the diamond market,' and that, if properly cultivated, this trend could provide fertile ground for diamond sales in the future.

Since the Ayer plan to romanticize diamonds required subtly altering the public's picture of the way that a man courts – and wins – a woman, the advertising agency strongly suggested exploiting the relatively new medium of motion pictures.

'Motion pictures seldom include scenes showing the selection or purchase of an engagement ring for a girl,' the Ayer proposal noted. 'It would be our plan to contact scenario writers and directors and arrange for such scenes in suitable productions.' Since movie idols were then paragons of romance for the mass audience, they would be given diamonds to use as their symbols of indestructible love.

In addition, the proposal suggested planting news stories and society photographs in selected magazines and newspapers that would reinforce the link between diamonds and romance. There would be stories about the size of diamonds that celebrities presented to their loved ones, and photographs that conspicuously focused on the glittering stone on the finger of a well-known woman. And there were to be radio programs where fashion designers talked about the 'trend towards diamonds.'

The Ayer plan also envisioned using the British royal family to help foster the romantic allure of diamonds. It observed, 'Since Great Britain has such an important interest in the diamond industry, the royal couple could be of tremendous assistance to this British industry by wearing diamonds rather than other jewels.' Subsequently, Queen Elizabeth did go on a well-publicized trip to the South

African diamond mines, and she accepted a diamond from Oppenheimer.

On 6 April 1939, H. T. Dickinson, a director of De Beers responsible for international diamond sales, arrived in New York on board the *Queen Mary*. At 4 p.m. that afternoon, he was in the offices of N. W. Ayer discussing the implementation of the advertising campaign. Initially, he found it difficult to believe that diamonds had steadily lost ground to other luxury goods in America, but after reviewing the data, he accepted the N. W. Ayer thesis: a new image for diamonds was needed. Within two months, De Beers authorized Ayer to begin its campaign.

The advertising agency wasted little time in approaching the film studios in Hollywood. In its 1940 report to De Beers, it noted, 'A long series of conferences with Paramount officials, capped by your own efforts, succeeded in changing the title [of a film] from "Diamonds Are Dangerous" to "Adventures in Diamonds".' It then reported that in another film called *Skylark*, it had succeeded in inserting a 'long scene' dealing with the selection of a diamond clip and bracelet for the star – Claudette Colbert; and that in the film, *That Uncertain Feeling*, Merle Oberon wore $40,000 worth of diamond jewelry. On the basis of these initial results, N. W. Ayer strongly recommended that continued efforts be made to manipulate Hollywood films. It reasoned that Americans 'have not been conditioned by their environment to diamond purchases. Aside from the engagement rings, they have no diamond tradition. But they are going to be influenced by . . . what they see their favorite movie star wear.'

To further advance the romantic image of diamonds, N. W. Ayer placed a series of lush four-colored advertisements about diamonds in the *New Yorker* and other magazines presumed to mold elite opinion. These advertisements featured reproductions of famous paintings by such respected artists as Picasso, Derain, Dali and Dufy, which were intended to convey the idea that diamonds were also unique works of art.

When the Second World War began in Europe, N. W. Ayer fed numerous stories to the press suggesting that the diamond market would not be adversely affected by these developments. Even though the war, in fact, virtually ended the gem diamond business, with mines being shut all over Africa and cutting centers in Europe being abandoned, the planted stories, which were widely circulated by the wire services, carried such optimistic titles as 'Diamond, King of Gems, Reigns Supreme Despite War,' 'Diamond Supply Unhurt by War,' 'War Gives Impetus to Diamond Cutting,' 'Marriage Increases Indicated by Rise in Diamond Sales,' and 'How Diamonds Spark the Wings of War and Peace.'

By 1941 the advertising agency reported to its client that it had already achieved impressive results in its campaign to alter the American public's perception of diamonds. Since its inception, the sale of diamonds had soared 55 per cent in the United States, reversing the previous downward trend in retail sales. N. W. Ayer stated in the accompanying memorandum to De Beers: 'the entire structure of your diamond organization for the duration of the war rests upon the ultimate sale of diamonds to consumers in the United States. . . . Your problem is to cultivate the desire to purchase diamonds for their own sake.' The advertising agency saw no reason to be overly modest in summarizing its own contribution. It noted in the report that its campaign required 'the conception of a new form of advertising which has been widely imitated ever since. There was no direct sale to be made. There was no brand name to be impressed on the public mind. There was simply an idea – the eternal emotional value surrounding the diamond.' It further claimed that 'a new type of art was devised . . . and a new color, diamond blue, was created and used in these campaigns. . . .'

As far as future campaigns were concerned, N. W. Ayer pointed out that paid advertisements themselves were not sufficient for solidifying the credibility of the diamond. 'It is the responsibility of the publicity effort to gain access to the editorial and news columns of magazines and newspapers, and thereby become part of the publication itself,' the report added. 'In this manner, it carries the authority of a disinterested source and consequently creates interest among readers.'

This technique of distributing its message disguised as a news story proved especially effective when it became necessary to foster the idea that diamonds were contributing to the war effort – and buying gems amounted to an act of patriotism. During the war De Beers also called on N. W. Ayer to defuse the charge that it was an international cartel. A penciled memorandum from De Beers in 1944 dealing with its public relations notes:

> Problem to convince American public that the Diamond Industry, though an admitted monopoly, operates fairly and in a manner that accords with American interests. This must be done in a way that will stand up under direct attack even from a government source.

It was not until after the war ended, when millions of soldiers returned to civilian life, that N. W. Ayer received an expanded budget from De Beers to proceed with the next stage of its campaign to make diamonds part of the romantic consciousness of the American public. In its 1947 strategy plan, the advertising agency strongly emphasized a psychological approach. 'We are dealing with a problem in mass psychology. We seek to . . . strengthen the tradition of the diamond engagement ring – to make it a psychological necessity capable of competing successfully at the retail level with utility goods and services. . . .' It defined as its target audience 'some 70 million people 15 years and over whose opinion we hope to influence in support of our objectives.' Since the point of the exercise was to cultivate a lasting image in the public mind, rather than merely to increase short-term sales, the advertising agency cautioned that 'the ordinary so-called "hard-hitting" techniques are not for you, for they are the very methods that helped to cheapen the diamond in the opinion of the public during the years before our association.'

Instead, N. W. Ayer outlined a far more subtle program which included arranging for lecturers to visit high schools across the country. 'All of these lectures revolve around the diamond engagement ring, and are reaching thousands of girls in their assemblies, classes and informal meetings in our leading educational institutions,' it explained in a memorandum to De Beers. The advertising agency also organized in 1946 a weekly service called 'Hollywood Personalities,' which provided 125 leading newspapers with descriptions of the diamonds worn by 'screen stars.' And it continued its efforts to focus news coverage on celebrities displaying their diamond rings as a symbol of romantic involvement. In 1947 the agency even commissioned a series of portraits of 'engaged socialites.' The idea was to create prestigious 'role models' for the poorer middle-class wage-earners. The advertising agency frankly explains in its 1948 strategy paper, 'We spread the word of diamonds worn by stars of screen and stage, by wives and daughters of political leaders, by any woman who can make the grocer's wife and the mechanic's sweetheart say "I wish I had what she has".'

Aside from the romantic connection, N. W. Ayer also found that it could subtly exploit the premarital insecurity women were found to have in their relations with men. Even though the tradition of diamond engagement rings was, at least in its popular form, mainly an invention of the late nineteenth century, the advertising agency decided to give it deep historical roots and establish it in the public's mind as an inseparable part of the marriage process. 'We keep people thinking of the diamond as the traditional symbol of the pledge to wed,' it explains in the 1948 memorandum. 'The tradition itself is kept before them – its origin, its meaning, its history. Told in different forms, in articles, in short "filler" items, in pictures, this story goes from our desks to appear in books, magazines and newspapers.' As evidence of the success of its campaign of surreptitious authoring of news stories, it cited the fact that 'newspapers have carried our items about the engagement diamonds of a list of women that range from Mrs [Harry S.] Truman to the "glamour girls" of Hollywood.' It suggested that these carefully constructed news stories were especially effective in planting ideas in the public mind, noting, 'Such items develop the feeling, more convincingly than mere repetition of the statement could do, that the diamond is in fact the only accepted symbol of engagement.'

De Beers needed a slogan for diamonds that expressed both the theme of romance and of legitimacy. Then in 1948 a N. W. Ayer copywriter came up with the caption 'A Diamond Is Forever,' which was scrawled on the bottom of a picture of two young lovers on a honeymoon. Even though diamonds can in fact be shattered, chipped, discolored or incinerated to an ash, the concept of eternity perfectly captured the magical qualities that the advertising agency wanted to impute to diamonds. Within a year, 'A Diamond Is Forever' became the official logo of De Beers.

In 1951, N. W. Ayer found some resistance to its million-dollar publicity blitz. It noted in its annual strategy review:

> The millions of brides and brides-to-be are subjected to at least two important pressures that work against the diamond engagement ring. Among the more prosperous, there is the sophisticated urge to be different as a means of being smart. . . . The lower-income groups would like to show more for the money than they can find in the diamonds they can afford. . . .

To remedy these problems, the advertising agency argued that 'it is essential that these pressures be met by the constant publicity to show that only the diamond is everywhere accepted and recognized as the symbol of betrothal.'

N. W. Ayer was constantly searching for new ways to influence American public opinion during this period. Not only did it organize a service to 'release to the women's pages [of daily newspapers] all the fresh material that we can find or create about the engagement ring,' but it set about exploiting the relatively new medium of television by arranging for actresses and other celebrities to wear diamonds when they appeared before the camera. It also established a 'Diamond Information Bureau,' which placed a quasi-official stamp of authority on the flood of 'historical' data and 'news' it released. 'We work hard to keep ourselves known throughout the publishing world as the source of information on diamonds,' it commented in a memorandum to De Beers, and added, 'Because we have done it successfully, we have opportunities to help with articles originated by others.' Among such successes, for example, the agency pointed to an article in the *National Geographic* exalting diamonds that it had helped prepare.

When sociologists such as David Resiman *(The Lonely Crowd)*, William White *(The Organization Man)* and Thorsten Veblen *(The Theory of the Leisure Class)* popularized the theory that Americans were motivated in their purchases, not by utility, but by 'conspicuous consumption,' N. W. Ayer proposed applying this sociological insight to the diamond market. 'The substantial diamond gift can be made a more widely sought symbol of personal and family success – an expression of socio-economic achievement.' To exploit this psychological need of Americans to conspicuously display symbols of their wealth, N. W. Ayer specifically recommended, 'Promote the diamond as one material object which can reflect, in a very personal way, a man's . . . success in life.' Since this campaign would require advertisements addressed to upwardly mobile men, the agency suggested that ideally they 'should have the aroma of tweed, old leather and polished wood which is characteristic of a good club.' In other words they were to evoke in men the sweet smell of success.

To further develop the diamond mind in America, N. W. Ayer asked both psychologists and sociologists to analyze 'basic human wants,' such as 'comfort,' 'freedom from fear,' 'longer life,' 'the ability to attract the opposite sex,' and 'social approval.' It justified this psychological investigation to De Beers in the following terms:

> An advertiser who can make a close and believable association between one or more of the 'basic human wants' and his product, can rouse a more vigorous and more universal demand for his product – and in the process tend to separate this demand from control by consumers' current economic situation.

The point of this manipulation was to create in consumers a desire for diamonds that had been subliminally linked through advertising with other 'basic human wants.'

Dr James Bossard, a professor of sociology at the University of Pennsylvania, observed in a report that he prepared for N. W. Ayer:

> The engagement ring . . . is a symbol of the ability to get your man in the competitive race. . . . It has the further features that it is not easily given (too expensive), it is visible (it sparkles), it is permanent (other things wear out), and it advertises the economic status of the giver. . . . Large-scale society makes for impersonal relations. One result of this is to place marked emphasis upon outward manifestations and visible evidence. . . . Conspicuous consumption becomes more impressive than quiet confidence. . . . Symbols are indicators of status. . . . A formal and visible symbol of approaching marriage becomes a vital necessity in a large office, a big university, a large plant.

In its strategy plan, N. W. Ayer strongly endorsed the professor's analysis. It added also that in terms of fashion 'women are conditioned to *want* what is shown in the fashion news.' It asserted that through psychologically designed advertising and public relations, women could be further conditioned to think of diamonds as a necessity of life.

For some sixteen years, N. W. Ayer carefully cultivated the romantic image in the public's mind that a diamond was a unique manifestation of nature and the rarest of all precious objects in the world. Then, in 1955, the General Electric Company announced with considerable fanfare that it had invented a process for manufacturing diamonds from ordinary carbon, which was the commonest element on earth. At the behest of De Beers, the advertising agency immediately began feeding stories to the press intended to dispel fears that the mass production of cheap diamonds was imminent. The crisis of synthetic diamonds soon passed from public attention. N. W. Ayer reported back to De Beers, 'At the time of the [General Electric] announcement there were, quite naturally, some expressions of uneasiness in the gem trade . . . but with each passing week the announcement is falling into perspective.' It added, 'We have fortunately been in a position to counsel trade organizations on communicating a relaxed point of view to their members.'

Toward the end of the 1950s, N. W. Ayer reviewed its achievements in fostering, if not wholly inventing, the diamond engagement tradition. It reported to its client in South Africa that twenty years of subtle but well-orchestrated advertisements and publicity had had a pronounced effect on the American psyche. 'Since 1939 an entirely new generation of young people has grown to marriageable age,' it noted with unmistakable pride of accomplishment. 'To this new generation a diamond ring is considered a necessity to engagement to virtually everyone.' The message had been so successfully impressed on the minds of this generation that those who could not afford to buy a diamond at the time of their marriage 'deferred the purchase' rather than forgoing it. Not only had the twenty-year advertising campaign helped De Beers 'sell current production' from its diamond mines, but, more importantly, it had elevated diamonds in the American mind to 'cherished possessions' which, according to N. W. Ayer, helped 'keep previous production in the hands of the consumer . . . and off the retail market.' Even in a severe economic pinch, diamonds would not be resold by consumers who had succumbed to the advertising pitch, 'A Diamond Is Forever.'

Indeed, N. W. Ayer proposed that instant engagement traditions should be invented for other countries. In its 1960 strategy plan it suggested, 'The idea of developing a public diamond engagement tradition in countries where it does not exist . . . has been volunteered by leading jewelers in those countries.' It noted that Germany and Sweden would be two outstanding targets for such an invention. Specifically, it said that an international engagement ring tradition would: 'enlarge the market for smaller diamonds . . .; insure regular growth by broadening the market base . . .; [and] help to keep diamonds in safe hands by making them cherished possessions of more people throughout the world.' The foreign-language editions of *Reader's Digest* were recommended as a means of introducing the diamond message abroad.

N. W. Ayer recognized in its analysis that some countries already had 'firmly rooted' traditions of exchanging simple gold rings to symbolize the engagement, and that in these countries it would not be possible to uproot instantly the existing tradition. Initially, it therefore suggested a campaign to associate diamonds with a 'gift of love.'

The campaign to internationalize the diamond mind began in earnest in the mid-1960s. The prime targets were Japan, Germany and Brazil. Since N. W. Ayer was primarily an American advertising agency, De Beers brought in the J. Walter Thompson agency, which had especially strong advertising subsidiaries in Japan, Germany and Brazil, to place most of its international advertising. Within ten years, De Beers succeeded even beyond its most optimistic expectations in creating a billion-dollar-a-year diamond tradition in Japan. In Germany and Brazil, De Beers met with more moderate success.

In America, which still remained the ultimate market for most of De Beers' diamonds, N. W. Ayer developed a plan for insulating diamond sales from the cyclical swings in the economy that affected most luxury goods. In 1960, it suggested a series of advertising messages which would gradually induce consumers into perceiving diamonds in terms of sentiments, such as love, instead of valuable gems which could be disposed of in hard times. Specifically, the 'engagement advertising strategy' for the 1960s involved three steps:

1. To attach to the diamond the meaning of the engagement period;
2. Conversely, to identify with the engagement period the romance, beauty, uniqueness, value and permanence of the diamond;
3. To express these ideas frequently to a clear majority of the US families capable of responding.

N. W. Ayer then outlined a 'psychology' for sentimentalizing diamonds:

The first time that a man spoke to a woman of his love, devotion, and expressed the wish never to be parted from her . . . the symbol of the first milestone was a diamond. The engagement diamond . . . This diamond ring . . . was a badge for the outside world to see. It gave the woman her status as a woman, the prestige of a woman. Nothing else could take the place of a diamond.

However, as the years go by, the woman needs further reassurance that her husband still loves her, according to this psychological profile. 'Candies come, flowers come, furs come,' the study continues, but such ephemeral gifts fail to satisfy the woman's psychological craving for 'a renewal of the romance.' A diamond, however, which originally symbolized the commitment of love, could serve to fill this emotional 'later-in-life' need. The advertising agencies therefore recommended that De Beers initiate a program of advertisements which would instill in the public's mind that the gift of a second diamond, in the later years of marriage, would be accepted as a sign of 'evergrowing love.'

N. W. Ayer argued that the development of a new 'later-in-life' diamond market would be necessary to absorb the increasing supply of diamonds from South Africa, because the number of engagement diamonds was more or less fixed by the number of marriages in America. Specifically, it recommended a campaign to 'reach deeper into the population to sell gift (later-in-life) diamonds in order to increase demand,' and in 1962 it asked authorization to 'begin the long term process of setting the diamond aside as the only appropriate gift for those later-in-life occasions where sentiment is to be expressed.' De Beers immediately approved the campaign.

The diamond mind had to be further restructured in the mid-1960s to accommodate the surfeit of minute Siberian diamonds that De Beers undertook to market for the Russians. Almost all these diamonds were under one-half carat in their uncut form, and there was no ready retail outlet for millions of such tiny diamonds. When it made its secret deal with the Soviet Union, De Beers had expected the production from the Siberian mines to gradually decrease. Instead, it accelerated at an incredible pace, and De Beers was forced to reconsider its sales strategy.

Up to this point, De Beers itself had been largely responsible for reducing the market for small, under one-carat diamonds. Through its twenty-year advertising campaign, it had encouraged American women to think of the size of a diamond as a status symbol or 'badge': the larger the diamond, the more status it represented. During this period, N. W. Ayer had surreptitiously authored film scenarios and news stories which constantly depicted women as measuring a man's commitment by the number of carats in the diamond he gave her. The engagement reports on celebrities that N. W. Ayer circulated also emphasized 'caratage,' or size, rather than quality. Diamonds were portrayed as 'a girl's best friend' if they were conspicuously large.

Now, however, De Beers ordered N. W. Ayer to abruptly reverse its theme: women were no longer to be led to equate the status and emotional commitment in an engagement with the sheer size of the diamond. Instead, a 'strategy for small diamond sales' was outlined which involved stressing the 'importance of quality, color and cut' over size, and in advertisement pictures substituting 'one-quarter carat' rings for 'up to two carat' rings. Moreover, the advertising agency began in its international campaign to 'illustrate gems as small as one-tenth of a carat and give them the same emotional importance as larger stones.' The symbolic content of the news releases was also to be manipulated so that women would be induced to think of diamonds, regardless of their size, as objects of perfection: a small diamond could be as perfect as a large diamond.

The new campaign met with considerable success. The average size of a diamond, which was one carat in 1939, fell to .28 in 1976, which coincided almost exactly with the average size of the Siberian diamonds that De Beers was distributing. However, as American consumers became gradually accustomed to the idea of buying smaller diamonds, they began to perceive the larger diamonds as 'flashy' and ostentatious. By the mid-1970s the advertising success was beginning to take on the aspects of a financial disaster. In its 1978 strategy report, N. W. Ayer noted, 'a supply problem has developed . . . that has had a significant effect on diamond pricing.' This problem, it explained, proceeded from its long-term campaign to stimulate the sale of small diamonds. 'Owing to successful pricing, distribution and advertising policies over the last fifteen years, demand for small diamonds now appears to have significantly exceeded supply even though supply, in absolute terms, has been increasing steadily.' But whereas there was an insufficient supply of small diamonds to meet the demands of consumers, N. W. Ayer reported that 'large stone sales [one carat and up] . . . have maintained the sluggish pace of the last three years.' Because of this, the memorandum continued, 'large stones are being . . . discounted by as much as 20 per cent.' In other words, by heightening the appeal of minute diamonds, the advertising campaign had inadvertently diminished the saleability of the larger diamonds. Since the larger stones were far more profitable to sell than the smaller ones, De Beers and its clients were being deprived of potential profits.

Despite this embarrassing 'supply problem,' N. W. Ayer argued that 'small stone jewelry advertising' should not be totally abandoned. 'Serious trade relationship problems would ensue if, after fifteen years of stressing "affordable" small stone jewelry, we were to drop all of these programs,' it pointed out.

Instead, it suggested a subtle change in 'emphasis' in presenting diamonds to the American public. In the advertisements, it planned such 'adjustments' as replacing smaller diamonds with one carat and over stones, and resuming both an 'informative advertising campaign' and an 'emotive program' which would serve to 'reorient consumer tastes and price perspectives towards acceptance of solitaire [single stone] jewelry rather than multi-stone pieces.' Other 'strategic refinements' it recommended were designed to restore the large diamond to being a visible symbol of conspicuous consumption. 'In fact, this [campaign] will be the exact opposite of the small stone informative program that ran from 1965 to 1970 that popularized the "beauty in miniature" concept. . . .' With an advertising budget for America of some $9,690,000, N. W. Ayer appeared confident that it could bring about this 'reorientation.'

N. W. Ayer further attempted to plumb the diamond mind in the mid-1970s by retaining the firm of Daniel Yankelovich, Inc., to poll a representative sample of the American public on its attitude toward diamonds. The study was continued over five years, and from this highly sophisticated analysis of public opinion emerged a rather surprising picture of a man, rather than a woman, as 'the key figure in the diamond jewelry acquisition process.'

In the case of engagement rings, men played a dominant role in 88 per cent of the purchases; indeed, in 46 per cent of the purchases, the man bought the ring without any participation whatsoever from his fiancée. In purchasing other pieces of diamond jewelry, the study found that women also only rarely participated in the decision. 'Not only is a woman unlikely to buy diamond jewelry for herself,' the study continued, 'she is also unlikely to buy diamonds for anyone else.' The essence of the diamond transaction was that it was a gift from a man to a woman.

The gift, moreover, contained an important element of surprise. 'Approximately half of all diamond jewelry that the men have given and the women have received were given with zero participation or knowledge on the part of the woman recipient,' the Yankelovich study pointed out. N. W. Ayer explored this 'surprise factor' in an analysis that observed:

> Women are in unanimous agreement that they want to be surprised with gifts. . . . They want, of course, to be surprised for the thrill of it. However, a deeper, more important reason lies behind this desire – "freedom from guilt." Some of the women pointed out that if their husbands enlisted their help in purchasing a gift, like diamond jewelry, their practical nature would come to the fore and they would be compelled to object to the purchase.

Women were not totally surprised by diamond gifts: some 84 per cent of the men in the study 'knew somehow' that the women wanted diamond jewelry. The study suggested a two-step 'gift-process continuum.' First, 'the man "learns" diamonds are O.K.' from the woman; then, 'at some later point in time, he makes the diamond purchase decision' to surprise the woman.

Through a series of 'projective' psychological questions, meant 'to draw out a respondent's innermost feelings about diamond jewelry,' the study attempted to examine further the curious, semi-passive role played by women in the diamond relationship. The man–woman roles seemed to resemble closely the sex relations in a Victorian novel. 'Man plays the dominant, active role in the gift process. Woman's role is more subtle, more oblique, more enigmatic. . . .' Like Victorian sex, women seemed to believe that there was something improper about receiving a diamond gift. They spoke about large diamonds as 'flashy, gaudy, overdone . . .' and otherwise inappropriate. Yet, through its psychological probing of the female mind, the study found, 'Buried in the negative attitudes . . . lies what is probably the primary driving force for acquiring them. Diamonds are a traditional and conspicuous signal of achievement, status and success.' It noted, for example, 'A woman can easily feel that diamonds are "vulgar" and still be highly enthusiastic about receiving diamond jewelry.' The element of 'surprise, even if it is feigned, plays the same role of accommodating dissonance in accepting a diamond gift as it does in prim sexual seductions: it permits the woman to pretend that she has not actively participated in the decision. She thus retains both her innocence – and the diamond.'

In projecting from this data a strategy for De Beers for the future, N. W. Ayer suggested that the objective of advertising was 'to perpetuate the positioning of diamond jewelry as the most special of all gifts, so that men will continue to "know" and women continue to "teach" that diamonds are acceptable and wanted.' While the advertising agency candidly recognized that 'available research has not shed light on how the man learns that a diamond gift would be acceptable to his wife,' it nevertheless pressed for a campaign of highly emotive advertising that would reinforce this cryptic male 'awareness' of female 'receptivity.' Specifically, it suggested that the 'tone of the copy' should project 'a strong sense of confidence in the voice of the giver that the gift will be especially well received.' Ideally, the male reader should be enabled 'to project himself into the situation [and] . . . play the role of the giver and anticipate the rewards associated with a gift of diamonds.' For example, an advertisement might depict a beautiful woman, gushing with love and admiration, as she is surprised by the diamond gift – while the male giver stands smugly by. No matter how uninterested men might be in diamonds themselves, these advertisements should convey 'the extraordinary reaction that can be expected from the gift.' The artwork in these advertisements should, N. W. Ayer further recommended, 'play to a known positive attitude in women that a gift of this sort is preferred as a surprise.' Finally, 'a significant male appeal implicit in the surprise situation is the strong implication that the gift will be a success.' N. W. Ayer concluded that such a campaign would provide 'an emotional appeal that is highly motivating to men.'

For manipulation of the diamond mind in the 1980s, the implications of this psychological research were clear. To induce men to buy women diamonds, advertising should focus not on the qualities and beauty of the diamond itself, but on the emotional impact of the 'surprise' gift transaction. In the final analysis, men were not moved to part with their earnings by the value, aesthetics or tradition of diamonds, but by the expectation that a 'gift of love' would enhance their standing in the eyes of their beloved. On the other hand, women accepted the gift as a tangible symbol of their status and achievement. Playing off the duality of the male–female relationship, N. W. Ayer helped De Beers expand its sales of diamonds in the United States from a mere $23 million in 1939 to over $2.1 billion, at the wholesale level, in 1979. In two-score years, the value of its sales had increased nearly a hundred-fold. In comparison, the expenditure on advertisements, which began at a level of only $200,000 a year and gradually increased to $10 million, seemed a brilliant investment by De Beers. It had, after all, helped evolve an American diamond mind capable of absorbing the plethora of diamonds from both Africa and Siberia.

Part Three

The Diamond Wars

The Smugglers | 14

Through the brillant financial maneuvers of Sir Ernest Oppenheimer, the diamond cartel had succeeded in gaining control of virtually all the diamond mines in the world by the early 1950s. It had made its arrangements with the government of South Africa, the colonial administrations in Angola, the Congo and Sierra Leone, and with Dr Williamson in Tanganyika. It was fully backed by the British, Belgian and the French governments, and it was recognized by every other government concerned as the official channel for the diamond trade. There were still unofficial channels, however, that the diamond cartel did not control: the smuggling routes that led from the diamond mines and diggings in southern and western Africa to entrepots such as Monrovia and Beirut. Since the African governments did not have either the techniques or resources at their disposal to interdict the diamond smugglers, Sir Ernest decided to recruit his own diamond soldiers. In December 1953, he instructed his London office to track down and contact Sir Percy Sillitoe.

Sillitoe had been, until November 1953, the head of the British counterespionage service known as MI5. During the Second World War, he had organized one of the most ingenious spy operations in the history of espionage. It was called the double-cross system, and it involved converting all the German spies in England into British double agents. Since the Germans accepted the reports of these spies as bona fide intelligence, Sillitoe and his double committee, which included Harry Oppenheimer's tutor at Oxford, Sir John Masterman, were able to feed the Germans a false picture of British activities. After the war, Sillitoe worked closely with American and French intelligence. In 1950, however, the British government was severely embarrassed by the defection of two of its diplomats from Washington – Donald Maclean and Guy Burgess – to Moscow, and the British security services came under increasing criticism. Sillitoe, who had in any case reached the age of sixty-five, was allowed to retire in the midst of the scandal. Since retired intelligence chiefs are expected to fade quietly away, Sillitoe moved to the seaside town of Eastbourne in southern England and worked in a local sweet shop owned by relatives, selling chocolates and other confectionery.

When Sillitoe received the invitation from Oppenheimer, he was behind the counter of his sweet shop. Within a matter of days, he had abandoned the confectionery, and was on a plane flying over Africa.

At the airport in Capetown, he was met by Oppenheimer's chauffeur and immediately driven to the village of Muizenberg on the Indian Ocean. He arrived at a beautifully landscaped estate where Oppenheimer and his family were spending their Christmas vacation.

At their initial meeting, Oppenheimer briefed Sillitoe on the smuggling problem. He explained that the smuggling of diamonds not only deprived De Beers of the value of the stolen diamonds but, far more serious, it threatened to undermine the monopoly prices for diamonds that De Beers had established. He estimated that somewhere between 10 and 20 per cent of all the diamonds reaching cutting centers were smuggled goods. These illicit diamonds were undercutting De Beers' prices. Moreover, if diamond dealers and cutters had an alternative source from which to buy their diamonds, they would be less willing to accept De Beers' rigid conditions for doing business in the diamond trade. Oppenheimer was emphatic: he wanted the smugglers stopped.

Sillitoe admittedly had no knowledge about the diamond business, but he suggested that the techniques of counterintelligence that he had employed during the war against the Germans could effectively be used against smugglers. If some of the individuals who illegally bought and sold diamonds could be identified, they could be 'turned' into double agents for the cartel. These agents then could be used to manipulate the diamond smugglers higher up the chain. To accomplish this for De Beers, Sillitoe suggested that he hire a half dozen top intelligence officers from the British secret service. These men would form the nucleus of a private intelligence service for the cartel.

After giving the matter some consideration, Oppenheimer accepted Sillitoe's proposal. De Beers would provide the financial support, and Sillitoe would have carte blanche to recruit an elite core of agents for the 'International Diamond Security Organization,' as it was eventually called.

Sillitoe's education in the diamond business began in 1954 with a tour of the mines. At the Kimberley mines, De Beers' security officers briefed him on the various ways in which employees had smuggled diamonds out of the mining areas in the past. The methods ranged from using rubber-band catapults to fling the diamonds over the barbwire fences to having a surgeon hollow out a niche in an ankle bone in which diamonds could be concealed under a bandage. The most common means was for individuals to simply swallow diamonds and then recover them once outside the compound. Because of the minute size of diamonds, it was virtually impossible to detect them except by X-raying the entire body. However, employees could not be subjected to constant X-rays without exposing them to lethal doses of gamma rays and thereby endangering their lives. X-ray examinations, therefore, could only be given to a small proportion of randomly selected workers each day. At best, the X-ray machine was a psychological deterrent to theft. Like the closed-circuit television cameras that conspicuously scanned back and forth at the mines, X-rays were another demonstration to black workers of the white man's magic. But once the employees understood that these electronic devices had only a relatively small chance of detecting smuggled diamonds, their value as deterrents was seriously impaired.

Sillitoe found that these security procedures were far too passive to prevent sophisticated thefts. He suggested instead that De Beers employ more aggressive and imaginative methods; for example, radioactive paints had been successfully used for the surveillance of enemy agents in England. (In one case, this paint had been applied to the shoes of a Soviet diplomat in London, and then his trail had been followed by means of a Geiger counter.) Sillitoe proposed that a few diamonds be radioactively 'labeled' with an invisible paint and then be conspicuously left around in areas where employees were likely to steal them. Assuming that the radioactive bait would be snatched up, a Geiger counter would click the moment the diamond passed through the gates of the compound. The thief then would not be arrested but followed, and in time the radioactive diamond would be sold to an intermediary. The intermediary could then be followed with the Geiger counter or arrested – and turned into an informer. Such exotic security measures resulted in the recovery of only a few diamonds, however.

Sillitoe next learned that the cartel's problem was not the trickle of diamonds being stolen from its South African mines but the flood of diamonds that were smuggled out of west and central Africa every year. With two of his staff assistants, Sillitoe traveled to areas outside South Africa from which most of the diamonds seemed to come. He went to Aquatia in Ghana, Freetown and Yengema in Sierra Leone, Bakwanga and Luluaburg in the Belgian Congo, and Dar-es-Salaam and Mwadui in Tanganyika. In each of these countries, he was able to make contact with the intelligence officers whom he had previously worked with in his capacity as head of British counterintelligence. Most of these countries were still British colonies in 1954, and his former comrades in arms were willing to extend him a good deal of unofficial cooperation. The first objective, as Sillitoe's deputy explained, was 'to set up an intelligence network which would penetrate this underground railroad round the world.'

In South Africa, most diamond mines were volcanic pipes, which could be isolated behind electrified ten-foot-high barbwire fences. In central and west Africa, however, most diamonds were 'mined' from streambeds that meandered over tens of thousands of miles of jungle. To recover these diamonds, natives needed only a shovel and a pan. Even though the governments had granted concessions to various diamond mining companies associated with De Beers, and had in theory banned anyone else from digging for diamonds, it was in practice impossible to enforce these regulations.

The problem was particularly difficult in Sierra Leone, where the river banks were littered with diamonds. Not only was the government unwilling to police this vast area to prevent illicit digging, but the local authorities explained to

Sillitoe that most natives believed 'the soil of Sierra Leone belonged to the Sierra Leoneans,' and not the diamond companies. At night, gangs of 'pot-holers,' as they were called, would dig up the river banks and disappear at daybreak with the diamondiferous gravel. The pot-holers would then either sell their diamonds to Lebanese traders or directly to Mandango tribesmen, who, in turn, smuggled them across the open border to Liberia. By one means or another, it was estimated that more than half of Sierra Leone's diamonds were sold in Monrovia as 'Liberian' diamonds. Even though Liberia had in reality no diamond mines of any significance, fictive 'mines' were created in the jungles to account for this enormous production of diamonds.

After carefully studying the situation, Sillitoe concluded that it would be futile to attempt to end the illicit mining in Sierra Leone by pot-holers. Even if Sierra Leone's understaffed colonial police could be induced to arrest thousands of these diggers, other natives would take their place panning the rivers and mudholes. Instead, he decided to concentrate his efforts on controlling Lebanese middlemen who were behind the illicit traffic.

Initially, Sillitoe's men recruited a number of clandestine agents in Sierra Leone and Liberia who would pretend to be independent diamond buyers. After making contact with the Lebanese, these agents offered to buy large quantities of smuggled diamonds at much higher prices than the cartel's real competitors were offering.

The quantity of diamonds available on the illegal market staggered Sillitoe. He found he needed more than $5 million in 'buy' money to maintain the intelligence operation, and to obtain such a large amount of hard currency in a British colony required the permission of the British government. Sillitoe managed, however, to persuade the British authorities that diamonds were an important factor in Britain's precarious balance of payments equation, and he was then quickly granted permission to spend hard currencies to buy up smuggled diamonds.

By making major purchases of diamonds in black markets, Sillitoe's agents were able to ferret out the middlemen trafficking in diamonds. Then, through surveillance and intercepted mail, they traced the traffic from the diamond fields of Sierra Leone through the entrepots of Liberia to the wholesale markets in Belgium. It turned out that reputable European merchants, who were also customers of the cartel, had been surreptitiously financing the African smugglers and one of the principal buyers of the smuggled goods was the Soviet Union, which then critically needed industrial diamonds to retool its factories.

Sillitoe realized that the illicit diamond traffic could not be ended decisively as long as the smugglers had high rewards for their goods and only minimal risks of being captured. He therefore decided to raise the stakes for the smugglers by hiring private armies of mercenaries to ambush their diamond caravans in the jungles. The most resourceful of these mercenaries was Fred Kamil, a Lebanese trader then in his twenties. Kamil had for years extorted money from smugglers on the route that led through the swamps from Sierra Leone to Liberia, and which was known as the 'stranger's trail.' With a group of gunmen, he also waylaid merchants and travelers who came down the narrow trail. In 1956, Sillitoe's organization offered Kamil a highly attractive deal. He would be supplied with information from undercover informers about the exact movements of diamond shipments from Sierra Leone to Liberia to facilitate his ambushes. In return, he would turn the diamonds over to a De Beers subsidiary, and he would receive one-third of their value in cash. Kamil agreed to the alliance, since it would also mean that he would have police protection in Sierra Leone.

Many of the ambushes were bloody affairs. A caravan of a dozen or so Mandango tribesmen would emerge from the jungle in Sierra Leone and head for the bridge across the Mao River, which was the Liberian border. Suddenly, mines and flares would be detonated all around them. Then Kamil's mercenaries would open fire with hunting rifles. The tribesmen, who were not hit, would instantly surrender and turn their diamonds over to the mercenaries. It was a 'diamond war,' Kamil later explained in his account of these exploits.

As the risks of smuggling diamonds to Liberia greatly increased, and caravan after caravan was intercepted and plundered by mercenaries, the Lebanese dealers saw little alternative but to sell their contraband diamonds in Sierra Leone. This meant that the dealers had to pay a tax on the diamonds. The Sierra Leone government facilitated these transactions by lowering the export tax on diamonds.

Once the illicit diamonds had been contained in Sierra Leone, De Beers established a string of buying offices in the jungle. Each buying office was no more than a corrugated iron hut, with a barred slit through which their agent did business with the pot-holers. Each agent was given a set of sample diamonds, with which he compared those diamonds offered for sale, and a strongbox full of Sierra Leonean currency. When he ran out of currency, he radioed the cartel's office in Freetown, and a plane was sent out to drop another box of currency next to his trading post. De Beers sent some of its most promising recruits in London into the jungles of Sierra Leone to train as diamond buyers. In short order, the pot-holers became fully accustomed to dealing with these well-tailored buyers in the strange huts.

By 1957, Sillitoe decided that he had successfully completed his mission for the cartel. He quietly disbanded his International Diamond Security Organization, though many of his agents and mercenaries continued working directly or indirectly for the cartel, and he returned to his chocolate shop in Eastbourne.

Sierra Leone, despite the counterintelligence successes of Sillitoe, again became in the late 1960s a serious threat to the De Beers' monopoly. In 1968, to muffled criticism about its dealings with the cartel, the government created a state-owned diamond company called Dominico to which all the diamonds found in that country had to be sold. Dominico, in turn, sold half its diamonds to a London corporation which in turn sold these diamonds to De Beers' Diamond Trading Company. The remaining half was in theory at least sold to three independent American dealers – Maurice Tempelsman, who received 27 per cent, Lazare Kaplan, who received 3 per cent, and Harry Winston, who received the other 20 per cent. In reality, however, both Tempelsman and Kaplan resold their share to the Diamond Trading Company in London, which effectively gave the cartel control of 80 per cent of the Sierra Leonean diamonds. Winston, who like Kaplan and Tempelsman was a major customer of the cartel, was temporarily permitted to sell his share in New York.

As part of the window dressing for this deal, Tempelsman

agreed to open a diamond-cutting factory in Sierra Leone's capital of Freetown. These cut and polished diamonds would then be sold to tourists as Sierra Leonean gems.

Even though the cartel and the Sierra Leone government were satisfied with this complicated arrangement for dividing the diamonds, a number of powerful Lebanese businessmen in Freetown believed that they were being unfairly cut out of the lucrative trade. They demanded a share of the diamonds but were turned down. The dispute came to a dramatic head on 13 November 1969, when a band of masked men with submachine guns brazenly held up the truck delivering the rich October shipment of diamonds to the sorting office in Freetown. The security officers from the mine put up no resistance, and the masked men walked off with the diamonds. A private plane at the airport then flew the cache of diamonds to Europe, where they were sold for an estimated $10 million to a consortium of diamond dealers.

In investigating this well-planned and professionally executed robbery, the cartel quickly established that the thieves had had inside information about the time and place of the delivery, and that the police had permitted them to escape from the country. The more they looked into the circumstances surrounding the crime, the more the cartel's investigators found abundant evidence of corruption in high places. The cover-up seemed to involve everyone from petty police officials to justices of the Supreme Court. From what the investigators could piece together from the cartel's network of informers, it appeared that a group of Lebanese businessmen were behind the robbery. Further inquiries showed, however, that these Lebanese had powerful connections with the highest officials in the government, and therefore there was virtually no possibility that any action would be taken against them.

Since De Beers could not easily eliminate the Lebanese from their positions of power in Sierra Leone, it decided to make a deal with some of them. The single most powerful Lebanese entrepreneur in Sierra Leone was Jamil Mohammed. He had an African mother and Lebanese father, and had made an immense fortune in diamonds, which he invested in real estate, rice and fishing. Then he became a partner with the Soviet Union in a lucrative venture that allowed their trawlers to fish in Sierra Leone's waters and operate out of Sierra Leone's ports. By 1969, he had become the richest man in Sierra Leone and more or less the godfather who looked after the interests of the Afro-Lebanese community. And he now became the man with whom the diamond cartel decided to deal directly in Sierra Leone.

Accordingly, the division of Sierra Leonean diamonds was suddenly revised in early 1970. The cartel would still receive, through its allies, 80 per cent of the total production. The remaining 20 per cent would, however, be taken away from Harry Winston, and most of this consignment would instead be given to Jamil Mohammed. Jamil Mohammed would then sell his share back to the cartel for a substantial profit. The net effect of this new arrangement was that the cartel received nearly 100 per cent of Sierra Leone's diamonds, and Jamil Mohammed, the cartel's new man in Sierra Leone, received a fixed percentage of the revenue from these diamonds. There were no more robberies in Sierra Leone and a marked decrease in smuggling.

The only problem that the cartel had in Sierra Leone now was that production was gradually decreasing. As riverbeds and mudholes were exhaustively panned, fewer and fewer diamonds were found. By 1978, Jamil Mohammed, vexed by the decline in output, made new demands on the cartel. He asked for a larger share of all the giant diamonds found in Sierra Leone (some weighed more than a hundred carats). These giant diamonds still could be sold directly to dealers in Antwerp and New York at enormous profits. When the cartel refused to increase his share of these giant diamonds, Jamil Mohammed threatened to sell his share of diamonds on the open market. The cartel now began to regard Jamil Mohammed 'as a monster of our creation,' as one of De Beers' executives put it.

It was, however, necessary to come to terms with strong men like Jamil Mohammed in Africa to preserve the diamond invention. Eventually, his share was increased, and he was given access to the great diamonds.

The smuggling problem was not restricted to Sierra Leone. Sir Ernest Oppenheimer had always considered the vast undeveloped diamond fields of the Congo to be the single greatest threat to the cartel. So long as the Belgians ruled this area, he was able to assure, through secret arrangements with the Belgian government and banking houses, that diamond smugglers would be ruthlessly stamped out in the Congo. The situation changed radically for the cartel after Belgium abruptly granted the colony independence in 1960 and it became the independent nation of Zaire. De Beers now had to persuade its president, Mobutu Sese Seko, that it also was in his interest to prevent diamonds from being smuggled out of the country. Working through intermediaries in the capital of Kinshasa, De Beers arranged a deal whereby Zaire would sell all its diamonds to a privately held corporation, which, in turn, would deliver these diamonds to De Beers' Diamond Trading Company in London. The corporation would pay an immense tax to the Zairean government and distribute an important share in the profits in the diamonds to Zairean stockholders who were closely associated with the Mobutu government. Consequently, Mobutu moved even more vigorously against the smugglers than his Belgian predecessor. He deployed hovercraft patrol ships, which could skim over the water at forty miles an hour, and armed helicopter gunships to police the diamond fields. These diamond soldiers tended to shoot first and ask questions only afterward. For example, in November 1979, they spotted a group of young Zaireans walking through a diamond digging, and ambushed them, killing some two hundred of them in a matter of minutes. They then learned that they were students on a camping trip, not diamond poachers.

Mobutu also moved to prevent diamonds from being pilfered in the sorting houses in Zaire. Since native sorters could not be effectively isolated from their family and friends, and therefore could easily pass along diamonds that they swallowed or palmed, Mobutu arranged with the Diamond Trading Company to employ European sorters rather than Zaireans. In a matter of months, the number of gem diamonds recovered – and turned in – in the Zairean sorting house increased by 30 per cent.

Most of Angola's diamonds were mined from meandering rivers in eastern Angola which allowed easy access to illegal diggers and smugglers. De Beers arranged for the rivers to be dammed and the riverbeds cordoned off behind barbwire. This prevented diamonds from being carried downstream. Then, to seal off the jungle border, De Beers arranged to hire the remnants of the Katanga gendarme, which had fled

Zaire en masse after its rebellion against Mobutu had failed in the 1960s. Led by mercenaries, these soldiers tracked down smugglers in the anarchic border zone, and received a bounty for the diamonds they recovered.

Even with the support of private armies and black governments, it was impossible for De Beers to eradicate native smugglers completely. To prevent even this trickle of gems from reaching Europe and competing with the cartel's prices, De Beers stationed undercover diamond buyers in Monrovia, Brazzaville, Burundi and other entrepots in Africa. Aside from buying back diamonds, this operation was designed to provide a constant flow of information that could be used against the diamond smugglers. One of the men chosen to head this undercover diamond buying was the Lebanese mercenary who had ambushed hundreds of smugglers in Sierra Leone, Fred Kamil.

In April 1965, Kamil was flown by De Beers to Johannesburg and then driven by a major in the South African police to Oppenheimer's headquarters at 44 Main Street to meet Colonel George Cloete Visser, head of security for the Anglo-American Corporation. According to Kamil's account, an agreement was 'hammered out' which included provisions that:

'[Kamil] would establish a network of investigators and informers which would operate secretly and independently, but under the direction of Anglo-American Corporation's Security.' The priorities were: '(a) the identity and activities of the Corporation's employees in positions of trust, involved in illicit diamond buying; (b) the discovery and closure of diamond leakages from the Corporation's mining and protected areas; (c) the recovery of stolen diamonds. . . .'

As compensation, Kamil was to be paid his expenses plus one-third of the value of all the diamonds recovered. It provided him with a powerful incentive to uncover stolen diamonds.

Kamil built a fairly extensive intelligence organization throughout southern Africa and made a small fortune recovering smuggled diamonds for the cartel. Then, in 1968, Colonel Visser abruptly terminated his arrangement with the cartel.

Angry and embittered, Kamil returned to Beirut, where

he wrote Harry Oppenheimer a series of letters demanding more compensation for his work. He received no response. Finally, in 1972, he devised a desperate plan to extort money from De Beers. He would hijack a South African airliner carrying Oppenheimer's son-in-law, Gordon Waddell, and demand that Oppenheimer personally meet with him and negotiate the ransom. With a Lebanese companion named Ajej Yaghi and a few hand grenades, Kamil managed to hijack a South African airliner – but the intended victim was not aboard it. Moreover, Oppenheimer refused to meet with him – or ransom the jet. Kamil finally ordered the pilot to land in Malawi, where army troops shot out the plane's wheels. After a twenty-four-hour siege, Kamil surrendered.

Kamil served only a short time in prison in Malawi and was pardoned. Shortly thereafter, the Anglo-American Corporation paid him £50,103 (about $100,000), supposedly in additional compensation for his past services. He came out of the diamond war a fairly rich man.

15 Infringement on the Patent

In 1950, De Beers had a worldwide monopoly on the production of natural diamonds. It directly controlled all the pipe mines in the world – there were only seven, and they were all in southern and central Africa – and it had arrangements, either direct or surreptitious, with the governments of all the major diamond-producing countries to buy whatever diamonds were found in these regions by native diggers or fortune hunters. Moreover, it had the financial and political resources to preemptively buy out any new diamond discovery in most parts of the world.

There was, however, another threat to the diamond invention that emerged that year: the possibility that diamonds could be produced in a laboratory or even a factory. A team of scientists at the De Beers Research Laboratories had come to the conclusion that it was only a matter of time before a process was found for synthesizing diamonds.They had received information that both the United States and the Soviet Union were encouraging research aimed at mass-producing industrial-grade diamonds, and they believed that converting carbon, which was one of the commonest of all substances on earth, to diamonds was merely an engineering problem. It required constructing a vessel strong enough to withstand the heat and pressure necessary for inducing the synthesis. In a meeting with Sir Ernest Oppenheimer, they argued that advanced metallurgic alloys and high-pressure physics made the solution of this problem inevitable. They proposed that De Beers itself take the lead in developing this diamond-making technology, then through patents and licenses attempt to control synthetic diamond production. They warned that if an outside party made the breakthrough, De Beers might lose its monopoly position.

Sir Ernest listened patiently to their arguments for a crash program on diamond synthesis. Then, after considering the matter, he turned them down, and said, 'Only God can make a diamond.' His dogma notwithstanding, his scientific assessment of the situation proved wrong. Within two years, a diamond was produced in a laboratory in Sweden.

For at least 300 years scientists had experimented with the conversion of carbon to diamonds – or vice versa. For example, as early as 1694, Florentine academicians gathered around a terrace to witness the following experiment: a magnificently cut diamond was placed in a crucible under a powerful glass lens. As the sun's rays focused on it, it began giving off acrid black vapors. A few minutes later, it disappeared in a cloud of smoke, leaving not a trace of diamond in the crucible. The academicians suggested that the diamond was pure carbon, and that under the fiery heat it had turned to the gaseous form – carbon dioxide. But they could not prove this assertion.

A century later, an English chemist, Smithson Tennant, burned a diamond in a sealed vessel filled with pure oxygen. It also decomposed into an acrid vapor. Through chemical analysis, Tennant was able to determine that this vapor was carbon dioxide, and that the weight of the carbon in the vapor exactly matched the weight of that of the diamond that had vaporized. From this and other experiments, it was scientifically established that a diamond was carbon.

If diamonds could be transformed through a simple chemical reaction into carbon, it followed that carbon, through a reverse process, could be converted to diamonds. From the nineteenth century onward, the idea that the commonest of elements, carbon, could be turned into rare diamonds in the laboratory intrigued both scientists and confidence men and led to a wide range of experiments – as well as dubious claims.

In 1880, a twenty-five-year-old Scottish chemist named James Ballantyne Hannay, working in a laboratory in Glasgow, attempted to achieve this sought-after synthesis by exploding carbonaceous material. He first sealed a mixture of powdered carbon, bone oil, and paraffin in coiled tubes, and then placed the tubes in a reverbatory furnace. When the heat and pressure built up sufficiently, the tubes exploded and splattered the furnace walls with white-hot debris. After waiting for the furnace to cool, Hannay carefully scraped a number of minute particles off the surface with a pair of tweezers and found that these specks scratched glass – one test of a diamond. Triumphantly, Hannay claimed that he had manufactured diamonds and sent about a dozen specimens to the British Museum of Natural History in London.

At the time, however, most of Hannay's contemporaries doubted that he had, in fact, achieved the synthesis of carbon to diamond crystals. Some scientists argued that he had misanalyzed the crystals that had resulted from his experiments as diamonds, and others openly insinuated that Hannay had himself put the diamonds into the tubes to fraudulently create a reputation for himself. Since the crystals that Hannay claimed were produced through his process were too minute to be used in either jewelry or industrial tools, the issue of whether or not these were authentic diamonds remained a purely academic one. (More than a half century later, however, Hannay's crystals were rediscovered by the British Museum and, under X-ray analysis, proved to be diamonds of an extremely rare variety called 'Type II.' The fact that Type II diamonds were not generally recovered from mines at the time of Hannay's experiments indicated that he had indeed manufactured them.)

Hannay was not the only experimenter in the nineteenth century who claimed success in synthesizing diamonds. In both Russia and France, scientists achieved similar results in the laboratory by applying heat and pressure to carbon. They were not able to persuade their peers, however, that the microscopic crystals their ingenious experiments yielded bore more than a passing resemblance to diamonds. The main effect of these early experiments was to induce an element of fear in the bankers who had invested heavily in natural diamonds. In 1905, for example, a self-styled French inventor named Henri Lemoine informed Sir Julius Werner that he had discovered a process for mass-producing gem-sized diamonds from lumps of coal. Sir Julius, a British banker who was one of the four life governors of De Beers Consolidated Mines, feared that unless such an invention were brought under control it would wreck the diamond industry. Even the mere rumor of its existence could cause a selling panic among the investors in De Beers. Under these circumstances, he decided that there was only one prudent course of action: he would demand a demonstration, and if the invention worked, he would buy it – and then delay or suppress it.

Lemoine proved most cooperative. He agreed to sell the invention in exchange for a royalty and money to further develop it. He also invited Sir Julius to his laboratory in Paris to witness personally the synthesis of gem-sized diamonds.

Several weeks later, Sir Julius arrived at the Paris laboratory, which was located in the basement of an abandoned warehouse. He was accompanied by Francis Oats, the top executive at De Beers, and two other associates. Lemoine seated the group around a huge furnace and then left the room.

A few minutes later, the French inventor reappeared stark naked. He said that he had removed all his clothes so that they could see that he was concealing no diamonds. Then, like some medieval alchemist, he proceeded to pour various unidentified substances into a small crucible and stir them together. After displaying the mixture to the four gentlemen from London, he placed it in the furnace and threw a number of switches.

As the furnace blazed away, the naked inventor stood in front of it, and explained that the key to the synthesis was the secret formula of the ingredients in the crucible, which he could not disclose. Then, after a quarter of an hour, he turned the switches off. Reaching into the furnace with a pair of tongs, he removed the white-hot crucible and placed it on a table in front of the men.

After it had cooled, he stirred the concoction with a pair of tweezers, and began plucking out from it well-formed though relatively small diamonds. In all, he produced some twenty gem diamonds, which he passed around for the group's inspection.

Peering at them, one after another, through his jeweller's loupe, Francis Oats found that they curiously resembled in color and shape the diamonds that were extracted from De Beers' Jagersfontein mine in South Africa. Highly skeptical of the demonstration, Oats then demanded that Lemoine repeat the procedure.

Without any objections, Lemoine mixed another batch of

ingredients in the crucible, and again cooked it for fifteen minutes in the furnace. This time he extracted from the smoldering brew thirty gem diamonds.

After examining this second batch of diamonds with their loupes, Sir Julius conferred with Oats in private. Oats suspected that the whole experiment was nothing more than a hoax. Sir Julius understood Oats' doubts, but believed that there was still some chance that this French inventor had stumbled on the secret formula for diamonds. He therefore offered to advance Lemoine money to develop his invention on the condition that its existence remain secret.

Over the next three years, Sir Julius gave Lemoine £64,000, an enormous sum of money. In return, Sir Julius received an option to buy the secret formula which had been deposited by Lemoine under seal in a London bank.

In 1908, however, a Persian jeweler admitted that he had sold Lemoine a supply of small, uncut diamonds from the Jagersfontein mine that exactly matched the description of the diamonds that had supposedly been manufactured in the furnace. Lemoine was then indicted and brought to trial for defrauding Sir Julius of £64,000. Despite his continued protestation that his invention worked, Lemoine was unable to duplicate his experiment for the court, and when his secret formula was unsealed by court order it was no more than a mixture powdered with carbon and sugar. Before the court could pass judgment on him, Lemoine fled the country.

In 1948, Soviet scientists began to experiment with the concept of growing diamond crystals from 'seeds,' just as rock candy crystals are grown from a single molecule of sugar. To accomplish this end, a minute fragment of diamond was bombarded by carbon iodine gas, and gradually carbon molecules attached themselves to the structure of the diamond 'seed,' thereby enlarging the crystal. These experiments were conducted at the time under a veil of complete secrecy.

Meanwhile, in Sweden, engineers at ASEA company focused their efforts on constructing a hydraulic press which could produce the enormous pressures necessary for the synthesis of diamonds. They used six cone-shaped pistons which, when they came together, formed a perfect sphere. Although the attempts to convert carbon in the form of graphite into diamonds in this press failed, the engineers succeeded, in 1953, in converting a mixture of iron and carbon into some forty diamond crystals. ASEA executives decided, however, to keep the results secret while they developed a more commercial process for directly converting graphite to diamonds.

The real engineering triumph came in the United States, however. In Schenectady, New York, a team of research scientists at the General Electric Company devised a hydraulic press which was far more powerful than the one in Sweden. It had the ability to generate pressures of more than a million pounds per square inch, and its tungsten-carbide walls could contain temperatures of over 5000 degrees Fahrenheit. (Equations worked out at Oxford by Sir Francis Simon and R. Berman had predicted that at these pressures and temperatures graphite would be directly converted into diamond crystals.) Then in 1954, the General Electric scientists began feeding graphite into the press. After enormous amounts of pressure were applied, they recovered minute diamonds – one millimeter in length. Under X-ray examination, it became clear that the amorphous carbon molecules in graphite, which resembled a hairnet, had been rearranged under the heat and pressure into a tetrahedron diamond structure. These were not false diamonds; they were the same as mined diamonds. The next problem for the General Electric scientists and engineers was to invent a commercial process through which these diamonds could be manufactured more cheaply than equivalent diamonds extracted from a mine. They began experimenting with different catalysts – nickel, iron, tantalum – which when placed in the press with the graphite would allow the reaction to take place faster and at less cost in terms of energy expended. By the end of the year, the engineers had designed a system of belts and presses that would continuously turn out diamonds at costs competitive with those of producing natural diamonds. Up to this point, the General Electric experiments had been a closely guarded secret, but in February 1955 General Electric decided to issue a press release outlining its achievements in diamond synthesis. Suddenly, the world knew that diamonds could be easily manufactured.

The shares of De Beers stock plummeted after the news of the General Electric invention. To be sure, General Electric's diamonds were too small and discolored by the catalyst to be used as gems, but as General Electric spokesmen had pointed out, they were perfectly suitable for industrial purposes such as grinding and shaping tools. Since these 'industrial' diamonds had accounted for one-quarter of its total profit, De Beers faced potentially disastrous competition from this American industrial giant. Even though General Electric had not yet claimed the capacity to synthesize larger and better quality diamonds, many investors feared they soon would.

De Beers outwardly attempted to maintain a façade of business as usual. It issued a statement congratulating the General Electric scientists on their successful experiment, and further suggested through its public relations officers that although this synthesis was of great academic interest, it would have no immediate effect on the diamond industry. They claimed that the production of diamond abrasive powder was years away, and that it was still impossible to synthesize gem-size and quality diamonds through the General Electric or any other known process.

Behind the scenes, however, the cartel was thrown into a state of near panic by the General Electric diamonds. Planners at De Beers began reevaluating their plans for the future development of diamond mines in light of the fact that the market would soon be flooded with man-made industrial-grade diamonds. If it became impossible to sell the natural, but flawed, diamonds from the mines, the economics of diamond mining would have to be radically revised. Moreover, there was now some question of whether the cartel could keep its mines in the Belgian Congo in operation, since more than 90 per cent of the diamonds from these mines were of industrial grade. In London, the cartel had also to reappraise the value of its stockpile of diamonds. And in Europe and the United States, the cartel's distributors of industrial diamonds demanded to know if and when De Beers intended to market its own synthetic diamonds.

Sir Ernest finally reversed his position: De Beers, if it were to retain control of the diamond market, had no choice but to begin manufacturing its own diamonds. Therefore, in March 1955, he ordered De Beers' Diamond Development Laboratories in South Africa to proceed with the program for synthesizing diamonds that he himself had rejected.

Under the direction of Dr J. H. Custers, a Dutch-born

physicist, the De Beers team moved into a building on the outskirts of Johannesburg and began developing the high-pressure presses and catalysts that they knew would be needed for the synthesis. At the same time, Harry Oppenheimer began negotiations with ASEA in Sweden to buy the crucial technology necessary to manufacture diamonds.

Meanwhile, the United States government, considering the technology for manufacturing diamonds strategically important, clamped a tight embargo on the publication of any further details of the General Electric experiments. The objective was to deny the Soviet Union any assistance in creating for itself a synthetic diamond industry. The General Electric Company was not even allowed to take out patents on its invention.

Initially, De Beers' engineers had to improvise hydraulic presses strong enough to contain the pressure and head required for the synthesis. Quite frequently their design failed. The laboratories were rocked by explosions and the walls covered with smoldering carbon. After much trial and error, they arrived at the same conical design as the General Electric engineers. In this press, the apexes of six cones came together like knife points.

In 1958, three years after they had embarked on the project, Dr Custers' team of scientists synthesized a diamond from graphite. Peering through a binocular microscope at the tiny crystal, Dr Custers confirmed the experiment and jotted down in his log, 'Eureka.' However, when the De Beers' scientist attempted to repeat the experiment, using identical heat, pressure and timing, no diamonds appeared in the crucible. These frustrations were now constantly interspersed with the eurekas of success; sometimes diamonds were produced, and sometimes they were not. To compete with General Electric, De Beers had to find a process that consistently produced diamonds.

On 8 September 1959, the De Beers' team finally found the mixture of catalysts, timing and other elements that resulted in the repeated synthesis of diamonds. This process worked 60 per cent of the time, which meant that more refining of the basic techniques was necessary before De Beers could seek a world patent on the invention.

Meanwhile, in America, General Electric executives, learning that De Beers was on the verge of cracking the secret of diamond-making, pressed the Eisenhower administration to lift the veil of secrecy, and allow them to file world patents before the South Africans did. In mid-September, the administration acceded to this urgent request, and General Electric took out the patents on its technology for synthesizing diamonds. The science of diamond-making was no longer secret.

De Beers, even though it was five years behind General Electric in perfecting the commercial manufacturing process for diamonds, was not yet defeated. It still possessed a worldwide marketing network for industrial diamonds and vast financial resources. After first attempting to litigate the patent rights, De Beers finally agreed to pay General Electric some $8 million plus royalties for the right to manufacture diamonds under the process invented by General Electric. It then entered into a series of cross-licensing agreements with General Electric which made it difficult, if not impossible, for other companies to compete in synthetic diamonds. To further enhance its position, Harry Oppenheimer arranged to buy the Swedish factory from ASEA, as well as all its patents and technology. By 1961, in addition to the Swedish presses, De Beers had seventy-five hydraulic presses in operation in South Africa squeezing out diamonds, and then it opened another factory in Shannon, Ireland. De Beers called its synthetic diamond division Ultra High Pressure Units, Inc.

While De Beers and General Electric were dividing up the markets in the Western world, the Soviet Union created its own massive synthetic diamond industry in Kiev. The Soviets used the basic General Electric process, but they built the hydraulic presses on a much larger scale. As a result, the Soviets had a capacity to manufacture over 10 million carats of diamonds a year.

By the mid-1960s, the diamonds pouring out of synthetic presses in South Africa, the United States and the Soviet Union were measured not in carats or ounces but in tons. Initially, man-made diamonds were no larger than bits of sand and were used almost exclusively as abrasive grit for grinding wheels and diamond saws. Gradually, however, techniques were developed for bonding the minute crystals of diamonds together into larger units that were used for a wide range of industrial purposes. Indeed, except for drilling bits and wire-drawing dies, which still required natural diamonds, synthetic diamonds were adapted for most industrial purposes.

Again the diamond invention was threatened. In October 1966, Harry Oppenheimer flew to New York where he met with William Courdier, the General Electric executive in charge of synthetic diamond production, and other senior General Electric executives. In the course of these meetings, Oppenheimer proposed that both companies should more closely coordinate their production of synthetic diamonds in accordance with prevailing market conditions. He explained that De Beers feared that a glut of diamonds might lead to price-cutting and other unpleasant consequences for the diamond-makers. Because of American antitrust laws, General Electric refused to go along with Oppenheimer's grand strategy. De Beers had to find new means of protecting its invention.

By 1970, more than half the diamonds produced in the world were manmade. Unlike prices for gem diamonds, which rose steadily during the postwar period, the prices of industrial diamonds dropped sharply. If it were not for the fact that the world's consumption of industrial diamonds had actually quadrupled between 1955 and 1970, and a host of new uses had been found for diamond abrasives, natural diamonds would no doubt have been wholly replaced by synthetic ones. Even with this vast expansion of the market for industrial diamonds, the price fell to less than 50 cents a carat for diamond abrasives.

Furthermore, in the midst of this heated competition, Dr Bernard Senior, one of the four scientists who achieved the diamond synthesis for De Beers, resigned from De Beers' laboratory with the intention of going into the diamond-making business himself. Since his employment agreement prevented him from competing with De Beers in South Africa, Dr Senior moved to the island of Mauritius and established there the Southern Cross Diamond Company for the purpose of manufacturing diamonds. In response to this new threat, De Beers quickly moved to impound Dr Senior's bank accounts in South Africa, and placed pressure on companies in South Africa not to ship Dr Senior the supplies he needed for his factory. In addition, it filed a large number of legal actions, and eventually the Southern Cross Company ceased to be a serious threat to De Beers.

There was, however, further disturbing news from America. General Electric announced in May 1970 that its scientists had accomplished what only a few years earlier was deemed unthinkable: they had synthesized gem-quality diamonds that weighed over one carat. Even the scientists conducting the experiment were surprised by the incredible results. The synthesis required, it was explained, two distinct phases. First, graphite was converted in an ordinary hydraulic press to diamond crystals no larger than a grain of sand and weighing only 1/500th of a carat. Then, in the second stage of the process, these crystals were put at either end of a metal tube which also contained a carbonaceous solution. The tube was left in a specially constructed hydraulic press that could maintain enormous heat and pressure for as long as a week. Under these conditions, the carbonaceous solution became unstable and released carbon atoms, which would eventually move to the cooler ends of the tube and attach themselves around the diamond 'seed.' Gradually, the crystals would begin to grow in size. After 167 hours, when the press was opened, there were blue-white diamonds of gem quality that weighed between .60 and 1.1 carats. Presumably, if the press had been kept closed longer, the crystals would have grown even larger. The General Electric vice-president for research and development summed up the achievement as a 'goal that has tantalized and frustrated scientists for nearly two centuries. . . . This comes very close to fulfilling the dreams of alchemists.'

Under closer scrutiny, it was found that the General Electric diamonds were not of perfect quality, but they were equal, if not superior, to most commercial-grade gems. After they were cut and polished, these man-made diamonds could not be differentiated from natural diamonds by the naked eye. In fact, even an expert, using a jeweler's loupe, could not necessarily discern any difference. (The only telltale difference between the General Electric diamonds and natural ones was that the former tended to *phosphoresce* under an ultra-violet lamp, whereas the latter tended not to.)

De Beers reacted to the synthesis of gem diamonds in the same calm tone in which it had reacted fifteen years earlier to the synthesis of industrial diamonds. It claimed that it had known for 'several years' that gem-sized diamonds could be created under laboratory conditions, but that since the cost of production would be 'many times greater than finding and obtaining the natural product,' it was convinced that such a synthesis would prove to be 'economically impractical.' Publicly, De Beers insisted that it would not alter its 'plans for the future.'

General Electric also attempted to reassure American diamond dealers that it was not about to flood the market with synthetic gem diamonds. Its spokesmen told dealers: 'Keep your diamonds. . . . We are not competing. We have no reason to harm the diamond industry.'

Despite these disclaimers, General Electric had evaluated the feasibility of manufacturing gem diamonds. It eventually decided against it for two reasons. First, there was a problem of what economists call 'opportunity costs.' Manufacturing gem diamonds required tying up the press for nearly a week. In that same period, the presses could produce batches of powdered diamonds for industrial purposes every three minutes. Even though diamond powder could be sold for roughly only 1/100th of what gem diamonds could be sold for, it would still be far more profitable to use the press for powder rather than gems.

To be sure, General Electric recognized that it would be possible to develop catalysts that would accelerate the time needed to produce gems and to engineer more efficient presses that would allow more diamonds to be grown in the same cycle. However, even if it were possible to mass-produce gem diamonds at costs comparable to those of industrial diamonds, there would be a more serious problem. If the public realized that diamonds could be manufactured in unlimited quantities in a factory, the entire market for diamonds might suddenly collapse. A senior General Electric executive who was involved in the decision not to manufacture gem diamonds explained to me, 'We would be destroyed by the success of our own invention. The more diamonds we made, the cheaper they would become. Then the mystique would be gone, and the price would drop to next to nothing.' General Electric decided not to invest hundreds of millions of dollars in presses to produce gem diamonds.

Although their chief rivals had decided not to go ahead

with manufacturing, it now became a war against time for the De Beers cartel. The science and technology that made it possible to manufacture real diamonds threatened to create a supply of diamonds that was beyond the control of De Beers. The diamond invention, which had given value to diamonds for more than a half century, could continue to survive only as long as this new invention – diamond synthesis – did not become commercially feasible. For the present, De Beers could retard it through secret agreements and financial interventions, but there was no certainty that it could prevent it from infringing on its basic pattern in the future.

16 | Warring with Israel

In the winter of 1978, diamond dealers in New York City were becoming increasingly concerned about the possibility of a serious rupture, or even collapse, of the pipeline through which De Beers' diamonds flowed from the cutting centers in Europe to the main retail markets in America and Japan. This pipeline, as every dealer knows, is a crucial component in the diamond invention made up of a network of brokers, diamond cutters, bankers, distributors, jewelry manufacturers, wholesalers and diamond buyers for retail establishments. Most of the people in this pipeline are Jewish, and virtually all are closely connected through family ties or long-standing business relationships. New York City's diamond district, where nearly half of all the gem diamonds in the world are bought or sold, is a key juncture in the pipeline.

The diamond district is located mainly in a single block on 47th Street between Fifth and Sixth avenues. If one walks along at street level, one sees retail stores with such enticing advertisements as 'We Buy Retail; Sell Wholesale.' These stores are meant mainly for tourists. The real diamond exchange, involving the sale of billions of dollars' worth of loose diamonds, takes place in 'clubs' and offices discreetly located on the upper floors of these buildings.

Most of the smaller dealers are members of the Diamond Dealers Club, at 30 West 47th Street.

Although the name evokes images of a plush and luxurious meeting place, the Diamond Dealers Club more closely resembles a tawdry cafeteria, with a linoleum floor and rows of bare tables. The 2000-odd members, many of whom are Hasidic Jews, sit across the tables from one another like players at a chess tournament, their gaze fixed on an assemblage of tiny diamonds spread out on a piece of paper in between them. Every few moments a diamond sale is made, and the diamonds on the table are sealed in the paper. In the center of the room is a glass booth where diamonds are officially weighed after the transaction is agreed upon. Meanwhile, a loudspeaker system pages members to the telephone where they conduct further business. (Most of the members have no other office than the 'club'). The club also provides a room for the afternoon prayer, and a kosher restaurant.

The larger dealers do their business not in the trading hall of the diamond club but in their own well-protected offices. Almost all these offices have closed-circuit television cameras to identify visitors, and at least three sets of locked doors through which the visitor must pass. The rule in the diamond district is that no stranger is ever admitted to these private offices. Since dealers commonly carry on their persons millions of dollars' worth of diamonds, such stringent precautions are an indispensable part of the profession.

What the New York dealers cannot guard against, however, is an interruption in supply. An important part of the pipeline goes from London to diamond-cutting factories in Tel Aviv and then to New York; but in Israel, in late 1978, diamond dealers were stockpiling supplies of diamonds rather than processing and passing them through the pipeline to New York. Since diamond prices were rapidly increasing at the time, and Israeli currency depreciating by more than 50 per cent a year, it became more profitable for Israeli dealers to retain the diamonds that they received from London than to cut and sell them for paper money. These Israeli dealers, moreover, could borrow money from the banks on their diamonds at relatively low interest rates. As more and more diamonds were taken out of circulation at the Tel Aviv end of the pipeline, an acute shortage began in New York, driving prices up. By 1979, these Israeli stockpiles began indeed to threaten the entire diamond invention. How had De Beers permitted such a dangerous situation to develop?

Until the Second World War, the diamond invention rested on three legs: production, centered in Africa; distribution, based in London; and diamond cutting, located almost exclusively in Antwerp. The German invasion of Belgium, however, knocked out one of the legs of the tripod

– Antwerp. Oppenheimer had provided the Belgian cutting factories there with the lion's share of De Beers diamonds, and he could count on them not to resell the diamonds to speculators or other 'weak hands.' With the fall of Antwerp, the diamond-cutting industry was suddenly taken out of De Beers' sphere of control.

Since many of the cutters in Antwerp were Jewish, the British-mandated territory of Palestine (Israel) became a natural focal point for the displaced industry. The birth of this new Israeli industry began in 1939 when two Jewish refugees in tattered clothes arrived at the port of Haifa in Palestine. When the customs officer on duty searched through their meager personal belongings, he discovered an envelope containing what looked like hundreds of tiny bits of broken milk glass. He puzzled over them for a moment, and then questioned the refugees about these strange fragments.

The refugees nervously explained that they were both diamond cutters from Antwerp, and the objects in the envelope were, in fact, rough diamonds which they hoped to cut and polish in Palestine. To do this, they told the customs officer, they would need a small loan to set up a rudimentary work shop. Did the officer know anyone who might help them?

The customs officer had never before seen an uncut diamond; indeed, few people in Palestine in 1939 had ever seen one. He therefore took the packet of diamonds to Oved Ben Ami, the mayor of neighboring Natanya.

Ben Ami, a short, sprightly man in his early thirties, was one of the most enterprising of the Jewish pioneers in Palestine. A decade earlier, Natanya was nothing but a marsh between Tel Aviv and Haifa, but Ben Ami, fearing that the Arabs might settle there and drive a wedge between the two Jewish cities, decided to found a Jewish settlement there. He put all his energy into raising money and recruiting settlers, and by 1939 he had succeeded in building a small city. It had, however, no industry. On seeing the diamonds, Ben Ami became interested in the possibility of establishing a diamond industry in his town of Natanya, and he asked to see the refugees.

The two men explained to Ben Ami that very little capital was necessary for cutting and polishing diamonds. All that was needed, in fact, was good sunlight, skilled labor, a few rudimentary tools and a supply of rough diamonds. They even demonstrated how a rough diamond was first cleaved, then cut and polished.

Ben Ami was impressed. He provided the men with a building in Natanya for their work and reached into his own pocket and lent them money for their personal expenses. He then did some further research into the diamond business.

Three requisites, sunlight, labor and tools, would be readily available in Palestine; the problem would be acquiring a steady supply of rough diamonds. He consulted a knowledgeable banker in Tel Aviv, and he found out that De Beers controlled virtually the entire world's supply of diamonds. Since the cartel had an agreement with the government of Belgium, which specified that most of the diamonds would be sent to Antwerp to be cut by Belgian labor, the banker advised him that there was little possibility that the cartel would ever allow Palestine to compete with Belgium.

Although discouraged, Ben Ami refused to give up. He knew that most of the world's diamond business, including the De Beers cartel, was, as he put it, 'in Jewish hands,' and he persuaded himself that most of these Jews would be sympathetic to the idea of creating a diamond industry in Palestine. He also realized that the Nazi armies were on the verge of overrunning Belgium and the Netherlands, and that many of the Jewish cutters, like the two refugees, might seek refuge in Palestine. He therefore dashed off a series of letters to the mayors of Antwerp and Amsterdam, as well as a number of guild officials in those cities, suggesting that they consider sending their Jewish cutters to Natanya for the duration of the war. He received, however, no reply until mid-1940.

Ben Ami finally received a letter from a Jewish industrialist in Antwerp. The industrialist, who had obtained Ben Ami's address from the mayor of Antwerp, offered to pay for the relocation of sixty Belgian diamond cutters in Palestine, if Ben Ami could arrange the necessary entrance visas.

Since the British authorities had placed strict limitations on the number of Jews allowed to enter Palestine, Ben Ami's first task was to persuade the British to waive their immigrant quotes. He asked Ben Gurion, then head of the Jewish Agency, for help. But Ben Gurion's first priority was saving Jews from nations that had already been overrun by the Germans, and not from neutral countries such as Belgium.

Ben Ami went to the British high commissioner for Palestine. In presenting his case, he argued that since most of the diamonds in the world came from the British Empire, it was in the national interest of Great Britain to make sure that the skilled diamond cutters in Europe were not all captured by the Germans. As there was a distinct possibility that Germany would invade Belgium and Holland in the months ahead, he proposed that the British facilitate the immediate transfer of sixty diamond cutters to Palestine.

After studying the memorandum that Ben Ami had prepared on the subject, the high commissioner agreed that some precautions should be taken to protect the diamond trade. Cutting the tangle of red tape surrounding Jewish immigration to Palestine, he issued Ben Ami with sixty visas for Belgian cutters.

The next problem for Ben Ami was to persuade De Beers to send a supply of diamonds to Palestine. In London, he consulted Harry Abrams, the managing director of De Beers' Diamond Trading Corporation.

Ben Ami made the case that De Beers was about to lose its cutting centers in Antwerp and Amsterdam and it should look to Palestine as an alternative. Abrams coldly replied, 'Don't worry about us. Mr Ben Ami. We have enough cut diamonds in our vault to last through the war . . . and then some.' Moreover, Abrams explained, De Beers had a binding agreement with the Belgian government that prevented it from sending diamonds to be cut anywhere else. Abrams shook his head definitively. Diamonds for Palestine were simply 'out of the question.'

Ben Ami was not so easily put off. He sought out the assistance of Otto Oppenheimer, the brother of Sir Ernest, and appealed to him as a Jew to assist not merely the diamond industry, but Palestine. Although Oppenheimer found Ben Ami outrageously aggressive and presumptuous, he finally wearily gave in and told Ben Ami, 'I will be your Ambassador and try to persuade De Beers.'

In fact, Oppenheimer was concerned that Ben Ami was stirring up the Colonial Office about the possible disruption of the diamond trade, and if he persisted, the British government might begin to scrutinize more closely the flow of diamonds around the world. To get rid of this persistent nuisance, Oppenheimer decided, with Abrams, to provide Ben Ami temporarily with a modest supply of diamonds that could be cut in Palestine.

Ben Ami then flew to Antwerp to recruit the sixty cutters. Even though war with Germany seemed imminent, he found it impossible to persuade the Jewish cutters to go to Palestine. They believed that the Germans might well capture Palestine, and they had no intention of leaving neutral Belgium. They were living in 'a paradise of fools,' he concluded, and in the end he managed to recruit only a half dozen cutters.

Ben Ami returned to Natanya considering his mission a failure. He had neither the master cutters nor the amount of diamonds he had hoped to obtain. However, within a week of his return, the Nazi armies blitzkrieged their way through the Low Countries. The British dispatched a destroyer to Antwerp in an attempt to seize the cutters' stocks of diamonds before they fell into German hands, and a few of the Jewish cutters escaped with the British raiding party. But the cutting centers of Antwerp and Amsterdam were lost to the Allies – and De Beers – and Palestine now became an expedient alternative.

In early 1941, Ben Ami received a message from George Prins, the broker who represented De Beers, saying that a consignment of diamonds had been allotted to Palestine. Before Ben Ami could receive them, however, he would have to pay £10,000, which was the value De Beers established for them. Even though this was an enormous sum of money in Palestine in 1941, Ben Ami managed to convince a leading bank to advance it to him for the diamonds, which would serve as collateral.

When the diamonds finally arrived in a small cardboard box, Ben Ami distributed them to the few trained diamond cutters. The diamonds themselves were relatively small stones, all less than a carat in weight, even in their uncut state. These melees, or medium-grade diamonds, required an enormous amount of labor to cut and finish, and had never been highly profitable goods in Antwerp or Amsterdam. With a flow of Jewish refugees from Europe, Palestine had, however, an abundance of cheap labor.

The diamond-cutting factories in Israel were organized along very different lines from those in Antwerp. Instead of assigning the task of cutting and polishing a diamond to a single master craftsman, it was divided among six men. This division of labor, called the 'chain of six,' made it far easier to train and employ diamond cutters and shortened the time involved in finishing the diamonds. Even though the process resulted in slightly inferior workmanship, the difference, especially on the small, medium-grade diamonds, was not noticeable to the naked eye.

By the end of the war, Palestine had suddenly become the world's largest manufacturing center for diamonds, in terms of quantity, if not quality. During the war years, no less than 5000 refugees had been trained as cutters, and De Beers had shipped more than $100 million worth of diamonds to Palestine. The rise of this Palestinian industry caused considerable concern in the more traditional cutting centers in Belgium.

After consulting the leading bankers and politicians in Belgium, De Beers decided that the only prudent policy for the cartel was to reestablish Antwerp as the world's manufacturing center. Antwerp was, after all, less than an hour's flight from London, and the dealers there had a long history of collaboration with the cartel. And Belgian interests still controlled the important mines in the Congo.

Between 1945 and 1948, De Beers reduced the number of diamonds consigned to Palestine by as much as 70 per cent. Moreover, the diamonds it continued to supply were smaller and of inferior quality to the medium-grade diamonds Palestine factories had received during the war. These sharp cutbacks had the intended effect of choking off the nascent industry.

In 1948, however, the Jewish state of Israel was established in Palestine. The new nation had only one viable industry – diamond manufacturing; and both the government and the Israeli banks decided that, despite the shortage of diamonds, the industry had to be aggressively supported. The major banks therefore extended virtually unlimited credit to diamond dealers to buy diamonds from the Belgian clients of De Beers. Since the Belgians preferred to manufacture the larger and more profitable stones, they were quite willing to make an instant profit on the smaller and less profitable stones in their consignments. The Israeli manufacturers made up for the higher prices that they paid for the diamonds by using cheaper labor. By the mid-1950s, Israeli manufacturers again dominated the melee, or small diamond, business – even though they had to buy most of their rough goods on the secondary market.

The cartel quickly adjusted to the reality of the situation. Since Israeli manufacturers were determined to get diamonds by one means or another, De Beers decided that it, rather than the Belgian manufacturers, should realize the profits on the Israeli transactions. In an abrupt reversal of policy, De Beers began to supply a number of carefully chosen dealers in Israel with an abundance of melee diamonds. One dealer, Joseph Goldfinger, the cartel's favored instrument in Israel, would be sent more than a hundred million dollars' worth of small diamonds a year. De Beers also created its own subsidiary in Israel, Diamondel, to deal in rough diamonds. By 1965, Israel was receiving more than five-sixths of De Beers' total allotment of melee diamonds.

In the 1970s, repeated devaluations of Israeli currency gave the Israeli diamond-cutting industry a competitive edge over its rivals in Antwerp and New York. Not only were the Israeli factories more efficiently organized to cut small diamonds but because of their devalued money, they also had vastly lower labor costs than the factories elsewhere. Not satisfied with dominating the melee diamond business, Israeli dealers began to bid for the larger stones. By 1975, diamonds accounted for nearly 40 per cent of Israel's non-agricultural exports, and nearly 20,000 workers were employed in the cutting factories. In Antwerp, by contrast, over one-fourth of all the diamond cutters were out of work, and hundreds of factories, unable to cope with the Israeli competition, faced bankruptcy.

De Beers became seriously concerned that the Israeli competition could disrupt the entire diamond trade. In early 1977, Sir Philip Oppenheimer dispatched his son Anthony to Tel Aviv, accompanied by other De Beers executives. Anthony Oppenheimer's mission was to persuade the Israelis to curtail their expansion. He met with De Beers' favored clients, the bankers who were extending credit to diamond dealers, and the government officials who supposedly regulated the Israeli industry. He discreetly warned them that De Beers would not tolerate unbridled competition between Israel and Antwerp, and announced that De Beers intended to cut the Israeli quota of diamonds by at least 20 per cent in the coming year.

This warning had the opposite effect of what had been intended. Rather than paring down production in line with this quota, Israeli manufacturers and dealers began building up their own stockpile of diamonds. They paid a premium of 100 per cent or more for the unopened boxes of diamonds that De Beers had shipped to Belgian and American dealers. (And by selling their diamonds to the Israelis, De Beers' clients could instantly double their money without taking any risks.) Israeli buyers also moved into Africa and began buying directly from smugglers. The Intercontinental Hotel in Liberia, which was then the center for the sale of smuggled goods, became a sort of extension of the Israeli bourse. After the Israeli dealers had purchased the diamonds, either from De Beers' clients or smugglers, they received 80 per cent of the amount they had paid from Israeli banks in the form of a loan. Because of government pressure to help the diamond industry, the banks charged only 6 per cent interest on these loans, well below the rate of inflation in Israel. By 1978, the banks had extended $850 million in credit to diamond dealers, an amount equal to some 15 per cent of the entire gross national product of Israel. The only collateral the banks had for these loans were uncut diamonds.

De Beers estimated the Israeli stockpile to be more than six million carats in 1977 and growing at a rate of almost a half-million carats a month. At that rate, it would be only a matter of months before the Israeli stockpile would exceed that of the cartel's in London. If Israel controlled such an enormous quantity of diamonds, the cartel could no longer fix the price of diamonds with impunity. At any time the Israelis could pour these diamonds onto the world market, destroying forever the carefully nurtured mystique of the value of diamonds. The cartel decided that they had no alternative but to force liquidation of the Israeli stockpile.

By 1977, however, the situation in Israel was almost completely out of De Beers' control. The Goldfinger organization, and other of De Beers' leading distributors in Israel, told De Beers that even if they cut back on their purchases, independent dealers and speculators would step in to take up the slack. The distributors warned the cartel that as long as the banks were willing to finance diamond purchases with artificially low interest rates, there would be no effective way of stopping Israelis from accumulating diamonds as a hedge against inflation. If it wanted to bring the diamond speculation under control, De Beers would have to clamp down on the banks.

De Beers was not without influence in Israeli banking circles. Harry Oppenheimer sat on the board of directors of Barclays International Bank, which controlled Barclays Discount Bank in Israel. And E. J. G. Daws, one of the managing directors of the De Beers operation in London, was on the board of directors of the Union Bank of Israel, which together with Barclays Discount Bank financed more than half of all the Israeli diamond purchases. De Beers made it clear to the Israeli bankers that it considered the present speculation to be extremely dangerous. Moreover, it warned that it was adopting a new strategy of imposing 'surcharges' on diamonds, which might be abruptly withdrawn at any moment. Since these 'surcharges,' which would range as high as 40 per cent of the value of the diamonds, were effectively a temporary price increase, they could be extremely risky to banks extending credit to diamond dealers. For example, with a 40 per cent surcharge, a diamond dealer had to pay $1400 rather than $1000 for a small lot of diamonds; however, if the surcharge was then withdrawn, the diamonds would be worth only a thousand dollars. Through this device, De Beers, in effect, announced that it was embarking on a policy of manipulating the prices of diamonds in order to trap speculators. Under these circumstances, the Israeli banks could not afford to advance 80 per cent of the purchase price, including the so-called surcharge. They therefore required additional collateral from the dealers and speculators. Further, they began, under pressure from De Beers, to raise interest rates on the already outstanding loans.

Within a matter of weeks in 1977, interest rates on diamonds went up 50 per cent. Moreover, instead of lending money based on what Israeli dealers paid for diamonds, the banks now would only lend money based on the official De

Beers price for diamonds. If a dealer paid more than the De Beers price for diamonds – and most Israeli dealers were paying at least double the price in 1977 – he would have to finance the increment from his personal funds.

To tighten the squeeze on Israel, De Beers abruptly cut off shipments of diamonds to forty of its clients who had been selling large portions of their consignments to Israeli dealers. This dramatic reprisal made De Beers' two hundred and fifty or so remaining clients aware of the risks involved in trafficking with Israel.

As Israeli dealers found it increasingly difficult either to buy or finance diamonds, they were forced to sell diamonds from the stockpiles that they had accumulated. As Israeli diamonds poured onto the market, prices began to fall at the wholesale level. This decline led the Israeli banks to put further pressure on dealers to liquidate their stocks in order to repay their loans. Speculators found themselves caught between rising financing charges and lower prices, and in a state approaching panic, began selling their diamonds regardless of the price they had paid. Hundreds of Israeli dealers, unable to meet their commitments, went bankrupt in the fall of 1980 as prices continued to plunge. The banks inherited the diamonds.

De Beers had clearly, at least temporarily, won the diamond war with Israel.

The Russians Are Coming | 17

The most ominous threat to the stability of the diamond invention, however, came from the Russians. For the Soviet Union, diamonds in the postwar years were a strategic objective of the highest priority. When the Cold War began in 1947, the Soviet Union had no secure source of industrial diamonds. It was entirely dependent on the De Beers cartel for the diamond drilling stones it needed in order to explore for oil and gas, the diamond die stones it needed to produce precision parts and draw out fine wire, and the diamond abrasives it needed to grind machine tools and armaments. Without a continuous supply of these industrial diamonds, it would be impossible for it to rebuild its war-wrecked economy – or to effectively rearm its military machine. Stalin, fully realizing that his crucial supply of diamonds could be cut off at any moment by an embargo, demanded that Soviet geologists and scientists develop a more dependable source of diamonds. Since no diamond mines had ever been found in the Soviet Union, there were only two possible ways of satisfying Stalin's order: either pipe mines had to be uncovered in the unexplored regions of the Soviet Union through a vast program of systematic prospecting, or industrial diamonds had to be manufactured through a laboratory procedure.

The search for diamonds focused on the Siberian plateau in Yakutia province that lay between the Lena and Yenisei rivers, which Soviet geologists concluded resembled geologically the 'shield' of South Africa. Both formations had remained stable for eons of geological time, and neither had been deformed or 'folded' by convolutions of the earth. Since kimberlite pipes had been found on the South African shield, Soviet geologists theorized that they might also exist in this Yakutian shield. The first party of diamond prospectors flew into Yakutia in late 1947. The expedition was ill-prepared for the punishing environment, however, and after suffering astounding privations on the tundra, it had to be abandoned. Moscow ordered the search to be continued, regardless of cost, and the following spring more geologists were flown into the wastelands of Yakutia. They were better equipped, with X-ray diamond detectors and other sophisticated prospecting gear, and they found a few microscopic diamond traces – but no pipe. Finally, in 1953, a young Russian geologist named Larissa Popugaieva, working in her laboratory in Leningrad, noticed that the prospecting samples from Yakutia contained an increasing percentage of tiny blood-red garnets called pyropes. Since she knew such garnets had been found in kimberlite ore formations in southern Africa, she proposed that prospectors, rather than searching for diamonds, follow the trail of the garnets. She then joined the diamond-hunting expedition in Yakutia and, intrepidly tracking the garnets, managed to find their source near the Vilyui River Basin within a matter of months. It was a volcanic pipe mine which she named 'Thunder Flash.' Unfortunately, however, the proportions of diamonds in the ore in Thunder Flash was not high enough for feasible production. Dozens of geologists, all looking for traces of blood-red garnets, then began scrutinizing the banks of the Vilyu River for more volcanic pipes (which the Russians call *trubkas)*. In the spring of 1955, another young geologist, Yuri Khabardin, came across a fox's hole in a ravine and saw outside it some freshly scooped-out blue earth. He found that it had a high diamond content, and excitedly began sending a message over his shortwave radio. It said cryptically, 'I am smoking the pipe of peace.' In Moscow, the prearranged code was immediately understood to mean that the geologist had discovered and tested a kimberlite pipe.

The volcanic pipe that Khabardin discovered was called appropriately the Mirny, or Peace, pipe. The blue ground at the mouth of the pipe was slightly more than a half mile wide, and covered some seventeen acres. Compared to kimberlite pipes in southern Africa, the Mirny was not an immense pipe. (It was less than one-quarter of the size of the Premier mine in South Africa.) But Soviet planners in Moscow ordered a crash program for getting diamonds out of it.

Before the Mirny pipe could begin producing diamonds,

Soviet engineers in Siberia had to find ways of overcoming the incredibly harsh conditions at the mine site. During the seven-month-long winter in Yakutia, they found that steel tools became so brittle that they broke like matchsticks, oil froze into solid blocks, and rubber tires shattered like fragile crackers in the subzero temperatures. Moreover, when the summer came, the top layer of permafrost melted into a swamp of uncontrollable mud.

Despite these natural impediments, Soviet engineers turned Mirny into an open-pit mine. Jet engines were used to blast holes in the permafrost, and enormous charges of dynamite were used to excavate the surface rock and loosen the underlying kimberlite ore. The entire mine had to be covered at night to prevent the machinery from freezing.

By 1960, huge steamshovels were loading the ore into trucks, which had to transport it some twenty miles to a separation plant (the permafrost at the site of the mine could not hold the weight of the plant). More pipes were later discovered on the very edge of the Arctic circle. To service these mines in the 'pole of cold,' as this region on the 112th meridian is called by the Russians, the Soviets erected an entirely new city – Aikhal. According to the descriptions in Soviet periodicals, Aikhal stands, like some giant centipede, on ten-foot-high steel legs. Each of these steel legs is embedded into the permafrost to prevent the city from sinking into a quagmire of mud during the summer thaw. Even in winter, when the temperature falls to 80 degrees below zero, giant pumps cool the air beneath the buildings to prevent the heat of the buildings from causing any melting in the permafrost. All the buildings are interconnected by elevated passageways and wrapped in a heavy shroud of translucent plastic. Aikhal is, as one journal puts it, 'a completely enclosed working environment.' This herculean effort had a single purpose: the production of Soviet diamonds.

Just as diamonds began to flow out of Siberia in the early 1960s, Soviet scientists in a laboratory in Kiev reported that they had found a commercial process for synthesizing minute diamonds that could be used as abrasive grit. The process, though similar to the one that General Electric had developed in the United States, was based on Soviet research in high-pressure physics.

In the Siberian diamond mine, the gem diamonds, which

had first been mined as a by-product of industrial diamonds, could now be sold abroad. In early 1962, the Soviet Union agreed to sell virtually all of its uncut gem diamonds to De Beers. Within a few years, diamond production was nearly 10 million carats a year, and the Soviet Union exported some 2 million carats as gems. Diamonds became the leading Soviet cash export to the West. In 1968, Viktor I. Tikhonov, the head of the Mirny Diamond Administration, said, 'We call ourselves the country's foreign exchange department.'

Meanwhile, in London, De Beers' executives were mystified by the progressively larger shipments of Soviet diamonds that they were receiving each year. In many ways, the Soviet outpouring of diamonds involved a number of enigmas that could nct be easily resolved on the basis of the sporadically available facts. First of all, the enormous production of diamonds from Mirny did not seem consistent with the relatively small size of the pipe mine.

Specifically, De Beers' geologists questioned how this Siberian pipe mine could produce five times the number of diamonds that comparable South African mines produced. For example, in 1978, the Finsch mine, which went into production in South Africa at about the same time as the Mirny mine in Siberia, produced some 2 million carats of diamonds. That same year the Soviets reported that Mirny produced well over 10 million carats of diamonds. Moreover, the Finsch pipe covered an area more than twice the size of Mirny, which suggested that Mirny was yielding more than ten times the number of diamonds per surface acre as its South African counterpart. This disparity became more puzzling when the different mining conditions in South Africa and Siberia were taken into account. The Finsch mine, which processes some 10,000 tons a day, 365 days a year, operates in an ideal arid climate. The machinery at the Mirny mine, on the other hand, must excavate ground that is frozen solid seven months of the year in subfreezing blizzards. Under these conditions, it seemed difficult to accept that the Soviets could be excavating the tonnage necessary to produce 10 million carats from a single pipe – or any quantity approaching that amount.

Soviet geologists, when asked about this mysterious production from Mirny, initially suggested that the Siberian ore had an extraordinarily high grade of four carats a ton. This greatly exceeded any grade of ore in the history of diamond mining in South Africa. The Finsch mine, which had the richest grade of any De Beers mine, was yielding in 1971 only about .8 carats a ton. The Soviet technical journals further confused the issue by reporting that the grade of Mirny ore was variable, and that at times it went as low as .05 carats a ton (which was inferior to any South African ore). The enigma of Mirny's overproduction was not therefore satisfactorily resolved.

The constantly accelerating production from Mirny in the early 1970s was another aspect of the mystery. Diamond pipes are shaped roughly like funnels, with the ore body tapering off below the surface of the earth. This means that in pipe mines the amount of ore excavated declines at deeper depths. In South Africa, after a few years of initially high production, all the pipe mines enter a phase of gradual decline. In Mirny, however, after ten years of intensive excavations, the production of diamonds, instead of leveling off, accelerated – according to Soviet statistics provided to De Beers. To be sure, part of these diamonds might have come from other Siberian mines, such as the Aikhal pipe and the Udachnaya pipe, which had gone into limited production. The sheer magnitude of the increased production, which went from 10 million carats in 1970 to 16 million carats in 1975, continued, however, to baffle De Beers analysts in London. Each year they predicted that Soviet shipments would decrease, but each year, despite the calculus of diminishing returns in diamond mining, the Soviet consignments to London continued to increase.

There was an equally inexplicable pattern during these years surrounding Soviet purchases of industrial diamonds in Europe from De Beers and its clients. Diamonds in a pipe occur in a wide spectrum of sizes, shapes and different qualities. Usually, a small proportion are sorted out for gems; a larger proportion of the twisted, deformed, and discolored diamonds are sorted out for drilling stones, dies, and industrial tools; and the balance is ground for abrasive grit. For the Siberian mines to produce some 3 million carats of gem-quality diamonds, which were exported to the West, they would also have to produce a substantially higher quantity of drilling stones, die stones and other industrial diamonds. On the basis of Soviet gem exports, De Beers analysts assumed that the Soviets would also have an enormous amount of industrial diamonds to export. Instead, they found to their surprise that the Soviets were heavily increasing their imports of almost all categories of industrial diamonds except for abrasive grit (which they manufacture). Since by 1975 the Siberian mines were assumed to be producing in excess of 10 million carats of industrial-grade diamonds – a quantity that could not possibly be entirely consumed by Soviet industry – De Beers' executives wondered what had happened to the millions of missing Siberian drill and die stones. When asked about this quirk in the diamond equation, Soviet geologists explained that Siberian diamonds could not be used for certain industrial purposes such as drilling and drawing out wire because they contained air bubbles that often explode under heat and pressure. In other words, Siberian diamonds were flawed for the very purpose they had originally been needed – industrial stones. This explanation raised more questions about the nature of Siberian diamonds than it answered.

The De Beers sorters in London also noticed that the Siberian diamonds had some extraordinary aspects. For one thing, they tended to have a greenish tint to them and sharp angular edges, which differentiated them from most other consignments of diamonds in the De Beers vaults. Secondly, the Soviet diamonds were remarkably uniform both in size and shape. With very few exceptions, the entire Soviet consignment consisted of melees, or medium-grade diamonds ranging from one-tenth to seven-tenths of a carat in weight. The vast preponderance of these diamonds weighed about a quarter of a carat and fitted through a sieve opening that was one to two millimeters wide. Whereas African diamonds came to London in a multitude of shapes – round, square, oblong, flat, triangular and twisted – the Siberian diamonds tended to be mainly octahedrons with eight sharp edges. The consistent regularity of these diamonds made separating and evaluating them far easier.

By 1976, De Beers was choking on the ceaseless flow of greenish diamonds that arrived each month in London on the Aeroflot jet from Moscow. De Beers had little choice but to accept the Soviet consignments. Otherwise the Soviets would almost certainly dump these diamonds, which now amounted to some 2 million carats a year of gems, on the world market, and cause a ruinous collapse in prices. There was, however, a limit to the number of small diamonds that De Beers could absorb. The De Beers board of directors was becoming increasingly concerned about the capacity of the Siberian mines. They wanted to know how many more millions of carats of Soviet diamonds would be produced; and also why previous De Beers estimates of waning production in Siberia had proved so wrong.

Before renewing its commitment to buy Soviet diamonds, De Beers asked the Soviet authorities to allow a group of executives to visit the Siberian mines and make their own appraisal. The Soviets agreed to the De Beers visit on the condition that Soviet geologists be allowed to observe De Beers' mines in southern Africa. (Subsequently, a Soviet geologist named Smernoff was dispatched to the Letseng mine in Lesotho as a 'consultant' to De Beers.)

Sir Philip Oppenheimer, who had conducted most of the negotiations with the Soviets in London, arrived in Moscow in the summer of 1976. He was accompanied by Barry Hawthorne, who was then De Beers' chief geologist in Kimberley, as well as a De Beers mining engineer, cost accountant and sales executive. Every night for nearly a week, the Oppenheimer party was taken to the best restaurants in Moscow by various Soviet officials for caviar-laden meals. They also met during the day leading Soviet geologists, mineralogists, engineers and mine managers. Despite these thorough briefings, Sir Philip insisted on personally inspecting the mines, some four thousand miles away in Siberia.

After some procrastination, the Soviet Diamond Administration finally organized air transportation to Yakutia for Oppenheimer and his associates. Fog delayed the flight for nearly a day, however, and by the time they had completed the arduous journey to Mirny, they had to begin preparing for the return journey to Moscow, which had been very tightly scheduled. 'We had about a twenty-minute tour of the mine,' Hawthorne recalled, 'and seeing any other mines in Siberia was out of the question.' Even in that brief period of time, the Oppenheimer party was able to get some picture of the Soviet mining operation.

The mine itself, which looked like any open-pit mine in South Africa, was far less deep than they had calculated.

This meant that less ore had actually been taken from this mine since 1960 than De Beers had assumed. How did the Soviets manage to produce the vast quantities of gem diamonds?

The Oppenheimer party was next taken for a whirlwind tour of the treatment plant itself. They were 'astounded,' as Hawthorne put it, to find that the Soviets did not use water to separate the ore from the diamonds. In all the other diamond mines in the world, centrifugal baths are used to remove the nondiamondiferous material. A Soviet engineer explained that because it is too cold during the Siberian winters to prevent water from freezing, the ore at Mirny was first crushed by machines to a standard size and was fed through a battery of X-ray sorting machines. As a kimberlite geologist experienced with pipe mines in South Africa, Hawthorne found this explanation difficult to understand. In the De Beers diamond mines, more than 99 per cent of the nondiamondiferous ore was washed away by the centrifugal baths, and thus only a minute fraction of the ore had to be processed through the X-ray machines. If the Soviets separated all the ore from the mine by X-ray machines, the separation would require over a thousand Sortex machines and millions of volts of electricity.

When I asked Hawthorne about this in 1978 in Kimberley, he was still puzzled by the 'problem' of Soviet production. He explained that he had not seen any of the Sortex machines or any evidence of power lines at the Soviet mine site. Moreover, judging from such standard mining parameters as the surface area of the open pit, the depth of the excavation, the height of the waste dumps, and the capacity of the earth-moving equipment and other machinery, he found it difficult to account for the vast quantity of diamonds that the Soviet Union had sold to De Beers. In 1978 alone, the Soviets delivered some 2.5 million carats of gem diamonds – almost one-quarter of the world's supply.

The enigma of the Soviet diamonds became all the more perplexing when De Beers received fragmented reports about Soviet advances in high-pressure physics. Even though the details of the Soviets' progress remained clouded in secrecy, it had become readily apparent to everyone in the diamond industry by the mid-1960s that Soviet scientists had developed the technology for mass-producing synthetic diamonds for industrial purposes. Soviet factories, located mainly in Kiev in the Ukraine, began to churn out a wide variety of diamond grit and other abrasives, which were offered for sale to European dealers; at international conferences, Soviet technicians claimed that they had developed synthetic diamonds ten times larger than any produced in the West.

In 1966, an English mineralogist named Henry Meyer attended a conference on crystallography in Moscow with Dr Kathleen Lonsdale, one of England's foremost crystallographers and a member of the Soviet Academy of Science. During the meeting, a Soviet scientist told of the enormous progress the Soviets had made in the field of high-pressure physics – including the construction of a hydraulic press some ten stories high – and offered to show the English scientists some crystals that had been produced in the laboratory. That afternoon, both Dr Lonsdale and Dr Meyer accompanied him to a research facility on the outskirts of Moscow where he produced a tray of some half dozen small, white gem diamonds, all perfectly shaped and weighing approximately a quarter of a carat apiece.

Dr Meyer, who specialized in analyzing the mineral inclusions in diamonds, closely examined the stones. They were not like any gem diamonds he had ever seen. The Soviet scientist then explained that all these gems had been synthesized from carbon in a hydraulic press. He boasted that manufacturing gems was no longer a scientific problem in the Soviet Union but an economic one. Both British visitors were astounded at this casual disclosure. No laboratory in the West had come even close to synthesizing a gem diamond. (The General Electric breakthrough occurred four years later.)

In Johannesburg, De Beers scientists soon heard of the Soviet breakthrough, but they assumed that Meyer and Lonsdale had merely witnessed an interesting laboratory experiment in crystal-growing, rather than any new technological invention.

The following year, however, there was further confirmation. Professor Bakul, the director of the Soviet Synthetic Research Institute in Kiev, recruited Jos Bonroy, one of the finest craftsmen in Antwerp, to cut and polish some highly unusual Soviet diamonds. Bonroy, who specialized in sawing distorted and awkwardly shaped stones, found these diamonds particularly difficult to penetrate. He saw that they were gem crystals of excellent purity and nearly ideal octahedron shape, but as he studied them, he found that they all tended to have very unorthodox sawing directions.

To assist Bonroy, Professor Bakul explained that all the diamonds, which weighed about one-half carat each and were slightly tinted, had been synthetically manufactured in Kiev. He asked the Belgian cutter to keep secret the fact that the Soviets had manufactured gem diamonds, since, as Bonroy later put it, 'the hypersensitive diamond market would be rocked by news such as this.'

Bonroy found the solution to cutting the synthetic gems. When he completed the work, and polished and buffed the synthetic diamonds, they looked exactly like gem diamonds.

Bonroy kept the secret of the Soviet diamonds for four years. In April 1971, he was asked to speak at a symposium in Kiev on the problems of cutting synthetic diamonds. Bonroy, concerned about the future of the diamond industry, asked Bakul whether the Soviet Union intended to mass-produce these synthetic gems.

The professor pondered the question for a moment and replied that the Russians still found it economically unfeasible to synthesize gem-quality diamonds. It was, however, not clear from his answer under what conditions the Soviets would use this technology to manufacture diamonds.

Even though the mysteries surrounding Soviet diamonds were never fully resolved, De Beers succeeded in absorbing the constantly expanding production. Although at one point in the mid-1970s it had to reduce its own production of diamonds from Namibia to accommodate Moscow's, De Beers gradually developed new markets for diamond jewelry in both Asia and America.

The De Beers arrangement with the Soviet Union was only for uncut diamonds. The Soviets had always reserved a small percentage of its production from Siberia for its own jewelry manufacturing. In the late 1960s, these Soviet-cut jewels began to appear in ever-increasing number in the grading halls of Antwerp. Cut and polished in Soviet factories in Moscow, Kiev and Swerdlosk, the diamonds were called 'silver bears,' and had some extraordinary features.

To begin with, most silver bears were almost exactly the same size in girth, and weighed approximately two-tenths of a carat each. Moreover, each of them had the same octahedron shape, and they were nearly identically faceted and polished. It was almost as if, as one Belgian trader observed, the silver bears, had all been cut from the same pattern.

Initially, diamond experts in the West were baffled by the inordinate regularity of these gems. How could miniature diamonds that could fit on the tip of a pencil point be so identically matched in size, shape and cut? Louis Asscher, one of the renowned master cutters of Europe, attempted to resolve the question by microscopically examining a sample of silver bears. He had a lifelong experience with diamonds; his father, the third generation of the house of Asscher in Amsterdam, had recut the crown jewels for the British royal family in 1907, and he himself had invented and popularized the Asscher Cut (the 'brilliant cut' of a triangular diamond). When he studied the silver bears, he found that they all contained a similar striation mark on certain facets. He concluded that this telltale mark came from a machine, and he suggested that the Soviets had invented an automated diamond-cutting machine that accounted for the silver bears.

A number of master cutters in Antwerp took issue with Asscher. They found that the Soviet cut on the silver bears was 'too good, too regular, too perfect,' as one of these cutters put it, to be anything but the work of skilled human hands. The Antwerp experts theorized that the Soviets had imposed draconian standards on their diamond cutters, and diamonds that failed to meet these criteria were simply ground to dust and used for industrial purposes. They recognized that in order to achieve such uniform diamonds, the Soviets would have to sacrifice a considerable portion of the average 'yield' – the weight of the finished gem – but they assumed that this was a cost the Soviets were willing to pay in return for standardization.

As the Soviets vastly stepped up their export of silver bears to Europe, the concern over Soviet cutting techniques was replaced with a much more urgent one about their marketing objectives. The Soviet diamond-trading organization opened up offices in rapid succession in 1981 in Antwerp, Zurich and Frankfurt. Italy began offering large discounts to American manufacturers, who needed a uniform product for their inexpensive assembly-line jewelry. In addition, reports reaching western Europe suggested that the Soviets were training thousands of new diamond cutters at a center in Kostrana, some 180 miles north of Moscow.

The Soviet trading organization itself conspicuously avoided releasing any meaningful data on the volume of its exports of polished diamonds to Europe. By 1970, however, diamond dealers in Antwerp reckoned that the Soviets were putting at least a half million silver bears on the market each year. Manufacturers in Tel Aviv, as well as Antwerp, became increasingly apprehensive about these Soviet diamonds. What they had first considered a novelty now seemed a threat to the very existence of their respective cutting centers.

The Soviet Union was already selling polished diamonds. For example, one New York dealer, Fred Knobloch, told me that he had been invited to Moscow on several occasions to buy cut diamonds by Russ Almaz, the Soviet diamond-trading company. He described being escorted to a glass skyscraper at 29 Kalinin Prospect, in Moscow, where he was ushered into an austerely furnished room full of diamond buyers from Asian and European countries. A Soviet official then emptied a canister of some 1500 small polished diamonds – all under a carat in size. The official explained that the rules were the same as those insisted upon in London by De Beers; there was to be no bargaining, and cash had to be paid in advance of delivery. When Knobloch agreed to buy the lot of diamonds on the Soviet terms, the Soviet official said – in perfect Yiddish – '*Mazel und Brucha*,' literally: 'Good luck and blessings,' the same phrase that is used to conclude a deal on 47th Street in New York – or in Tel Aviv or Antwerp. A few feet away, at another table, he heard another Soviet official saying '*Mazel und Brucha*' to a Japanese buyer. He realized then that the Russians were as capable as De Beers of conducting an international diamond business – right down to giving the traditional Jewish blessings.

In its public statements, De Beers desperately attempted to calm fears in the trade. In its 1971 issue of the *International Diamond Annual*, it went to considerable lengths to explain:

There has been no indication that the Soviet Russian authorities have the slightest intention of 'dumping' their polished goods on Western markets. On the contrary, the Soviet authorities appear to accept that the industry they have been at great pains to develop and establish would founder if the market for diamonds in the Western world were undermined or were not held in strong hands.

In their private deliberations, however, De Beers' executives were far less certain in whose 'strong hands' the Soviets wanted control of the diamond trade. They certainly did not want to afford the Soviets the opportunity of establishing direct relations with the American, Belgian and Japanese jewelry wholesalers. If the Soviets succeeded in bypassing the diamond distribution chain that De Beers had ingeniously devised over a half century, they obviously would be a step closer to taking over the diamond cartel from De Beers.

The silver bear offensive raised a more immediate practical problem: the excess of silver bears had to be drained from the market and brought under control. De Beers therefore strongly encouraged a number of its own dealers to buy silver bears directly from the Russians and then, when market conditions were tight, redistribute them through their own marketing channels. The chief operative in this endeavor was Joseph Goldfinger, De Beers' man in Tel Aviv.

Goldfinger had been born in Lithuania, and studied to be a rabbi at the Yeshiva before emigrating to Palestine in the mid-1930s. When the diamond industry began in Natanya during the Second World War, he trained as a cutter, and then began dealing in both uncut and cut diamonds. In 1949, he was invited by De Beers to attend their sight in London, and quickly proved himself to be both resourceful and dependable. Because the Israeli industry was expanding at a breakneck pace, De Beers needed a subdistributor in Israel who could shrewdly apportion its supply of melee diamonds among the hundreds of small manufacturers scattered around Tel Aviv. Goldfinger, who had demonstrated that he had both the requisite energy and judgment, was given a 'dealer's sight' in 1962, which meant that he received diamonds not only for manufacturing himself, but also for redistributing to other Israeli dealers. By 1973, he was receiving up to $20 million worth of diamonds in his box at the London sights, and he had become De Beers' third largest client.

With this enormous sight from De Beers, Goldfinger became known as 'Mr Diamond' in Israel. He became heavily involved in every phase of the Israeli diamond industry and built up a network of wholesalers of polished diamonds that extended from Tel Aviv to Hong Kong and Tokyo. When the silver bear crisis arose, Goldfinger was logically the man that De Beers turned to. Not only did he have vast experience in marketing small polished diamonds but he also had a strong interest in preventing the Soviets from making inroads into this market.

The original plan, in 1973, was for Goldfinger to go to Moscow and to buy from Russ Almaz, the Soviet diamond-trading organization, the selections of silver bears most in demand by American and Japanese manufacturers. Together with the uncut diamonds which De Beers was itself buying from the Soviets, these purchases of polished diamonds would help reduce the Soviet exports to Europe to manageable proportions.

The Soviet Union, however, in deference to Arab demands for a boycott against Israel, preferred not to deal directly with Goldfinger. Instead, it was arranged that I. Hennig, the broker next to De Beers on Charterhouse Street, would buy the diamonds in Moscow for Goldfinger's account, and turn them over to Goldfinger in London. In early 1974, representatives of I. Hennig traveled to Moscow and were lavishly entertained by Dolnitsov, the head of AmRuz. The London brokers purchased substantial quantities of the silver bears for Goldfinger's account, effectively withdrawing them from the market. On a subsequent trip to Moscow, the brokers were surprised to find that Dolnitsov had been replaced by a more dour official. No explanation for the change was offered. The arrangement remained intact, though, and the brokers were able to arrange delivery of some $2 million worth of silver bears a month. These preemptive buys succeeded in stabilizing the polished diamond market.

Even as De Beers extends its alliance with the Russians into the 1980s, however, it is extremely vulnerable to any Soviet policy change. For example, in September 1980, the Soviet trading company without warning, slashed its price, on its silver bears in Antwerp by 15 per cent. (Reportedly, it needed additional foreign exchange to finance its war in Afghanistan.) To prevent prices from falling, De Beers compensated by distributing fewer such diamonds to its own customers. Like the Goldfinger preemptive buyout, this was, however, only a temporary expedient. If the Soviet Union continues to expand its own production of both uncut diamonds and silver bears De Beers will be unable to stockpile or sell the increment. It remains in the power of the Soviets to preserve or destroy the diamond invention.

18 The American Investigation

The diamond invention was an ingenious mechanism for restraining any free trade or competition in diamonds. This brought it directly into conflict with the laws of the United States, where most of the diamonds in the world are sold to American customers. The Sherman Anti-Trust Act states unambiguously that 'any combination or conspiracy in restraint of trade' is a criminal offense in the United States punishable by fines and prison sentences. The Justice Department first became aware of the extent of the mechanism to stifle competition in the diamond trade in the early 1940s, when the FBI conducted a series of interviews with American diamond dealers concerning their wartime supplies. It learned that De Beers systematically restricted production, fixed prices, and allocated markets – which, if De Beers had been an American company, would all have been offenses under federal antitrust law. Even De Beers' largest clients confirmed these operations. Harry Winston, for example, acknowledged to federal investigators that it was 'a most vicious system,' and characterized De Beers as 'an outstanding monopolistic concern.'

In 1945 the Justice Department at last filed an antitrust case against De Beers and its associates. The court found that, despite the evidence, it lacked jurisdiction. Since De Beers was a South African corporation that distributed its diamonds in London, and the title for the diamonds changed hands outside the United States, the judge ruled that De Beers could not be held accountable under the laws of the United States. The Justice Department thus had to abandon the 1945 conspiracy case against De Beers.

The legality of the diamond invention depended on De Beers maintaining a modicum of distance from its American customers. Yet the continued effectiveness of the invention required that it exert a measure of control – albeit invisible control – over the crucial American market. This tension between the laws of the United States and the requisites of an international cartel forced refinements in the system.

Some came abruptly. For example, in the fall of 1973, the owner of a well-known diamond firm in New York City found that Monty Charles, at De Beers' Diamond Trading Company in London, would not accept any overseas calls from him. Before the war, his father had dealt directly with Sir Ernest Oppenheimer, and for twenty years or so he had always discussed by phone with Monty Charles the diamonds his firm needed for the coming year. Never before had Monty Charles refused to come to the telephone. Finally, after days of placing trans-Atlantic calls, and arguing with the soft-spoken operator at Number Two Charterhouse Street, he was put through. Without giving the owner any opportunity to talk about diamonds, Monty Charles warned him, 'This is the last time that I or anyone else here will speak to you. Do not, under any circumstances, call here again'.

The diamond dealer was dumbfounded. How was he supposed to communicate with his main supplier of rough diamonds? Monty Charles suggested that he engage I. Hennig and Company, a London diamond broker, to act as an intermediary in his future dealings with De Beers.

The New York dealer could not understand why his long-standing relationship with De Beers had changed so suddenly. He quickly retained I. Hennig, which is owned by Hambros Bank, a financial adviser to Harry Oppenheimer and De Beers. The new arrangement required the dealer to order his consignment of diamonds from I. Hennig, who would purchase them from De Beers. In return for handling these transactions, the broker received 1 per cent of the value of the consignments.

Eventually, the broker explained that De Beers had changed its policy, not merely toward him, but toward all its American clients. Direct negotiations between De Beers and its American clients was no longer possible.

The reason for this sudden alteration in its dealings with American customers in 1973 was that De Beers again found itself under investigation for violating the American antitrust laws. Indeed, a new grand jury had been convened, and a long list of American dealers subpoenaed to testify about their relations with De Beers.

The antitrust division of the Justice Department reopened its investigation because it received a series of complaints indicating that De Beers might be secretly participating in the industrial diamond business inside the United States. Most of these reports came from tool and drill bit manufacturers, who believed that they were paying too much for industrial diamonds because of De Beers' manipulation of the market. As early as April 1967, the Justice Department received an unsubstantiated report implying that Harry Oppenheimer had personally attempted to buy a controlling interest in a small diamond tool manufacturer in Verona, New Jersey. The American owner rebuffed him. The Justice Department also received word that a number of key men who had worked for the Oppenheimer interests were being placed in strategic positions in American diamond firms. There was, of course, nothing illegal about Oppenheimer buying corporate interests in the United States, or in his ex-employees working in America; but these unconfirmed reports, if true, seemed to signal a change in De Beers' strategy.

In late 1970, there was a new development in the case. An anonymous caller, speaking from a pay phone in a muffled voice, began providing the lawyers in the antitrust division with evidence that suggested that De Beers was attempting a secret takeover of the industrial diamond business in the United States. The mysterious caller rattled off a list of names, places, transactions, bank accounts and subterranean corporate connections in the diamond trade. He also gave detailed accounts of secret meetings between American dealers and agents of the cartel, and the names of witnesses who could confirm these charges.

The allegations he made went as follows: before General Electric began mass-producing synthetic industrial diamonds, De Beers had been able to manipulate diamond prices from its offshore bases in London and Johannesburg. Now, however, with General Electric pouring out a virtually unlimited supply of industrial diamond abrasives, major dealers and users of industrial diamonds were no longer dependent on De Beers. De Beers had decided to intervene directly in the United States by covertly buying control of companies that distributed diamond grit and diamond drill stones. Through these companies, it could both guarantee itself a share of the American market and control prices.

Although Justice Department lawyers were initially skeptical of this furtive source, they found that many of his leads checked out. Moreover, the specific details he provided could only have come from someone who had access to the inner workings of the international diamond cartel. Gradually, other witnesses began to confirm the story. (Nevertheless, the informant adamantly refused to meet with the lawyers of the federal investigators, or to disclose his identity.)

Even with the help of other informants, the task of tracing a connection between De Beers and its putative American coconspirators was extraordinarily difficult. To even approach the problem of establishing jurisdiction, the Justice Department lawyers had to weave their way through a bewildering maze of some 300 interlocking corporations, registered in Luxembourg and other convenient nations, which were either partly or fully controlled by the Oppenheimer interests. The lawyers also found that industrial diamond users, who were heavily dependent on De Beers and its subsidiaries for their supply of diamonds, were extremely reluctant to discuss openly their relations with De Beers.

Finally, in December 1971, the lawyers requested that a grand jury be convened so that potential witnesses could be compelled to testify and, if necessary, granted immunity in return for their testimony. To break through the walls of the corporate labyrinth, they decided to focus their investigation on the activities of two American firms closely allied to the Oppenheimer interests. The first was Engelhard Metals and Minerals, Inc., a diversified company incorporated in Delaware and based in New York City; the second was Christensen Diamond Products, a manufacturer of diamond drills serving mainly the oil industry, based in Salt Lake City.

The founder of Engelhard Minerals and Metals, Charles Engelhard, was a well-connected American entrepreneur who had inherited a small metal fabricating company from his father. In the late 1940s, he had journeyed to South Africa to make his fortune. South African mines had a surplus of gold, but government regulations prohibited the exporting of gold bullion from South Africa without permits from the central bank, which were very difficult to obtain.

Great Britain, which still controlled the financial affairs of South Africa, wanted to retain as much gold as possible within the sterling bloc. Engelhard found a loophole in the regulations: while it was illegal to export gold bars, it was legal to export objets d'art made of gold. Engelhard formed a company called Precious Metals Development that bought gold from the mines and cast it in the form of statues and other religious items. He then exported these religious objets d'art to Hong Kong, where they were melted down and turned back into gold bullion, which could then be sold on the free market. (This ploy was later used by Ian Fleming, who was a business partner of Engelhard, in his novel *Goldfinger*; and indeed the title character was supposedly modeled on Engelhard himself.)

While living in Johannesburg, Engelhard became a close friend of Harry Oppenheimer. Both men were approximately the same age and came from the same German–Jewish background. Both men were born millionaires, who later owned and controlled their own family businesses. And both men also shared a passion for racehorses (at one point, Engelhard owned 250 thoroughbred horses). Oppenheimer invited Engelhard to join the board of the Anglo-American Corporation, and for his part, Engelhard invited Oppenheimer to participate in a number of mutually profitable joint ventures.

The Justice Department investigators were especially interested in the relationship between Harry Oppenheimer and Charlie Engelhard. They theorized that Oppenheimer relied on Engelhard Minerals and Metals to provide the services, credit terms, and contacts necessary to keep its American clients from buying their synthetic diamond grit from General Electric. They concluded in a memo that, 'Oppenheimer turned to Engelhard to take up the GE challenge.' Specifically, Oppenheimer had arranged for Engelhard's holding company, called Engelhard Hanovia, to become the American distributor for De Beers' abrasive grits. 'The idea was that grit sales needed a new "American look," with the old De Beers monopoly image less exposed,' the lawyers noted. They concluded that the entire scheme was intended by De Beers to avoid 'exposing gem monopoly to antitrust sanctions.'

In reconstructing this complicated arrangement, the investigators found that it was based on a quid pro quo. In return for acting as an intermediary for De Beers, Engelhard received all the costs for setting up a Swiss company called Prometco, plus a guaranteed profit of £100,000 a year. It was a fairly lucrative deal for Engelhard, and it also accommodated his friend Oppenheimer.

The deal provided far-reaching benefits. In the mid-1960s, Engelhard intervened on behalf of Oppenheimer to prevent the United States government from dumping its vast stockpile of industrial diamonds on the world market. Engelhard, one of President Lyndon Johnson's chief fundraisers and highly influential in the Democratic party, offered to buy up one and one-half million carats of diamonds from the stockpile (which he planned to sell to De Beers) on condition that the government promised not to sell any more diamonds for five years. Not only did Engelhard personally make a tidy profit from the exchange but as a Justice Department review notes, 'The commitment by the United States not to sell any more of the stockpile would be for the very purpose of protecting the monopoly of the diamond syndicate.' If the government entered into such an agreement, it would become increasingly difficult to bring an antitrust action against the monopoly at a later date. For this reason, the Justice Department vehemently protested against the deal, and despite Engelhard's personal influence with President Johnson, its protest prevailed.

Engelhard had also begun to buy control of some important users of industrial diamond abrasives, including Supercut, Inc., then the third largest consumer of diamond grit in the United States, and Concut, Inc., a Midwest manufacturer of diamond tools and abrasive grinding wheels. These acquisitions provided Oppenheimer with leverage in the competitive battle, shaping up between General Electric and De Beers, for control of the synthetic market in America.

Just as the Justice Department was about to file antitrust actions, Engelhard relinquished his right as exclusive distributor of De Beers' abrasive diamonds in the United States and devolved the distributorship to three industrial diamond dealers in New York, all of whom had close ties with De Beers. These new De Beers distributors all agreed to abide by the ground rules that De Beers had previously established in return for this valuable concession.

Engelhard arranged for Oppenheimer to buy a controlling interest in his far-flung empire, since he had no male heirs to take over (he died in 1971). To do this, Oppenheimer set up HD Development Corporation, which was jointly owned by Oppenheimer and Anglo-American.

Despite this whirl of corporate maneuvers, Justice Department lawyers learned that, when Engelhard was involved in the diamond business, Oppenheimer owned no part of it; when Oppenheimer bought control of Engelhard, it was no longer directly in the diamond business.

Moreover, as the grand jury investigation gathered momentum, Engelhard Minerals and Metals severed all its visible connections with the diamond business. It not only disposed of the abrasive manufacturers it had bought, but locked away in its vaults all the records of its previous dealings with De Beers, its subsidiaries and its agents. Harry Oppenheimer and other South African directors of Engelhard, who were also directors of De Beers and the Anglo-American Corporation, stopped attending board meetings of Engelhard in the United States. The concern was that they would be subpoenaed to appear before the grand jury. The Justice Department heard from one of its sources that 'the General Counsel for Engelhard . . . had a fit' when this possibility was divulged to the American members of the board. Justice Department lawyers also received reports that the 'Rothschild on the De Beers' board, upset at being told that he could not come to the US because of the diamond investigation, has now resigned from the De Beers board'; and that 'Harry Oppenheimer is extremely upset at not being able to come to the US.'

In order to accommodate Oppenheimer and the other South African directors, Engelhard Minerals and Metals agreed to hold meetings in London and elsewhere outside the United States. In September 1974, Engelhard directors flew to London and met with Oppenheimer and a number of De Beers executives.

While one group of antitrust lawyers was at work trying to unravel the criss-crossing web of corporate ownership among firms dominating the distribution and sales of diamond grit, a second team of lawyers was actively investigating an alleged conspiracy by De Beers to control the market for drilling stones. These industrial diamonds, ten to twenty times the size of abrasive grit, are crucially important for drilling for oil and other minerals. A single petroleum drilling bit, in which the block-shaped diamonds are inlaid in the metal cutting surface, may require more than $20,000 worth of diamonds; and without diamond drill stones, it would be practically impossible to drill many offshore and deep oil wells.

Unlike diamond grit, drill stones cannot be economically synthesized, and therefore the drilling industry is heavily dependent for its diamond drilling bits on the natural stones excavated from the De Beers-controlled mines in Africa. (The Soviet Union, it will be recalled, imports rather than exports drill stones.)

In tracing through the subpoenaed records of the major drilling companies in the United States in the early seventies, the antitrust lawyers found that a single American company and its subsidiaries supplied most of the diamonds for petroleum drill bits: the Christensen Diamond Products Company. Moreover, through informants and other sources, they learned that Christensen and his company had a long-standing involvement with the Oppenheimer interests.

Frank L. Christensen, a former football player from Detroit, had built up during the 1950s a firm that specialized in providing diamond-cutting dies to the automotive industry. When he visited Johannesburg, he developed a friendship with E. T. S. Brown, a robust De Beers executive, who headed its Industrial Diamond Division. Ted Brown, as he was called, spent considerable time showing Christensen around South Africa and he soon found in the ex-football star the sort of hard-driving entrepreneur he had been looking for to expand De Beers' sales in the United States. Brown's division had just developed a specially treated diamond that was especially efficient as a drilling stone, and he encouraged Christensen to use it to make drilling bits for the petroleum industry. Since De Beers itself could not operate in America, Brown began channeling the better quality bits to Christensen's firm, which rapidly increased its share of the American market.

In 1960, Brown made Christensen an offer he apparently could not refuse. A De Beers subsidiary in Luxembourg, called Boart International SA, would buy a 50 per cent share of Christensen's stock; working together, Christensen and De Beers would dominate the drilling business throughout the world. Christensen agreed, and in conjunction with Brown, who was also managing director of Boart International, he bought shares in other drilling contract companies in the United States and Venezuela. By 1970, Christensen and his silent partners at De Beers controlled well over 50 per cent of the petroleum drilling business in the United States; through subsidiaries his firm also attained a dominant position in most other kinds of large-scale drilling industries all over the world. A Justice Department analysis noted that 'a key feature of the plan has been the formation of a worldwide network of companies jointly owned by Boart and Christensen Diamond Products to consume De Beers processed diamonds . . . [and] the acquisition of stock interests in Longyear and Boyles Bros., two of the largest consumers of diamond drill bits in the United States, and the foreclosure of the substantial purchase of diamond drill bits by these competitors to competitors.' Since ownership of these companies was concealed through a tangle of corporations registered in Luxembourg and the Netherlands, the Justice Department concluded: 'Much of this conduct was done so as to be secret and misleading.'

Just as the Justice Department lawyers were proceeding in 1971 to assemble the final pieces in their case against De Beers and its American associates, they learned of a startling new development. De Beers had relinquished its entire interest in Christensen Diamond Products by having its Boart International subsidiary sell back to Christensen Diamond Products all the stock that it owned in the company. This timely reorganization effectively undercut the entire antitrust case by legally divorcing De Beers from the American company, the main target of the long grand jury investigation. There was little that the Justice Department could do. As one of the antitrust lawyers on the case explained to me, 'After all, the remedy we had been proposing all along was to compel De Beers to sell its stock in Christensen, and when it did it of its own accord, it left us without much ground for proceeding against it.'

In the end, the Justice Department had to settle for a token victory. Two distributors of diamond grit, Anco and DAC, both of whom had their De Beers' distributorships devolved on them by Engelhard, were indicted for price-

more far-reaching, De Beers was held not to control legally the rights to the submerged portion of the 200-mile-long forbidden zone.

While De Beers attempted to redress this definition of the forbidden zone in the appellate courts, a brash, young oil-pipeline lawyer named Sammy Collins persuaded the authorities in Namibia to grant him a prospecting concession for the underwater portion on the diamond beach. He then, in 1961, sold shares in a company called the Marine Diamond Corporation, and with the proceeds equipped a barge with giant suction hoses, pumps, and other dredging gear. By August 1962, Barge 77, as it was called, began recovering small diamonds from the ocean floor. A few weeks later, Barge 77 sank in a storm, and Collins had to build a second one.

In 1964, Collins was back in full production. The pumps on his barges were sucking 30,000 carats of diamonds a month out of the sea. Although these diamonds were of gem quality, most were extremely small, averaging about .45 carats apiece. Collins predicted that when the dredging system was perfected, it would yield much larger diamonds. He informed his financial advisers that he planned ultimately to have fourteen barges operating in the ocean off the Namibian coast, and that these ships would recover more than one million carats' worth of gem diamonds a year. If realized, this production would in the mid-sixties be equivalent to nearly one-fifth of the world's gem diamonds.

De Beers obviously could not afford to have such a competitor working alongside its most lucrative mines in the forbidden zone. To succeed in his ambitious venture, Collins had to demonstrate to his financial backers that he could sell the diamonds at a profit as well as recover them. And De Beers still had some influence on the market for small diamonds. In 1964, most of the factories that could cut and polish diamonds less than a half carat in weight were located in Israel and were, directly or indirectly, clients of De Beers' Diamond Trading Company. Suddenly, these Israeli manufacturers found that the boxes they were receiving at the London sights were brimming over with the same categories of small diamonds that Collins was producing in Namibia. Moreover, it was made clear to at least one of Israel's leading manufacturers that if he bought any of Collins' diamonds, his supply from De Beers would be cut off.

Collins discovered that despite his enterprise in dredging diamonds from the ocean, there was no ready market for them. Despite the shortage of immediate revenue from the sale of diamonds, Collins was committed to an ambitious program of building and outfitting barges. By 1965, he found that the Marine Diamond Corporation was drained of all its cash resources and faced with bankruptcy. There was, moreover, little possibility of raising additional capital from outside banks, since it was clear to everyone concerned that the market for these diamonds was controlled by the diamond cartel. Under these conditions, Harry Oppenheimer offered to buy the Marine Diamond Corporation. Collins had no choice but to accept, and, within months, his company became a subsidiary of a De Beers subsidiary. De Beers then gradually reduced the dredging operation and closed it entirely in 1971. Collins, the would-be competitor, died in retirement in South Africa in 1978.

De Beers was confronted with another potential competitor in the mid-1970s, Albert Jolis. Jolis, a resourceful American, who had served in the OSS during the Second World War, headed an international diamond firm called Diamond Distributors, Inc., or DDI. His father, Jac Jolis, had once worked for De Beers, and for three generations the Jolis family had had a close business relationship with the Oppenheimers. Indeed, in the late 1940s, Sir Ernest had encouraged Jolis's father to establish a diamond-cutting factory in Los Angeles, and he had promised him a supply of uncut diamonds for the venture. Then, without any prior warning Sir Ernest decided against the Californian venture and refused to provide any diamonds for it. No explanation was ever tendered, and the Jolis family was expected to take the loss without asking any questions. From that point on, Albert Jolis was eager to break the dependence his family had on De Beers. He negotiated a deal in the French territory of Ubangi, which became the Central African Republic, and set up diamond-buying offices in Venezuela and Brazil. These countries provided only a small fraction of the diamonds his firm sold, and so he still had to rely on De Beers' sights in London for the lion's share of his diamonds.

In 1975, however, Jolis saw a golden opportunity to acquire a major diamond concession in Angola. Until then, Angola had been a Portuguese colony, and its diamond fields, which produced 1.5 million carats of diamonds a year, had been under control of a Portuguese-based company, Diamondco, which was partly controlled by De Beers' stockholders. Diamondco sold all of its diamonds under long-term contract to the Diamond Trading Company in London. When Portugal decided to withdraw from Africa in 1975 after more than 200 years of colonial rule, the diamond concession was again up for bidding. Angola itself was at the time on the brink of civil war.

Three rival factions shared positions in the transitional government. Each was determined to seize power for itself; and each was secretly receiving arms and mercenary assistance from foreign intelligence services. The MPLA, which had spearheaded the guerrilla war of independence against Portugal, was backed by the Soviet Union and Cuba. The FLNA, whose forces had been given sanctuary and training in neighboring Zaire, was supported by the odd combination of the United States, North Korea, China and Zaire. And UNITA, which was allied to the dominant Ovambo tribes in southern Angola, had an even more curious medley of sponsors – Zambia, Tanzania and South Africa. (A fourth faction, FLEC, not represented in the government, advocated the secession of the oil-rich enclave of Cabinda and was backed by French oil interests.) In this maelstrom of international intrigue, even De Beers, with all its resources, could not immediately exert influence over the diamond fields. It was first necessary to pick the eventual winner in the power struggle.

Jolis saw the possibility of obtaining the Angolan concession – and dealing with the cartel from a position of strength. Flying to the Angolan capital of Luanda, Jolis made contact with Jeremias Kalandala Chipanda, minister of natural resources in the transitional government. A mining engineer by training, Chipanda turned out to be extremely well-informed about the diamond business. He had personally inspected the diamond fields, and he suspected that the De Beers cartel had deliberately retarded the development of new riverbed mines in order to hold down the world supply of diamonds. He reasoned that if these riverbeds were more aggressively mined, diamonds could earn more foreign exchange for his country.

In their negotiations, Jolis managed to persuade the Angolan minister that his company, unlike De Beers, would have a competitive incentive to develop the fields as rapidly as possible. Moreover, he promised to train black technicians (De Beers had trained only eight in all of Angola). Jolis also flew in a geologist, who prepared a comprehensive report on Angola's mineral wealth.

After weeks of wining, dining, and briefing the minister and his staff in Luanda, an agreement was finally reached. Jolis's firm would be given a large portion of the concession formerly held by a De Beers subsidiary on the condition that it would accelerate the development of the diamond fields. Jolis returned to New York that spring and began making arrangements to hire personnel and to market the Angolan diamonds. Although he realized that the final outcome of his venture in Angola would depend on how the political crisis there was resolved, he had high hopes of success.

That summer, however, the political situation changed radically. The Soviet-backed MPLA faction seized Luanda in July, initiating a full-scale civil war. The transitional government was quickly deposed – with Minister Chipanda, a supporter of the UNITA faction, fleeing into the jungle. With the assistance of Soviet rockets and Cuban troops, the MPLA forces quickly routed the other two rival factions (despite aid to them from the CIA). By the year's end, the MPLA was in almost complete control of Angola.

Early in 1976 Jolis learned that his diamond concession had been cancelled by the new MPLA regime. Moreover, his geologist and staff had been denied visas. When he attempted to make contact with government officials his calls went unreturned.

Jolis finally arranged for someone in Angola with connections with the MPLA to investigate the loss of this concession. In Luanda, his intermediary made inquiries at the Ministry of Natural Resources and eventually obtained an internal staff report that cleared up the mystery. According to this document, the Soviet Union had specifically instructed its MPLA allies to cancel all agreements and negotiations with Jolis's Diamond Distributors, Inc. Adding insult to injury, the Soviets had further advised the Angolans that Diamond Distributors, Inc., was an established front for De Beers. Since the MPLA had strictly forbidden Angolans from trading with South African companies, this piece of misinformation linking Diamond Distributors, Inc., to De Beers effectively precluded the former from doing any business in Angola.

When Jolis read the contents of this report, he realized that he had been driven out of Angola. The only remaining question was what would happen to the Angolan output of diamonds, which, though severely diminished by the chaos of civil war, still had to be disposed of.

Under Soviet guidance, the MPLA arranged to sell the entire production of its diamond fields to a supposedly independent firm in London innocuously named the Diamond Development Corporation. (With the assistance of Soviet arms and experts, and Cuban troops, the Angolans also managed to close down the smuggling routes between the diamond fields and the Zairean border.)

The Angolan diamonds actually went to the offices of the Diamond Development Corporation in Chichester House, near Holborn Circus on the fringes of London's financial district. The Diamond Development Corporation, putatively in the business of sorting and selling African diamonds, was in turn owned by the Chichester Corporation, which itself is controlled by subsidiaries of De Beers. Both corporations were established by De Beers to provide a double cover for its dealings with African nationalists. (As one former De Beers executive explained, 'If the Angolans ever demanded an interest in the Diamond Development Corporation, the assets and profits could be shifted to Chichester.')

The shipments of Angolan diamonds were then driven around Holborn Circus to Number Two Charterhouse Street, headquarters of the Diamond Trading Company. Through this circuitous route, Angola's diamonds again entered the De Beers stockpile.

Of all the competitive threats to De Beers, the most potentially dangerous came from Harry Winston in New York. A short, determined man, Winston had made his own fortune in the diamond business. He had been born in 1900 in a walk-up tenement apartment in New York City, and by the age of fourteen had quit school to join his father in the jewelry business. He quickly discovered a diamond 'mine' in estate jewelry. Buying up diamonds from estates, with financing from the banks, he found he could recut and sell them at a profit. He arranged to mass-merchandise these diamonds through chain stores. By 1940, he was America's largest diamond dealer, and he also was given by De Beers the largest consignment of uncut diamonds.

After the Second World War, Winston rapidly expanded his American business. He opened up his own diamond factories in New York City, Puerto Rico (then offering tax advantages) and Israel. He also became the dominant wholesaler in America, supplying the major department stores and chain stores with their diamonds. Indeed, by the early 1950s, he was distributing more than one-quarter of all the engagement diamonds in the United States. He dreamed of acquiring his own diamond mine and bypassing the diamond cartel entirely.

He first negotiated with Dr Williamson for the Tanganyika concession, but he realized that the British colonial authorities would never allow him to jeopardize De Beers' control of the diamond trade. Tanganyika was then a British colony.

In 1953 Winston saw a more promising opportunity in Angola. De Beers, attempting to renegotiate its contract for the diamonds with the Portuguese, had run into a snag over foreign exchange. The conflict concerned whether the Portuguese would be paid in dollars for their diamonds, as they preferred, or in British pounds, which De Beers preferred.

Winston flew to Lisbon to make his offer. There he made contact with Spiros Assantos, a well-connected banker who was influential in the Salazar government then ruling Portugal, and worked out with him a detailed plan to outbid De Beers for the diamonds. Since he could provide Portugal with a guaranteed market in the United States, which accounted for the sale of three-quarters of all gem diamonds in 1953, and could also pay in dollars, which Portugal desperately needed to balance its foreign exchange deficit, Spiros Assantos was confident that his bid would prevail.

Unfortunately, at a critical point in the negotiations, Spiros Assantos died on the operating table in a Lisbon hospital. Winston was left without a contact in the Salazar government. Soon afterward, he received a telephone call from Sir Ernest Oppenheimer warning him that if he persisted in his efforts to interfere in the negotiations, he would be entirely cut off from De Beers' diamonds. On the other hand, Sir Ernest suggested, if he withdrew from the negotiations, his consignment in London would be substantially increased at the sights. While he was still mulling over this offer, he received an ultimatum from the Foreign Office. He had forty-eight hours to leave Portugal. He then decided, as he later explained to his son Ronald, that 'he had a business to run in New York,' and boarded the next plane to the United States.

Winston learned several months later from his financial associates in Lisbon why the government had issued this ultimatum. They told him that the British ambassador had intervened directly with the Salazar government, warning that the entire diamond system would collapse if Portugal bypassed De Beers and sold diamonds direct to Winston. The British government threatened that unless the Salazar government ended the negotiations with Winston and restored its contract to De Beers, it would place an embargo on all port wine imports. Since port was a crucially important export for Portugal, and England was its main market, the Salazar government ordered Winston to leave the country.

Winston, still seeking a diamond concession, next went to the West African country of Sierra Leone, also a producer of diamonds. He again tried to undercut the existing arrangement De Beers had with the British mining company that held the concession. This time, however, Oppenheimer made Winston an irresistible offer. Aside from his regular consignment of diamonds, Oppenheimer promised Winston 22 per cent of all the diamonds produced from mines along the Atlantic Ocean beaches of South-West Africa, now Namibia. These ocean mines were the richest single source of gem diamonds in the world, and the clear crystals found there were sought after by all of De Beers' clients. By guaranteeing himself 22 per cent of these highly prized diamonds, Winston would have a virtually unassailable position in the American diamond market. Moreover, Oppenheimer offered to give Winston the right to choose the diamonds he wanted from the West African fields. In return for granting him these advantages, Oppenheimer expected Winston to abandon his search for his own diamond mines. Winston agreed to these terms.

The uneasy truce between De Beers and Winston prevailed for almost a decade. De Beers, however, saw the arrangement as only a temporary expedient; and Winston still sought to sever his dependence on De Beers. In the early seventies Winston saw yet another possible source of diamonds: Siberia. He quietly opened up negotiations, through the Soviet trade delegation in London, to acquire a major share of the uncut diamonds coming from Siberian mines. He had, after all, his own cutting factories and the main distribution network for diamonds in the United States. Despite these assets, Winston underestimated the strength of the silent partnership between the Soviet Union and De Beers. In 1975, his overtures were flatly turned down.

De Beers, meanwhile, began a maneuver that would severely curtail the ambitions of Harry Winston. It began providing a large number of diamonds at its sights to Star Diamonds, owned by Sali Klagsbrun, a close friend and golfing partner of Monty Charles. Star Diamonds began to sell its diamonds in direct competition with Winston. In 1978, Harry Oppenheimer told Winston on the telephone that he would no longer receive the consignment of diamonds from Namibia that his father had arranged for him to receive at each sight. Winston reportedly became furious, and told Oppenheimer that Sir Ernest would never have gone back on his word.

Winston died soon afterward. Star Diamonds rapidly expanded its market share in America, and in 1979 hired some thirty additional salesmen in California. It then made an offer to Ronald Winston, who had succeeded his father, to buy his business. Ronald Winston refused to sell.

In 1980, Ronald Winston found his allotment progressively smaller at each sight. Whereas only five years earlier his father had received the largest single sight – worth over $20 million – Ronald now was receiving only a small fraction of his firm's needs. At one sight, the value of the diamonds fell to less than $2 million. Winston's pleas to Monty Charles to increase his allotment fell on deaf ears. Meanwhile, Star had received more than $20 million in its box at a single sight. On an annual basis, it was getting nearly 10 per cent of De Beers' total allocation. Winston was forced to buy most of his diamonds on the secondary markets in Antwerp and Tel Aviv. Although he managed to keep a large share of the American wholesale business, he found it increasingly difficult to compete with the cartel. If nothing else, his profits were tightly squeezed.

Despite De Beers' success in suppressing individual competitors, major refinements in the design of the diamond invention were necessary to preempt challenges from the Soviet Union and other producing nations. The diamond cartel could no longer sustain the value of diamonds merely by controlling the production of the mines in southern Africa; it now needed to extend its reach 'downstream' to the cutting, distributing, wholesale and even retail elements of the diamond trade to prevent the Soviet Union and others from establishing their own sales network. De Beers, in effect, had to compete with its own clients.

In 1975, De Beers opened up a small cutting factory in Lisbon. To allay the fears of clients, De Beers spokesmen stressed that the purpose of this factory was to monitor market conditions and keep track of smuggled diamonds that were arriving in Lisbon from Angola. They stressed that they had no intention of using the Lisbon factory to compete with clients. The following year, De Beers organized and financed Lens Diamond Industries in Antwerp (though the ownership remained in the hands of De Beers' shareholders rather than with De Beers itself). Lens built a huge factory, initially employing 545 workers, who sawed De Beers' rough diamonds into basic shapes, then distributed them to the cutting factories in Antwerp for faceting and polishing. It was the largest such facility in the world, and with it, De Beers had the potential for completely dominating the cutting industry in Antwerp. When a number of Antwerp manufacturers voiced their concern that De Beers was taking over an important part of their trade with this factory, De Beers' head of public relations, David Neil-Gallagher, answered that De Beers' sole purpose in building this factory was to give stable employment to Belgian sawers who might otherwise be tempted to leave Antwerp's diamond industry for more lucrative opportunities in the automotive industry.

Yet, even as De Beers rationalized its entry into the sawing business in Antwerp, it began construction of a second sawing factory in Tel Aviv. Clearly, a part of the new design was to take over the task of sawing uncut diamonds into their basic shapes.

In South Africa, De Beers provided financial assistance to small and supposedly independent diamond-cutting factories in and around Capetown. It sent a large number of 'Pieromatic' automatic diamond-cutting machines to these factories, and by 1980 some 20 per cent of the world's diamond-cutting machines were operating in Capetown. It also trained workers of racially mixed origins, classified under South Africa's apartheid laws as 'coloreds,' to polish the diamonds, which provided the Capetown factories with the cheapest labor force outside of India.

As the Capetown factories went into production, De Beers made arrangements for them to contract to sell their entire production to major Hong Kong dealers. Ho Pak Tao, one of Hong Kong's leading *diamantaires*, told an American trade journal in 1979, 'We used to depend on Israel for small goods but now we are using "coloreds" and automatic machines to cut small goods in our South Africa factory. . . .' Aside from the Hong Kong-to-Capetown connection, De Beers initiated a program of supplying selected Hong Kong manufacturers with presawn diamonds from its Lens factory in Antwerp. In 1979, for example, it shipped some 40,000 carats of these Belgian-sawn diamonds to Casey Diamonds Ltd, a Hong Kong polishing factory that employed over 100 Chinese workers and a number of Pieromatic cutting machines.

The developments in Capetown and Hong Kong were viewed with considerable consternation by Israeli manufacturers who had previously considered the $300 million Hong Kong polishing market their private preserve. With these embryonic cutting factories, De Beers now had considerable leverage over the Chinese dealers and, through them, access to the entire Southeast Asian market for polished gems.

In India, De Beers also sought to expand its sphere of influence over the manufacturing of diamond chips. In October 1979, it set up the Hindustan Diamond Corporation as a partner. Since the Indian government preferred not to be openly associated with a South African corporation, De Beers accommodatingly arranged that two Bermuda corporations, in which it owned substantial shares, be nominal owners of its interests in the Hindustan Diamond Corporation. Under this arrangement, the Hindustan Diamond Corporation became a distributor of De Beers' diamonds in India. It contracted to buy large quantities of diamonds, most of them less than a tenth of a carat apiece, and allocate them among manufacturers in the Bombay area. The Indian manufacturers, in turn, farmed these minute diamonds out to a cottage industry of some 300,000 workers, mainly women. With the support of the government in this venture, De Beers established a modicum of quasi-official control over this segment of the polishing industry.

De Beers also became a major dealer in polished diamonds through an Antwerp subsidiary called Diatrada. Diatrada had buying agents purchase large quantities of polished diamonds from manufacturers and resell them to wholesalers. A similar operation was opened in Tel Aviv, which by 1979 became the single largest purchaser of diamonds in Israel. Among other things, De Beers uses these buying offices to maintain the price of polished diamonds during periods of recession and glut. When a certain size or quality of diamond becomes excessive and cannot be easily disposed of on the trading bourses of Antwerp and Tel Aviv, Diatrada steps in and buys up the surplus. At the same time, De Beers deletes or heavily reduces the category of uncut diamonds that yielded this particular type of polished diamond at its sights in London. The net effect of these coordinated actions is to create an artificial shortage of this type of diamond and drive up the price. Diatrada then gradually resells its inventory of polished diamonds at the higher price.

To further solidify its position in polished diamonds, De Beers began holding regular sights for major dealers in polished diamonds in Lucerne, Switzerland. In 1978, De Beers pressed these clients into doubling their annual purchases of polished diamonds, and most of them agreed to the larger consignment. The following year, De Beers distributed over $300 million worth of finished gems at these sights.

Despite the fact that De Beers captured nearly one-quarter of the entire polished diamond business by the end of 1979, according to trade estimates, its executives continued to minimize its role in this area. Harry Oppenheimer, for example, said, in an interview published in *Jewelers' Circular Keystone* in September 1979: 'Our polished dealing operations were begun some years ago, principally to give us a better insight into the functioning of the market – they act as a market listening-post, if you like. The polished division [of De Beers] conducts its activities as does any other dealer in polished goods, by buying and selling in the cutting centers governed by the state of the market.'

Independent dealers are not entirely satisfied by Oppenheimer's assertion. De Beers, after all, is in a very different position from others in the diamond trade: it has cash reserves of over $1.5 billion for buying diamonds, and almost total control of the allocation of uncut diamonds to factories around the world. It can force manufacturers to buy its presawn diamonds, and it can cut off the supply from any cutting factory that fails to subscribe to its policy. 'The handwriting is on the wall,' one of De Beers' leading brokers explained to me. 'By 1985, De Beers will run the entire polished diamond show, just as it runs the uncut diamond trade now. It has to, if only to keep the Russians out.'

In Antwerp, the manufacturers treat De Beers' move into the polished diamond business as a fait accompli. 'They are already competing with their own clients in polished goods,' a governor of the Antwerp Diamond Club stoically observed. 'They have the diamonds, the capital and the connections. Those are the facts of life.'

Part Four

Diamonds Are Not Forever

Have You Ever Tried to Sell a Diamond? | 20

De Beers' advertising slogan, 'A Diamond Is Forever,' embodied an essential concept of the diamond invention. It suggested that the value of a diamond never diminishes and that therefore a diamond never need be sold or exchanged. This precept, of course, is self-fulfilling: as long as no one attempts to sell their diamonds, they retain their value (especially since the cartel tightly controls the supply of new diamonds). When, however, an individual is forced to defy this principle by attempting to sell diamonds, the results prove to be both unexpected and illuminating. Consider the following cases.

In the fall of 1978, a thirty-two-year-old Californian computer wizard named Stanley Mark Rifkin discovered an ingenious way to become a multimillionaire overnight. While working as a consultant for the Security Pacific National Bank in Los Angeles, he had learned the secret computer code that the bank used to transfer funds to other banks telegraphically at the end of each business day. With this information and his mastery of the bank's computer, he realized that he could transfer tens of millions of dollars to any bank account in America. The problem would be withdrawing the money from the system. In early October, he devised a complicated plan for siphoning this money out of the bank and converting it into Russian diamonds. The first step was to establish an alias identity. Under the pseudonym, 'Mike Hanson,' Rifkin opened a bank account at the Irving Trust Company in New York, arranged a phony passport and other documentation, and retained a respected diamond broker, Lon Stein, to acquire for him a multimillion dollar consignment of diamonds from the Soviet Union. The Soviet diamond organization, Russ Almaz, agreed to sell 'Hanson' at its fixed wholesale price 115,000 perfectly cut, round, brilliant silver bears for $8,145,000. For arranging this low price, the broker took a standard 2 per cent commission, or $162,000. For the deal to be consummated, Rifkin only had to arrange for the cash to be wired to the Soviets in Zurich.

On 25 October, Rifkin coolly entered the bank's transfer room under the pretext of inspecting the computer. He picked up a telephone connected to the computer and dialed a long series of digits. Instantly, the computer withdrew $10,200,000 from a nonexistent account and transferred it to the account of 'Mike Hanson' at the Irving Trust Company in New York. Rifkin then had the New York bank transfer $8,300,000 to the Zurich account of Russ Almaz.

A few days later, using his phony passport, Rifkin flew to Switzerland, took delivery of the diamonds, which weighed under five pounds, and smuggled them through customs into the United States. He then began contacting dealers in Los Angeles, but none was willing to buy the diamonds.

Meanwhile, on 2 November, the Security Pacific National Bank finally discovered that more than ten million dollars was missing. It was possibly the largest bank robbery in history, and the FBI immediately began investigating the loss. Within a few days, it received a tip about Rifkin, and arrested him in Carlsbad, California, on 8 November. The cache of Russian diamonds, as well as the remaining cash, were simultaneously recovered.

Initially, bank officials seemed elated that most of their money had been prudently invested in diamonds by the computer thief. Only a few weeks earlier *Newsweek* had reported in a cover story, 'The Diamond Boom,' that diamonds were 'the ideal asset' and that quality diamonds were soaring in price. To be sure, the diamonds that Rifkin had bought from the Soviets were not quality-grade investment diamonds but commercial-grade melees used in jewelry. Even so, the London-based Economist Intelligence Unit had reported that these small diamonds had increased by at least 50 per cent in value in 1978, and projected a further increase for them in 1979. Independent appraisers estimated that the Soviet diamonds, which Rifkin had bought at a low price, were worth at least $13 million at the retail level, and the bank foresaw that it might make a profit of some $5 million on the appreciation in value of the diamonds. In anticipation of this windfall, they agreed to pay the 10 per cent customs duty on the diamonds (which Rifkin had evaded) as well as the cost of the FBI investigation. Before this expected profit could be realized, the bank had to await the outcome of the trial, since the diamonds were important evidence.

Finally, in September 1978, the bank announced that it would sell its hoard of diamonds to the highest bidder. More than twelve major dealers were invited to the bank's vault to inspect the 115,000 Soviet diamonds. They were instructed to submit sealed bids by the end of the business day on 18 September. A minimum price of $7.5 million was established to encourage high bids, though independent appraisers assured the bank that the diamonds would fetch a far higher price than that.

On the day of the auction, bank officials anxiously waited to see how much profit they would garner from the Soviet hoard. By the end of the day, however, only a single bid had been submitted, and when it was opened, it was for several million dollars less than the floor price. The bank officials were amazed and disappointed at this turn of events. Even though the diamonds had been purchased through a reputable broker at wholesale price, and no customs duty had been paid, no American dealer would pay anywhere near this price nearly a year later.

The bank offered to sell the Soviet diamond sales organization back their own diamonds at the original 1978 price. The Soviets flatly refused to buy the diamonds back at any price.

The bankers learned that two Israeli banks were also trying to sell large quantities of diamonds received as collateral from Tel Aviv dealers, and this might make it far more difficult, if not impossible, for the Security Pacific National Bank to unload its 115,000 diamonds. They decided not to wait any longer.

During the episode, Walter S. Fisher, the vice-president of Security Pacific charged with the responsibility of selling the 115,000 diamonds, made some discoveries about the nature of the diamond business. First of all, he realized that diamonds were not a standardized, or 'fungible' commodity, as were gold, silver and platinum. Different appraisals of the same diamonds had varied widely, ranging between some $13 million to $6.5 million. Indeed, the value seemed wholly dependent, not on any fixed price but on what the buyer thought he could sell them for. Moreover, even though all these diamonds were commercial-grade stones destined for the mass market, Fisher found that it was extraordinarily difficult to find a buyer. All the distribution channels seemed to be controlled by De Beers, and, as it turned out, none of the dealers in the United States were willing to buy such a large consignment of diamonds from an irregular source. The bank therefore found it necessary to deal through De Beers' main broker in London, I. Hennig. Finally, Fisher found that he had no choice but to accept the terms dictated by the buyer, if he wanted to sell the diamonds. He literally had to deliver the 115,000 diamonds to an unknown corporation in Liechtenstein, G. S. G. Investments, without receiving any money for them for eighteen months. These were terms that the bank probably would not have accepted in selling any other commodity. With a flourish of understatement, the banker concluded, 'Selling diamonds is far more difficult than I had anticipated.'

To be sure, the Security Pacific National Bank's problem was made worse because it had to dispose of the diamonds quickly. However, even when individual diamonds are held over long periods of time, selling them at a profit can prove to be surprisingly difficult. For example, in 1970, the London-based consumer magazine called *Money Which?* decided to test diamonds as a decade-long investment. It bought two gem-quality diamonds, weighing approximately one-half carat apiece, from one of London's most reputable diamond dealers for £400 (or about $1000). For nearly nine years, it kept these two diamonds sealed in an envelope in its vault. During this time, Great Britain experienced rampant inflation, which ran as high as 25 per cent a year. For the diamonds to have kept pace with this inflationary spiral, they would have had to increase in value at least 300 per cent. If this had indeed happened, the magazine's two diamonds should in fact, by 1978, have been worth some £1400. When the magazine's editor, David Watt, attempted to sell the diamonds in 1978, he found that neither jewelry stores nor wholesale dealers in London's Hatton Garden district would pay anywhere near that price for the diamonds. Most of the jewelry stores refused to pay any cash for the diamonds, and the highest bid that Watt received was £500, which amounted to a profit of only £100 in over eight years, or less than 2 per cent a year at a compound rate of interest. If the purchase price was calculated in terms of 1970 pounds, it would amount to only £167. David Watt summed up the magazine's experiment by saying, 'As an eight-year investment the diamonds that we bought have proved to be very poor.' The problem again was that the buyer, not the seller, determined the price.

The magazine conducted a further experiment to determine the extent to which larger diamonds appreciate in value over a one-year period. In 1970, it bought a 1.42 carat diamond for $1800. In 1971, the highest offer it received for the same gem was $900. Rather than sell it at such an enormous loss, Watt decided to extend the experiment and held it until 1974 when again he made the rounds of the jewelers in Hatton Garden to have it appraised. During this tour of the diamond district, Watt found that the diamond had mysteriously shrunk in weight to 1.02 carats. One of the jewelers had apparently switched diamonds during the appraisal.

Watt, undaunted, attempted another such experiment in 1974, buying another 1.4 carat diamond from a reputable London dealer. This time he paid $6300. A week later, he decided to sell it. The maximum offer he received was $2400.

In 1976, the Dutch Consumer Association also attempted to test the price appreciation of diamonds. They bought a perfect, over-one-carat diamond in Amsterdam, held it for eight months, and then offered it for sale to the twenty leading dealers in Amsterdam. Nineteen refused to purchase it, and the twentieth dealer offered only a fraction of the purchase price.

In 1972, financial speculators in California had a very expensive lesson in the value of diamonds. In January, the West Coast Commodity Exchange began trading diamond contracts. Each contract contained twenty carats of cut and polished diamonds that were certified by diamond appraisers to be in flawless condition. On the first day of trading, speculators, assuming that the value of diamonds would increase with inflation, paid $660 a carat for the diamonds, or $13,200 per contract. Immediately thereafter, diamond dealers began selling contracts on the exchange, and the price plummeted down to the limit allowed by the exchange for the next six days. The following week, the price was down more than 40 per cent. The diamond dealers, who had offered the packets for sale at more than $600 a carat, made a vast profit within days on the falling prices. The speculators, who could not afford to keep putting up cash to meet the collapsing prices, lost everything. By the end of the second week, the West Coast Exchange ended trading in diamond futures. The value of diamonds, it turned out, could not be established through an open market.

Even among experts, the valuation of a diamond depends on highly subjective criteria. In 1979, for example, William Goldberg, the president of the Diamond Club in New York City, was offered a six-carat diamond in my presence by a reputable New York dealer. Both Goldberg and the dealer agreed that the diamond had excellent clarity, with no defects visible under a ten-power magnifying glass, had a highly desirable blue-white color, and had been expertly cut. The only disagreement was, in fact, over the price of the diamond. The dealer believed it was worth $4000 a carat, or $24,000. Goldberg believed it was worth considerably less than that. He then showed the diamond to a South African dealer who was visiting his office and asked his opinion. After carefully inspecting it, the South African said he wouldn't pay $8000 for the diamond, because it 'lacked any fire or life.' Goldberg nodded, took another look at the six-carat diamond, and returned it to the New York dealer without making an offer. He explained to me, 'It was a good stone, but it might not be that easy to resell.'

Selling diamonds can also be an extraordinarily frustrating experience for private individuals. In 1978, for example, a wealthy woman living in New York City decided to sell back a diamond ring that she had bought from Tiffany two years earlier for $100,000, and use the proceeds to buy a necklace of matched pearls that she fancied. She had read about the 'diamond boom' in news magazines, and hoped that she might make a profit on the diamond. Instead, the sales executive with whom she dealt explained, with a touch of embarrassment, that Tiffany had 'a strict policy against repurchasing diamonds.' He assured her, however, that the diamond was extremely valuable and suggested another Fifth Avenue jewelry store. The woman went from one leading jeweler to another, trying to sell her diamond. One store offered her the opportunity to swap it for another jewel, and two other jewelers offered to accept the diamond 'on consignment,' and pay her a percentage of what they sold it for, but none of the half-dozen jewelers she visited that day offered her cash for her $100,000 diamond. She finally gave up trying to sell the diamond and kept it.

Retail jewelers, especially the prestigious Fifth Avenue stores, generally prefer not to buy back diamonds from customers because the offer they would make most likely would be considered ridiculously low. The 'keystone,' or markup, on a diamond and setting may range from 100 to 200 per cent, depending on the policy of the store. If they bought diamonds back from customers, they would have to buy them back at the wholesale price. Most jewelers would prefer not to make a customer an offer that not only might be deemed insulting but would also undercut the widely held notion that diamonds go up in value. Moreover, since retailers generally receive their diamonds from wholesalers on consignment and need not pay for them until they are sold, they would not readily risk their own cash to buy diamonds from customers. Rather than offer customers a fraction of what they paid for diamonds, retail jewelers almost invariably recommend their clients to firms that specialize in buying diamonds 'retail.'

Perhaps the firm most frequently recommended is Empire Diamonds, on the 66th floor of the Empire State Building in midtown Manhattan. Empire's reception room, which resembles a doctor's office, is usually crowded with elderly women who sit nervously in plastic chairs waiting for their name to be called. One by one, they are ushered into a small examining room where an appraiser scrutinizes their diamonds and makes a cash offer. 'We usually can't pay more than 60 per cent of the current wholesale price,' Jack Braud, the president of Empire Diamonds, explained. 'In most cases, we have to pay less since the setting has to be discarded and we have to leave a margin for error in our evaluation (especially if the diamond is mounted in a setting).' Empire removes the diamonds from their settings, which are sold as scrap, and resells them to wholesalers. Because of the steep markup on diamonds between the wholesale and retail levels, individuals who buy retail and, in effect, sell wholesale often suffer enormous losses on the transaction. For example, Braud estimated that a half-carat diamond ring that might cost $2000 at a retail jewelry store could only be sold for $600 at Empire.

The appraisers at Empire Diamonds examine thousands of diamonds a month but only rarely turn up a diamond of extraordinary quality. Almost all the diamonds found in jewelry are slightly flawed, off-color, commercial-grade diamonds. The chief appraiser explained, 'When most of these diamonds were purchased, American women were concerned with the size of the diamond, not its intrinsic quality.' He pointed out that the flaws were commonly concealed by the setting, and added, 'The sort of flawless, investment-grade diamond one reads about is almost never found in jewelry.'

Many of the elderly women who bring their jewelry to Empire Diamonds and other buying services have been the recent victims of burglaries or muggings and fear further attempts. Thieves, however, have an even more difficult time selling diamonds than their victims. When suspicious-looking characters turn up at Empire Diamonds, for instance, they are asked to wait in the reception room, and the police are called in. In January 1980, for example, a disheveled youth came into Empire with a bag full of jewelry that he called 'family heirlooms.' When Braud pointed out that a few pieces were imitations, the young man casually tossed them in the wastepaper basket. Braud buzzed for the police.

When thieves bring diamonds to underworld fences, they usually get a pittance for them. In 1979, for example, New York City police recovered stolen diamonds with an insured value of $50,000 which had been sold to a fence for only $200. According to the assistant district attorney who handled this particular case, the fence was unable to dispose of the diamonds on 47th Street, and was eventually turned in by one of the diamond dealers whom he had contacted.

While those who actually attempt to sell diamonds often experience disappointment at the low price they are offered, the stories circulated in the press by N. W. Ayer continue to suggest that diamonds are resold at enormous profits. This is because the accounts they select to distribute to the gossip columns are not of the typical diamond ring that a women desperately tries to peddle to small stores and diamond-buying services like Empire, but of truly extraordinary diamonds that movie stars sell, or claim to sell, in a publicity-charged atmosphere. The legend created around the so-called 'Elizabeth Taylor' diamond is a case in point. This pear-shaped diamond, which weighed 69.42 carats after it had been cut and polished, was the fifty-sixth largest diamond in the world, and one of the few large-cut diamonds in private hands. Except for the fact that it was a diamond, it had little in common with the millions of small stones that are mass-marketed each year in engagement rings and other jewelry. When Harry Winston originally bought the diamond from De Beers, it weighed over 100 carats. Winston had it cut into a fifty-eight-faceted jewel, which he sold in 1967 to Harriet Annenberg Ames, the daughter of publisher Moses Annenberg, for $500,000. Mrs Ames found it, however, extremely costly to maintain: the insurance premium just for keeping it in her safe was $30,000 a year. After keeping it for two years, she decided to resell it and brought it back to Harry Winston.

Winston advised Mrs Ames that he could not buy it back for the price at which she had purchased it from him, and suggested that she might do better auctioning the diamond at Park Bernet. She called Ward Landrigan, the head of Park Bernet's jewelry department, and explained that because she did not want any publicity, the diamond should be auctioned without her family's name attached to it.

This caveat gave the publicist whom Parke Bernet retained for the auction the idea for a brilliant gambit. The huge diamond, which would appear on the cover of the catalogue, would be called 'The No Name Diamond,' and the buyer would have the right to rechristen it. In August 1969, Ward Landrigan brought the diamond to Elizabeth Taylor's chalet in Gstaad, Switzerland, and assured her that it was the finest diamond then available on the market. She expressed interest in it, and shorly thereafter items were planted in gossip columns suggesting that Elizabeth Taylor planned to bid up to a million dollars for the No Name Diamond.

At that point, Robert H. Kenmore, whose conglomerate had just acquired Cartier in New York, saw the possibility of gaining considerable publicity for Cartier by buying the No Name Diamond, renaming it the Cartier Diamond and reselling it to Elizabeth Taylor. He preferred to pay a million dollars for it, so that the sale would be indelibly impressed on the public's mind as the most expensive diamond ever purchased. He arranged to borrow the million dollars from a bank, and took the $60,000 interest cost on the loan out of his conglomerates' public relations budget.

The auction was held on 23 October 1969, and after sixty seconds of excited bidding, the diamond was sold to Cartier for $1,050,000. Harriet Ames received from Parke Bernet, after paying their commission and sales tax, $868,600, and Cartier acquired the diamond. Four days later, Elizabeth Taylor and her husband, Richard Burton, bought the diamond from Cartier for $1,100,000 (which meant that Cartier took a slight loss on the interest charge), and a few days later the diamond was transferred to Elizabeth Taylor's representative on an international airliner flying over the Mediterranean to avoid any further sales tax on the diamond.

Some ten years later, when she was married to John Warner, the United States senator from Virginia, Elizabeth Taylor decided to sell this well-publicized diamond. She announced that the minimum price was $4 million, and to cover the insurance costs for showing it to prospective buyers, she further asked to be paid $2000 for each viewing of the diamond. At this price, however, there were no buyers. Finally in 1980, she agreed to sell the diamond for a reported $2 million to a New York diamond dealer named Henry Lambert who, in turn, planned to sell the stone to an Arabian client. The profit Miss Taylor received from the transaction, after paying sales taxes and other charges, was barely enough to cover the eleven years of insurance premiums on the diamond; and if inflation were taken into account, and the return Miss Taylor received calculated in 1969 dollars, she suffered a considerable loss on buying and holding the fifty-sixth largest diamond in the world for over a decade.

Most knowledgeable diamond dealers believe that the value of extraordinarily large diamonds, such as the one bought and sold by Elizabeth Taylor, depends more on cunning publicity than the intrinsic quality of the stone. An extreme example of this is the seventy-carat diamond given to the Emperor Bokassa in 1977 by Albert Jolis, the president of Diamond Distributors, Inc. The Jolis family first negotiated a concession to mine diamonds in 1947 in what was then the French colony of Ubangi. Jolis's father, Jac Jolis, had made the case to the State Department that an American company should have the mining rights for diamonds in French Central Africa, thus assuring the United States a supply of industrial diamonds. He even hired William Donovan, the wartime head of the OSS, to represent his firm in the negotiations. According to a declassified memorandum from the American embassy in Paris, State Department officials were persuaded that it was important for the United States to gain 'direct access to strategic materials such as industrial diamonds.' Eventually, with the assistance of Donovan, Jolis's firm gained control over the alluvial deposits of diamonds in Ubangi. In 1966, Bokassa, then a colonel in the provisional gendarme, seized power in a military coup d'etat and proclaimed himself president of what was then the Central African Republic. President Bokassa agreed to continue the Jolis concession in return for the government receiving a share of a profit. A decade later, however, when Bokassa decided to become emperor and rechristened the country the Central African Empire, Jolis was given to understand that he was expected to provide a 'very large diamond' for the coronation.

As the coronation date approached, Jolis found himself caught in a difficult situation. His firm could not afford to spend millions of dollars to acquire the sort of supersized diamond that would put the emperor-to-be in a league with the shah of Iran or the British royal family; yet if he presented him with a small diamond, Bokassa might well withdraw his firm's diamond concessions. Finally, Jolis hit upon a possible solution to this dilemma. One of his assistants had found a large chunk of industrial diamond bort, weighing nearly seventy carats, which curiously resembled Africa in shape. This piece of black, poorly crystallized diamond would ordinarily have been crushed into abrasive powder, and as such would have been worth about $2 a carat, or $140. Jolis instead ordered that this large diamond be polished and mounted on a large ring. He then had one of his workmen set a one-quarter carat white diamond at the point in the black stone that would coincide with the location of the capital of the Central African Empire. Finally, Jolis placed the ring in a presentation box with a certificate stating that this diamond, which resembled the continent of Africa, was unique in all the world.

The following week, though understandably nervous about how it would be received by the mercurial Bokassa, Jolis flew to the Central African capital of Bangui and presented the ring. Bokassa took it out of the box, examined it carefully for a moment, and took Jolis by the hand and led him into a room where his entire cabinet was assembled. He paraded around the table, jubilantly displaying to each and every one of his ministers this huge black diamond. He proudly slipped it onto his ring finger. Jolis's mining concession was secure, at least temporarily, in the Central African Empire.

A few days later, the emperor proudly wore the black diamond during the coronation ceremony. The world press reported that this seventy-carat diamond, which had cost Jolis less than $500, was worth over $500,000. A piece of industrial bort was thus elevated to being one of the most celebrated crown jewels in the world. When the Emperor of Central Africa met Giscard D'Estaing, the president of France, he extended his black diamond to him as proof of his royalty.

The Bokassa empire ended unceremoniously in 1979 when French paratroopers, on orders from Paris, staged a bloodless coup d'etat and put the former emperor and his retinue on a jet headed for France. From there, Bokassa went into exile on the Ivory Coast with his prize diamond ring.

When Jolis heard that he retained among his crown jewels the industrial diamond he had presented him two years earlier, he commented, 'It's a priceless diamond – as long as he doesn't try to sell it.'

The value of the emperor's diamond, like that of most other diamonds, depends heavily on the perception of the buyer. If it is accepted as a unique gem and a crown jewel, it could be auctioned off for a million dollars. If, on the other hand, it is seen as a piece of industrial bort, it will be sold for $140 and used as grinding powder. It is, as Jolis observed, 'a two-tier market.'

Caveat Emptor | 21

In 1977, in Los Angeles, a film producer, who had just closed his account with his stockbroker, received an unexpected call from a stranger with a distinct English accent. The caller, identifying himself as a representative of 'De Beers Diamond Investments Ltd,' began by commending the producer on his acumen in withdrawing from the stock market. 'You obviously are aware of the fact that stocks and bonds can't keep pace with inflation,' he continued in a soft voice, 'but have you considered diamonds as an alternative?' He explained that diamonds had appreciated '700 per cent over the last ten years,' and that they were the 'most prudent investment available, since the supply is tightly controlled by a private monopoly.' Without further ado, the caller offered to sell the film producer a selection of 'investment diamonds' for $5000.

'But how can I buy diamonds over the phone?' the producer asked incredulously.

'All the diamonds are sealed in plastic with a certificate guaranteeing their quality,' the caller responded. 'And of course you have heard of De Beers.' The more hesistant the producer became, the more determined the caller became. 'We can register these diamonds under your wife's name, which might be helpful for your taxes,' the caller went on. 'Think of how surprised she will be when the diamonds arrive . . . and you are buying them below wholesale.'

The caller, it turned out, was one of dozens of salesmen seated around a bank of telephones in Scottsdale, Arizona. Like the rest of the men in this 'boiler room,' as it was called, he was making a 'pitch' to sell diamonds and had been supplied with a list of names of individuals around the country who had recently closed brokerage accounts. For every order he sold, he received a commision of 10 to 20 per cent, depending on the purchase price. Since the prices were in reality far above wholesale prices, the company could afford to pay its salesmen, most of them 'telephone pros,' large commissions. And despite the similarity of its name, De Beers Diamond Investments Ltd was in no way connected with De Beers Consolidated Mines. Like a host of other recently formed diamond 'boiler rooms,' with names like Diamond Selection Ltd, Kimberlite Diamond Resource Company, and Tel-Aviv Diamond Investment Ltd, this firm was formed to promote 'investment diamonds.'

When the mail-order diamonds finally arrive at the purchaser's home, they are sealed in plastic with the certificate guaranteeing their quality. The customer is then advised of what amounts to a catch-22 situation: the quality of the diamond is only guaranteed as long as it remains sealed in plastic; if the customer takes it out of the plastic to have it independently appraised, the certificate is no longer valid. When customers broke the seal, many found diamonds of inferior or even worthless quality. Complaints to the authorities proliferated at such a rate in New York that the attorney general was forced to mobilize a 'Diamond Task Force' to process the hundreds of allegations of fraud.

'It is incredible,' William R. Raikin, the assistant attorney general said in the *New York Times* in 1979. 'These crooks will get outwardly rational people to buy a sealed bag containing supposed gems. . . . And they have the nerve to tell their victims not to unseal the packet for two to three years, after which they promise to buy back the stones at much higher prices.' He added, 'It never fails to amaze me how . . . professional people like lawyers [and] medical practitioners will send checks for thousands of dollars to people they never met or heard of after being contacted by these boiler-room operators.'

Apart from selling tens of thousands of diamonds a month over the telephone, many of these newly created firms hold 'diamond investment seminars' in expensive resort hotels. At such events, they present impressive graphs and data, and typically assisted by a few well-rehearsed shrills in the audience, they proceed to sell sealed packets of diamonds to the audience. (Not uncommonly, in dealing with elderly investors, diamond salesmen play on their fear that their relatives might try to seize their cash assets and have them committed to nursing homes. They suggest that the investors can thwart such attempts by putting their money in diamonds and hiding them.)

Some of these entrepreneurs were relative newcomers to the diamond business. Rayburne Martin, who went from De Beers Diamond Investments Ltd to Tel-Aviv Diamond Investments Ltd – both domiciled in Scottsdale, Arizona – had a record of embezzlement and security law violations in Arkansas and was a fugitive from justice during most of his tenure in the diamond trade. Harold S. McClintock, also known as Harold Sager, had been convicted of stock fraud in Chicago, and had been involved in a silver bullion caper in 1974 before he helped organize De Beers Diamond Investments Ltd. Don Jay Shure, who arranged to set up another De Beers Diamond Investments Ltd in Irvine, California, had also formerly been convicted of fraud. Bernhard Dohrmann, the 'marketing director' of the International Diamond Corporation, had served time in jail for security fraud in 1976. Donald Nixon, the nephew of President Richard M. Nixon, and Robert L. Vesco, the fugitive financier, were, according to the New York State attorney general, allegedly participating in a high-pressure telephone campaign to sell 'overvalued or worthless diamonds' by employing 'a battery of siken-voiced radio and television announcers.' Among the diamond salesmen were also a wide array of former commodity and stockbrokers who specialized in attempting to sell sealed diamonds to pension funds and retirement plans.

Meanwhile, in London, the real De Beers, unable to stifle all the bogus entrepreneurs in Arizona and California using its name, decided to explore the potential market for investment gems. It announced in March 1978 a highly unusual sort of 'diamond fellowship' for selected retail jewelers. Each jeweler who participated would pay a $2000 fellowship fee. In return, he would receive a set of certificates for investment-grade diamonds, contractual forms for 'buy-back' guarantees, promotion material, and training in how to sell these unmounted diamonds to an entirely new category of customers. The target was defined by De Beers as 'men aged fifty-five and over with inherited or self-made wealth to spend.' Rather than sell fine jewels, as they were accustomed to, these selected retailers would sell loose stones with a certificate for $4000 to $6000.

De Beers' modest move into the investment diamond business caused a tremor of concern in the trade. De Beers had strongly opposed retailers selling 'investment' diamonds on the grounds that because there was no sentimental attachment to such diamonds customers would eventually attempt to resell them and thereby cause sharp price fluctuations. Indeed, De Beers executives expressed concern that retailers would not be able to cope with the thousands of distressed investors who would try to resell their loose diamonds back to them. In response to this new 'diamond fellowship' scheme, the authoritative trade journal *Jewelers' Circular Keystone*, observed: 'Besides giving De Beers an unusually direct role in retail diamond sales, the program marks a softening of its previous hard-line stand against gem investing.' Eric Bruton, the publisher of *Retail Jeweller* in London, added, 'De Beers is standing on the edge of a very slippery slope. . . . They say it is unwise to sell diamonds directly as an investment, then [they] go ahead with this diamond investment scheme.'

If De Beers had changed its policy toward investment diamonds, it was not because it wanted to encourage the speculative fever that was sweeping America and Europe. Its marketing executives in London fully realized that speculators could panic at any moment, and by precipitately flooding the market with diamonds they had hoarded, burst the price structure for diamonds. They had, however, 'little choice but to get involved,' as one De Beers executive explained. Even though the 'De Beers Diamond Investments' in Arizona, which had pioneered selling diamonds over the telephone, had gone bankrupt in late 1978, more than 200 firms had by then entered the business of selling sealed packets of diamonds to the American public over the phone. And aside from these proliferating boiler rooms, many established diamond dealers rushed into the field to sell diamonds to financial institutions, pension plans and serious investors. It soon became apparent in the Diamond Exchange in New York that selling unmounted diamonds to investors was far more profitable than selling them to jewelry shops. By early 1980, David Birnbaum, one of the leading dealers in New York, estimated that in terms of dollar value, nearly one-third of all diamond sales in the United States were for these unmounted investment diamonds. 'Only five years earlier, investment diamonds were only an insignificant part of the business,' he added. Even if De Beers did not approve of this new market in diamonds, it could hardly ignore one-third of the American diamond trade.

The phenomenon of mass-marketed investment diamonds was made possible in the 1970s by the invention of the diamond certificate. Diamonds themselves cannot be valued by any single measure, such as weight, and the factors involved in such an assessment – clarity, color, and cut – cannot be made by an individual investor or financial institution.

Moreover, since diamonds are not fungible in the sense that one diamond can be exchanged for another diamond of the same weight, some means had to be found of standardizing the quality of diamonds. Certificates, which guarantee the color, clarity, and cut of individual diamonds, provided this medium.

In the late 1960s, the Gemological Institute of America, a privately owned company established to service jewelers, developed a convenient system for certifying the quality of diamonds. For ascertaining the 'cut' of the diamond, the Gemological Institute devised in 1967 a 'proportionscope.' This contraption casts a magnified shadow of the stone in question over a diagram that represents the ideal proportions for a diamond of that size. By comparing the overlap between the image of the diamond and the diagram, the deviation from the ideal can be easily measured – and recorded on the certificate. For determining the 'clarity' of the diamond, the Gemological Institute developed a 'Gemolite' microscope, which has an attachment for rotating a diamond under ten-power magnification against a dark background. If no blemishes can be seen in the diamond under this magnification, it is graded 'flawless'; if there are blemishes, but they are very difficult to find with this lens, it is graded 'VVS,' and with imperfections visible at lower magnifications, it is further downgraded. Finally, to establish the exact color of the diamond, the Gemological Institute introduced the 'Diamondlite': a boxlike machine with a window in it which allows a diamond to be compared with a set of sample stones that span all the color gradations from pure white to yellow. The purest white on this scale is classified as 'D,' the next grade of white is classified as 'E.' Gradually, by grade 'I,' the white is tinted with yellow; and by grade 'K,' the color is considered to be yellow and of much lower value.

By 1978, diamonds were being routinely certified through these methods, not only by the Gemological Institute of America, but also by other gemological laboratories in Antwerp, Paris, London and Los Angeles. Since dealers needed certificates for selling investment diamonds, and customers were usually willing to pay a hefty premium for such a document attached to the diamond, the laboratories found it difficult to keep up with the demand. Long lines of diamond dealers usually formed in front of the laboratories and, in many cases, stand-ins were hired to wait in line for impatient dealers.

The certification mechanism, despite all the Rube Goldberg sorts of inventions employed, did not entirely remove the subjective element from diamond evaluation. Not uncommonly, dealers would resubmit the same diamond to the Gemological Institute and receive a different rating for it. It did, however, facilitate the trading of rare diamonds. A diamond certified as D, flawless, was an extreme rarity, and since very few such stones existed, or would ever be extracted from mines, they could be bought and sold on the basis that they were in short supply. The price of these near-perfect diamonds rose from $4000 a carat in 1967 to $22,000 a carat in 1978 to $50,000 in 1980. Even though such extravagant prices for D, flawless, diamonds are frequently cited by the press in stories about the appreciation of diamonds, they are in fact no more representative of diamond prices in general than the prices paid by philatelists for misprinted postage stamps are representative of the value of ordinary stamps. In all the world, there are probably fewer than one hundred diamonds mined that can be cut into one-carat, D, flawless, stones, and only a small proportion of these are ever certified and sold to investors. Moreover, very few diamonds are ever sold for the prices reported in the news stories. 'No dealer I know has ever sold a one-carat investment diamond for $50,000,' a New York dealer stated in 1980. 'It may of course be the asking price.'

The high prices quoted for the few available D, flawless, stones do not necessarily hold for diamonds of a slightly inferior grade. For example, in 1978, when D, flawless, diamonds were quoted at $22,000 a carat, an H grade white diamond, without any visible imperfections, was valued at only $2750. Once mounted in a ring or piece of jewelry, it would be extremely difficult for the untrained eye to differentiate between a D and H color (especially since the setting reflects through the diamond). But while this subtle difference is of little importance in the sale of jewelry, it creates nearly 90 per cent of the value in an investment diamond. For what is measured by this grading system is not beauty, but the comparative rarity of a given class of diamonds.

Most investors have no choice but to rely on the piece of paper that comes attached to the diamond to specify the grade, and hence the value, of their investment. Not all certificates, however, emanate from the Gemological Institute of America. Many certificates have been issued by less reputable – or even nonexistent – laboratories, and the diamond might be of a much lower grade than that certified. Even if the certificate comes from a bona fide laboratory, its evaluation of the diamond may later be disputed by another assessor. Robert Crowningshield, the New York director of the Gemological Institute, observed, 'I've never seen two experts agree on the quality of a particular diamond.'

The extent to which the value of diamonds is determined by the eye of the beholder was demonstrated in 1981 by an experiment conducted under the sponsorship of *Goldsmith* magazine. In this test, four leading diamond evaluators were handed 145 diamonds which had previously been graded by the Gemological Institute of America, the European Gemological Laboratories and the International Gemological Institute. The team of experts was not told how each of the diamonds had previously been graded. After the team had reached its own consensus on the grade of each stone, the results were compared with those of the gemological institutes. In 92 out of 145 cases, the team of evaluators disagreed with the grades previously given on the certificates. Despite all the scientific paraphernalia surrounding the process of certification, diamond grading remained, according to this test, an extraordinarily subjective business.

To make a profit, investors at some point must find buyers who are willing to pay more for their diamonds than they did. Here, however, investors face the same problem as those attempting to sell their jewelry: there is no unified market on which to sell diamonds. Although dealers will quote the prices for which they are willing to sell investment-grade diamonds, they seldom give a set price at which they are willing to buy the same grade diamonds. In 1977, for example, *Jewelers' Circular Keystone* polled a large number of retail dealers and found a difference of over 100 per cent between different offers for the same quality investment-grade diamonds. Moreover, even though most investors buy their diamonds at or near retail price, they are forced to sell at wholesale prices. As *Forbes* magazine pointed out in 1977, 'Average investors, unfortunately, have little access to the wholesale market. Ask a jeweler to buy back a stone, and he'll often begin by quoting a price 30 per cent or more *below* wholesale.' Since the difference between wholesale and retail tends to be at least 100 per cent in investment diamonds, any gain from the appreciation of the diamonds will probably be lost in the act of selling them.

Many New York dealers feared that despite the high-pressure telephone and seminar techniques, the diamond bubble could suddenly burst. 'There's going to come a day when all those doctors, lawyers and other fools who bought diamonds over the phone take them out of their strong boxes, or wherever, and try to sell them,' one dealer predicted.

The Great Overhang | 22

Except for those few stones that have been permanently lost, every diamond that has been found and cut into a jewel since the beginning of time still exists today. This historic inventory, which overhangs the market, is literally in the public's hands. Some hundred million women wear diamonds on their person, while millions of others keep them in safe deposit boxes or strong boxes as family heirlooms. It is conservatively estimated that the public holds more than five hundred million carats of gem diamonds in this above-the-ground inventory, which is more than fifty times the number of gem diamonds produced by the diamond cartel in any given year. Since the quantity of diamonds needed for engagement rings and other jewelry each year is satisfied by the production from the world's mines, this prodigious half-billion carat overhang of diamonds must be prevented from ever being put on the market. The moment a significant portion of the public began selling diamonds from this inventory, the price of diamonds could not be sustained. For the diamond invention to survive, the public must be psychologically inhibited from ever parting with their diamonds.

In developing a strategy for De Beers in 1953, the advertising agency N. W. Ayer noted, 'Diamonds do not wear out and are not consumed. New diamonds add to the existing supply in trade channels and in the possession of the public. In our opinion old diamonds are in "safe hands" only when widely dispersed and held by individuals as cherished possessions valued far above their market price.' The advertising agency's basic assignment was, in other words, to make women value diamonds far more than they are actually worth on the market. N. W. Ayer set out to accomplish this task by attempting through subtly designed advertisements to foster a sentimental attachment to diamonds which would make it difficult for a woman to give them up. Indeed, women were induced to think of their diamonds as their 'best friends.' As far as De Beers and N. W. Ayer were concerned, 'safe hands' belonged to those women psychologically conditioned never to sell their diamonds.

This conditioning could not be attained solely by placing advertisements in magazines. The diamond-holding public, which includes individuals who inherit diamonds, had to remain convinced that diamonds retained their monetary value. If they saw price fluctuations in the diamond market and attempted to dispose of them to take advantage of these changing prices, the retail market would become chaotic. It was therefore essential that at least the illusion of price stability be maintained.

The extremely delicate positioning of the 'overhang' provides one of the main rationalizations for the cartel arrangement. Harry Oppenheimer explained the unique situation of diamonds in the following terms: 'A degree of control is necessary for the well-being of the industry, not because production is excessive or demand is falling, but simply because wide fluctuations in price, which have, rightly or wrongly, been accepted as normal in the case of most raw materials, would be destructive of public confidence in the case of a pure luxury such as gem diamonds, of which large stocks are held in the form of jewelry by the general public.' During the periods when production from the mines temporarily exceeds the consumption of diamonds, which is determined mainly by the number of impending marriages in the United States and Japan, the cartel can preserve the vital illusion of price stability by either cutting back the distribution of diamonds at its London sights or by itself buying back diamonds at the wholesale level. The underlying assumption is that as long as the general public never sees the price of diamonds fall, they will not become nervous and begin selling the hundreds of millions of carats' worth of diamonds that they hold from prior production. If this overhang ever reached the market, even De Beers and all the Oppenheimer resources could not prevent the price of diamonds from plummeting.

Before the advent of the twentieth century and the mass-marketing of diamonds, the 'overhang,' though it existed, was far less of a danger. Diamonds were then considered to be the almost exclusive possession of aristocrats and the wealthy elite, who were not expected to precipitately sell their jewels – except under the direst circumstances. In times of revolution, however, this stock did threaten to come cascading onto the market. When the Czar of Russia was deposed in 1917, the Bolsheviks announced that they were selling the mass of diamonds that his family had accumulated over the centuries. The fear that this stockpile of diamonds would come onto the market depressed world diamond prices for over a year. Then Solly Joel, the nephew and heir of Barney Barnato, who controlled the diamond syndicate in London, offered the Bolsheviks one-quarter million pounds for the entire hoard sight unseen. The Bolsheviks, desperately in need of cash to finance their revolution, accepted the offer, and delivered the diamonds in fourteen cigar boxes to London. Joel then assured the other diamond merchants that he would keep these diamonds off the market for years, and panic subsided.

With the bulk of the diamonds in the hands of the general public, the problem of the overhang became much more difficult to handle. When the demand for diamonds almost completely abated after the crash of 1919, De Beers shut down the supply of diamonds by closing its mines and buying the production of independent mines for its stockpile in London. It could not, however, prevent diamonds from the overhang seeping into the market. Prices for small gems fell to $5 a carat. De Beers, already heavily in debt, continued through the 1930s to borrow money to buy back as many of these diamonds as it could absorb. But despite all these efforts, enough of the overhang came onto the market to make it impossible for jewelers to buy back diamonds. Public confidence in diamonds as a store of value was nearly destroyed, especially in Europe, and it required more than a generation before diamonds were again to reach their 1929 price level.

In the 1960s, the overhang again threatened to pour onto the market when the Soviet Union began to sell its polished diamonds. De Beers and its allies now no longer controlled the diamond supply. De Beers realized that open competition with the Soviets would inevitably lead to 'price fluctuations,' as Harry Oppenheimer gingerly put it. This, in turn, would undoubtedly weaken the public's carefully cultivated confidence in the value of diamonds. Since Oppenheimer assumed that neither party could afford risking the destruction of the diamond invention, he offered the Soviets a straightforward deal – 'a single channel' for controlling the world supply of diamonds. In accepting this arrangement, the Soviets became partners in the cartel, and coprotectors of the diamond invention. De Beers then devised the 'eternity ring,' made up of hundreds of tiny Soviet-sized diamonds, which could be sold to an entirely new market of married women. The advertising campaign designed by N. W. Ayer was based on the theme of recaptured love. Again, sentiments were born out of necessity: American wives received a snake-like ring of miniature diamonds because of the needs of a South African corporation to accommodate the Soviet Union.

As the supply of Soviet diamonds continued to flow into London at an ever-increasing rate, De Beers' strategists came to the conclusion that this production could not be entirely absorbed by 'eternity rings' or other new concepts in jewelry. They began looking for diamond markets for miniature diamonds outside the confines of the United States. Even though they succeeded beyond their wildest expectation in creating an instant diamond 'tradition' in Japan, they were unable to create similar traditions in Brazil, Germany, Austria or Italy. Despite the cost involved in absorbing this hoard of Soviet diamonds each year, De Beers prevented, at least temporarily, the Soviet Union from taking any precipitate actions that might cause the diamond overhang to start sliding down onto the market.

Another threat came in 1977. Sir Philip Oppenheimer and other De Beers executives became concerned about the buildup of Israeli stockpiles of uncut diamonds in Tel Aviv. Most of these diamonds had been pledged as collateral for loans with which the dealers bought still more diamonds. The Israeli banks, who had lent some $850 million – or nearly one-third of all of Israel's foreign exchange – on the diamonds, began asking the dealers to repay the loans. To do this. however, dealers would have to sell their diamonds, which could cause an abrupt drop in the price. And if the price began dropping, the banks themselves might be forced to liquidate the remaining stockpiles of diamonds, causing the sort of panic in the diamond market that could conceivably unsettle the overhang.

After establishing liaisons with the Israeli banks, De Beers executives worked out, what one of its chief brokers termed, 'a billion dollar squeeze play.' First, De Beers reduced the number of diamonds provided to the Israeli dealers at the London sights. Then, through a special surcharge, De Beers actually increased the price the dealers had to pay. To get the cash for these diamonds, the latter were forced to reduce their inventories. Meanwhile, De Beers' publicity department churned out a series of press releases about new surcharges and rising prices that distracted attention from the fluctuation in wholesale prices. Before the year ended, according to *Jewelers' Circular Keystone,* about 350 Israeli dealers, unable to repay their loans, were forced into bankruptcy. The wholesale price, cushioned by De Beers' buying operations, wavered but did not collapse. By 1979, the Israeli stockpile had been successfully dispersed.

The most serious threat to the stability of the diamond overhang came in 1980 from the sale of 'investment' diamonds to speculators in the United States. De Beers had methodically nurtured the idea in America that diamonds were not subject to the vagaries of price that affected other consumer luxuries. To maintain this illusion in the public's mind, De Beers made it a *sine qua non* of its marketing strategy that retail prices should never fall. Price competition between major retailers of diamonds was prohibited by the rules of the game prices. *Jewelers' Circular Keystone*, which interviewed dozens of leading retailers in 1979, explained:

> If the giant retailers ever declared a predatory price war on 'mom and pop' competitors and each other, they could destroy the image of diamonds as a commodity that always appreciates in value. . . . So a tacit unwritten agreement with De Beers forbids such privileged retailers from engaging in predatory price wars.

Under this system, nationwide jewelry chains, though they get their diamonds either directly from De Beers or a De Beers sight-holder at a lower price, do not attempt to undercut the small jewelry shop (which acquires its diamonds on consignments at much higher prices). What varies is the profit and markup, not the retail price. As long as individuals do not attempt to resell their diamonds and thereby discover the enormous difference in markups, or 'keystones,' as they are called in the trade, it is possible to retain the appearance of stable and gradually increasing prices.

The situation radically changed in the late 1970s when the more unsavory sales organizations began selling millions of carats of 'investment' diamonds to men who had no sentimental attachment to the diamonds themselves and acquired them solely for the purpose of reselling them at a higher price. They were not even mounted as jewelry. By 1980, it was estimated that American investors had paid more than a billion dollars for these diamonds. Moreover, many of the companies that had sold the diamonds with the guarantee of a 'buy-back' at a fixed price had either gone bankrupt or simply closed their offices and disappeared.

Unless the diamond cartel managed somehow to absorb or get control of these private stockpiles, they could come cascading onto the market and unhinge the entire overhang. One New York diamond dealer gave a gloomy scenario of what would happen if this accumulation of diamonds was suddenly sold by speculators.

> Investment diamonds are bought for $30,000 a carat, not because any woman wants to wear them on her finger, but because the investor believes they will be worth $50,000 a carat. He may borrow heavily to finance his investment. When the price begins to decline, everyone will try to sell their diamonds at once. In the end, of course, there will be no buyers for diamonds at $30,000 a carat or even $15,000. At this point, there will be a stampede to sell investment diamonds, and the newspapers will begin writing stories about the great diamond crash. Investment diamonds constitute, of course, only a small fraction of the diamonds held by the public, but when women begin reading about a diamond crash, they will take their diamonds to retail jewelers to be appraised and find out that they are worth less than they paid for them. At that point, people will realize that diamonds are not forever, and jewelers will be flooded with customers trying to sell, not buy, diamonds. That will be the end of the diamond business.

Whether this pessimistic scenario unfolds in the 1980s remains to be seen. De Beers would no doubt commit billions of dollars of its cash reserves to buying back diamonds and attempting to stabilize prices, and the Soviet Union might even join in the effort to rescue the diamond invention. Nevertheless, the time is past when De Beers could manipulate prices merely through the expedient of shutting down mines, and putting pressure on cutting factories and large dealers. Its own success in mass-marketing diamonds in America and Japan has expanded the overhang to proportions which cannot be easily controlled. Each year's production from the mines of Africa and Siberia adds some 10 million carats of diamonds in the overhang.

Meanwhile, in the laboratories of the United States, Japan, China and the Soviet Union, scientists are developing new methods and techniques to manufacture larger diamonds more economically in hydraulic presses. In the late 1960s, scientists from both General Electric and Soviet laboratories demonstrated that it was possible to 'grow' from a carbon solution diamonds of gem quality that could not easily be distinguished from diamonds mined from the earth. Diamond dealers already envision the possibility that gem diamonds will be manufactured commercially in the laboratory in the future. And, if this occurs, the diamond craze of the twentieth century, like the tulip mania of the eighteenth century, might disappear overnight.

In any case, the diamond invention is neither eternal nor self-perpetuating. It survived for the past half century because two critical conditions were satisfied: the production of diamonds from the world's mines was kept in balance with world consumption; and the public refrained from attempting to sell its inventory back onto the market. De Beers satisfied the first of these conditions by owning and controlling the major sources of diamonds and the second of these conditions by fostering the illusion in the public's mind that diamonds are forever. Both achievements may prove to be temporary phenomena, however. As De Beers enters the 1980s, it no longer owns or monopolizes the world's diamond mines, and it now must depend on the Soviet Union and Black African nations to impose discipline on production. Moreover, the massive diamond inventory in the public's hands now hangs over the market like the proverbial sword of Damocles, and diamond speculators have already altered the delicate balance between supply and demand.

The Coming Crash of 1983 | 23

In the spring of 1981, executives of the Diamond Trading Company made an emergency trip to Tel Aviv. They had been informed that three Israeli banks were now holding \$1.5 billion worth of diamonds in their vaults – an amount nearly equal to the annual production of all the diamond mines in the world – and that the banks were threatening to dump the colossal hoard of diamonds onto an already depressed market. The Israeli banks themselves were caught in a financial squeeze over the diamonds that threatened the entire economy of Israel. The problem had really begun in the mid-1970s when the Israeli government had attempted to greatly expand the diamond cutting industry in and around Tel Aviv. The government then arranged for the banks to lend Israeli diamond manufacturers as much money as they needed to acquire uncut diamonds at very low rates of interest. In effect, Israeli diamond manufacturers could buy a stock of diamonds either from De Beers or on the open market in Antwerp and then take these diamonds to a bank, leave them there as collateral and receive in a low-interest loan the full amount they paid for the diamonds. They could then use the money they received from the bank to purchase more diamonds. Since Israel was suffering from runaway inflation and currency tended to depreciate drastically in value every month, manufacturers continued to add diamonds to their growing stockpiles held by the banks. Then when the world recession of 1979/80 made it more difficult for manufacturers to sell diamonds, the price of diamonds began to fall. Hundreds of manufacturers, unable to put up more collateral for their debt, went bankrupt. By 1981 the manufacturers had forfeited virtually all their stockpiles to the Israeli banks.

When the banks investigated the possibility of reselling

the diamonds in Europe or the United States they found there was little market for their holdings. The entire pipeline was choked with uncut and unsold diamonds. The only alternative to dumping these diamonds on the market was reselling them en masse to De Beers itself.

De Beers, however, was in no position to absorb such a huge cache of diamonds. During the recession it had to use a large portion of its cash reserves to buy diamonds from Russia or Black Africa which it could not immediately resell. This was necessary to preserve the cartel arrangement. As it added diamonds to its stockpile, De Beers depleted its cash reserves. Moreover, in 1980 it found it necessary to buy back diamonds on the wholesale markets in Antwerp to prevent a complete collapse in diamond prices. Therefore, when the Israeli banks approached De Beers about the possibility of buying back the diamonds, De Beers, possibly for the first time since the Depression of the 1930s, found itself severely strapped for cash. It could, of course, itself borrow the billion and half dollars necessary to bail out the Israeli banks, but this would strain the financial structure of the entire Oppenheimer empire.

De Beers, unfortunately, had few alternatives if the diamond invention was to be saved. It could not allow the banks to flood the market with diamonds. The sharp fall in prices could trigger a panic and the entire diamond overhang could come into the market. As the Soviet Union and other silent partners of De Beers watched to see whether the De Beers system could survive this crisis, Sir Philip Oppenheimer, Monty Charles, Michael Grantham and other top executives from De Beers and its subsidiaries feverishly attempted to prevent the Israeli banks from dumping their hoard of diamonds. However, despite their best efforts, the situation grew increasingly precarious. In September 1981, Israel's major banks quietly informed the Israeli government that they faced losses of disastrous proportions on defaulted accounts that were almost entirely collateralized with diamonds. The extent to which the solvency of these banks was dependent on diamonds was staggering. Three of Israel's largest banks – the Union Bank of Israel, the Israel Discount Bank and Barclays Discount Bank – had loans of some $660 million outstanding to diamond dealers, which constituted a significant portion of the bank debt in Israel. To be sure, not all these loans were in jeopardy, but according to bank estimates, defaults in diamond accounts now had risen to 20 per cent of the loan portfolio at some of these major banks. The crisis had to be resolved either by selling the diamonds that had been put up as collateral, which threatened to precipitate a worldwide selling panic and a total collapse of prices, or by some sort of outside assistance from the Israeli government or De Beers – or both. The negotiations provided only stopgap assistance: De Beers would buy back a small proportion of the diamonds and the Israeli government would not force the banks to conform to banking regulations that would result in the liquidation of the stockpile.

'Nobody took into account that diamonds, like any other commodity, can drop in value,' Mark Mosevics, chairman of First International Bank of Israel, explained to the *New York Times*. According to industry estimates, the average one-carat flawless diamond had fallen 50 per cent in value since January 1980. In March 1980, for example, the benchmark value for such a diamond was $63,000; in September 1981, it was only $23,000. This collapse of prices forced Israeli banks to sell diamonds from their stockpile at enormous discounts. One Israeli bank reportedly liquidated diamonds in its inventory valued at $6 million for $4 million in cash in late 1981. It was now becoming abundantly clear to the diamond trade that there was a major stockpile of large diamonds that De Beers did not control. And, without such control, diamond prices could not be maintained in the market place. It was this very possibility that the diamond invention sought to obviate.

De Beers was now confronted with the fact that after some ninety years of brilliant manipulations and maneuvers, it was losing control over the powerful levers that had established the value of diamonds.

In August 1981, De Beers took drastic measures. To begin with, it reduced the sale of diamonds at its August sight, which is ordinarily the second largest distribution of diamonds in the year, by some 95 per cent. Then it informed its leading dealers throughout the world that in the foreseeable future, and at least until mid-1982, they would be receiving few new diamonds of size and quality. It further requested these dealers to reduce the number of cut diamonds that they were selling on the market. According to one New York dealer, Monty Charles explained in private conference that 'they faced a crisis that was unprecedented in modern history.'

Even though De Beers still had the power to cut back on the diamonds it released from its own stockpile (and mines), it could not control either the quantity or quality of diamonds released from the Israeli stockpiles. It still had an enormous cash reserve, which had by mid-1981 fallen to just over $1 billion, but even this was not enough to buy up all the Israeli diamonds. Moreover, as interest rates soared into double figures, De Beers found it increasingly costly to buy diamonds in the open market for cash and then hold them in its vaults. De Beers had thus effectively lost control over the demand lever for diamonds as 1982 approached.

There was an even more serious threat to De Beers' control over the production of diamonds. Ever since Cecil Rhodes and his group of European bankers had assembled the components of the diamond invention at the end of the nineteenth century, the managers of the diamond cartel shared a common nightmare – the nightmare that a giant new source of diamonds would be discovered outside their purview. Sir Ernest Oppenheimer, using all the colonial connections of the British Empire, succeeded in weaving all the later discoveries of diamonds in Africa into the fabric of the cartel; and, when diamonds were discovered in Siberia in the late 1950s, Harry Oppenheimer managed to negotiate a secret agreement that effectively brought the Soviet Union into the cartel. However, all these brilliant efforts did not end the nightmare. In the late 1970s vast deposits of diamonds were discovered in the Argyle region of western Australia near the town of Kimberley (which coincidentally had been named after Kimberley, South Africa). Test drillings in 1981 then indicated that these Australian diamond pipe mines could produce up to 50 million carats of diamonds a year. This staggering quantity was larger than the entire production of the De Beers cartel in 1981. Even though only a small percentage of these Australian diamonds were of gem quality, the total number produced would still be sufficient to change the world geography of diamonds. Either this 50 million carats would be brought under control or the diamond invention would be finished.

De Beers rapidly moved to get a stranglehold on these

Australian diamonds. It began by acquiring a small indirect interest in CRA, the Australian company which controlled most of the mining rights to this venture. Then, in 1980, it offered a secret deal to CRA through which it would gain the right to market the total output of Australian production. This agreement might have ended the Australian threat if Northern Mines, a minority partner in the venture, had accepted the deal. Instead, Northern Mines leaked the terms of the deal to a leading Australian newspaper, which reported that De Beers planned to pay the Australian consortium 80 per cent less than the existing market price for the diamonds. This immediately led to a furore in Australia. The opposition Labour Party charged not only that De Beers was seeking to cheat Australians out of the true value of the diamonds, but that the deal with De Beers would support the policy of apartheid in South Africa. It demanded that the government impose export controls on the diamonds rather than allowing them to be controlled by a South African corporation. Prime Minister Malcolm Fraser finally acceded to the storm of public protest and announced to Parliament that his government would oppose any deal through which De Beers, or any of its subsidiaries, got control of Australia's diamonds. De Beers' failure in Australia was now complete. Ironically, it had been able to negotiate secret deals with the authoritarian regimes in the Soviet Union and Black Africa, even though they professed to be the archenemies of South Africa's apartheid policy, but it had failed to come to an arrangement with a democratic government that had been in the Commonwealth with South Africa. Even if De Beers somehow manages to buy up Australia's entire production, it still will not control the quantity of diamonds that pour out of Australian mines. De Beers will therefore have to buy for its stockpile a plethora of diamonds on Australia's terms, and the vast sums of money necessary for this enterprise will no longer be available for supporting the rest of the diamond market. The Australian diamonds place an especially difficult strain on De Beers' finances, since in 1982 De Beers' surplus of cash finally ran out and it became a net borrower.

De Beers also saw its empire begin to crumble in Zaire. Sir Ernest Oppenheimer had concluded more than a half century ago that control over the diamond mines in Zaire (then called the Belgian Congo) was the key to the cartel's control over world production. De Beers, together with its Belgian partners, had then instituted mining and sorting procedures to maximize the production of industrial rather than gem diamonds. Since there was no other ready customer for the massive quantities of industrial diamonds the Zairean mines produced, De Beers remained its only outlet. In 1981, however, President Mobuto abruptly announced that his country's exclusive contract with De Beers' subsidiary would not be renewed. Mobuto had reportedly been influenced in this decision by offers he had received from both Indian and American manufacturers for Zaire's diamond production. According to one New York diamond dealer interested in importing diamonds from Zaire, 'Mobuto simply wants a more lucrative deal.' Whatever his motives, the sudden withdrawal of Zaire from the cartel further undercuts the stability of the diamond market. With increasing pressure for the independence of Namibia and a less friendly government in neighboring Botswana, De Beers' days of control in Black Africa seem indeed to be numbered.

Even in the midst of this crisis, De Beers' executives in London still maneuvered to save the diamond invention by buying up loose diamonds. By 1982 the inventory of diamonds in its vault had swollen to a value of over a billion dollars – twice the 1979 inventory. To rekindle the demand for diamonds, De Beers launched a new multimillion-dollar advertising campaign (which included $400,000 spent for television advertisements during the royal wedding of Prince Charles and Lady Diana in July 1981), yet this campaign could realistically be expected to buy only a few months of time for the cartel. By the mid-1980s the avalanche of Australian diamonds will be pouring onto the market and unless the resourceful managers of De Beers can find a way in the interim to bring this plethora of diamonds under their control, it will probably signal the final collapse of world diamond prices. Under these circumstances, the diamond invention will disintegrate and be remembered only as a historical curiosity, as brilliant in its way as the glittering, brittle, little stones it once made so valuable.

Epilogue

On 9 March 1982 – a day which is likely to be remembered in the diamond trade as Black Tuesday – De Beers announced that it was cutting the dividend on its shares. It was the first time there had been such a reduction in thirty-eight years, but De Beers had little alternative: world diamond sales were plummeting and its operating profit had decreased by 55 per cent in a single year. Meanwhile the stockpile of diamonds in its vault had doubled. More ominously, De Beers was rapidly running out of cash: As the *Financial Times* commented: 'Two years ago De Beers had cash resources of $1.2 billion which were earmarked for supporting the diamond market. . . . Now the company has more or less exhausted its cash and . . . it has raised a short-term loan of $240 million from an associated company believed to be Anglo-American.'

To hold the cartel together, however, De Beers will have to borrow a much larger amount of cash. In 1982 the Soviet Union is scheduled to deliver to De Beers its spring and fall production, valued at $600 million, and there are also impending shipments from Zaire, Sierra Leone and Angola which have to be preemptively paid for. Even De Beers' credit is not limitless; and at interest rates of over 15 per cent, financing the Siberian and African mines is an exceedingly expensive proposition. If the diamond surplus continues, it is only a matter of time before De Beers will have to refuse the excess, if only to avoid bankruptcy, and then these glittering pebbles will flood onto the markets of the world.

Endnotes

Prologue

The Diamond Invention had its origins in a casual meeting that I had with a diamond broker named Ben Bonas in June 1978. Bonas casually explained that he was an intermediary between the Diamond Trading Company in London and diamond dealers all over the world. In this capacity, he had handled about one-third of the world's uncut diamonds. When I heard that he was in the diamond business my initial response was to assume that it was all part of a very ancient trade. 'Not at all,' he said. 'The diamond business was only really invented in the last hundred years.' He pointed out that although diamonds had been precious gems for centuries, the business of mass-marketing them as engagement rings, and controlling the price, was a comparatively recent phenomenon. The 'invention' that he referred to intrigued me; it was the system for restricting the supply of diamonds and maintaining the price in the world market.

It was, in brief, a complete monopoly. The possibility that the value of diamonds was artificially sustained intrigued me, and I decided to look further into this mechanism. The investigation took two and a half years.

The success that the diamond cartel had in creating a market in Japan was explained to me by Hugh Dagnell, one of the chief marketing strategists for the Diamond Trading Company in London. The statistics on the Japanese and other markets come from a private study done by the Diamond Trading Company called *The Retail Diamond Market for Nine Marketing Countries* (1978). I also did a series of interviews with the advertising personnel at N. W. Ayer and J. Walter Thompson who were working on a diamond account. The series of full-color advertisements were supplied to me by the Diamond Trading Company in London.

Chapter One

The Diamond Invention began as a project for the German magazine, *Geo,* which in 1978 was planning an American edition. The editor, Harold Kaplan, wanted a long report on the mining of diamonds, and he offered to finance a trip to the world's diamond mines. I first went to the offices of De Beers' Diamond Trading Corporation in London at Number Two Charterhouse Street on 28 November 1978. After receiving an initial briefing on diamond production from Richard Dickson, the public relations officer in charge of visiting journalists, I flew directly to Johannesburg, South Africa. From there I proceeded to diamond mines in Botswana, Lesotho, Namibia and Kimberley. Then I went to the diamond-cutting centers in Antwerp and Israel, and back to De Beers' headquarters in London. The trip took eight weeks.

The section on New York was logistically the easiest, since I live in New York and have many friends in the diamond business. The magazine *Jewish Living* (which lasted only three issues) arranged many of the interviews that I had with Jewish diamond dealers on the New York Exchange. I interviewed the president of the Diamond Dealers Club, William Goldberg, in his office in the Diamond Exchange. Fred Knobloch was kind enough to tell me in detail of his trips to Moscow to buy Soviet diamonds. The articles in the *Jewelers' Circular Keystone* detailing concern for the diamond market were written by David Federman, who was kind enough to share his sources with me.

In Johannesburg, I spent a good deal of my time at the offices of the Anglo-American Corporation at 44 Main Street. I was especially struck by the genteel and very English atmosphere that prevails in this part of South Africa. At lunch, for example, the service begins with an English butler serving drinks. Then everyone is ushered to a long table with fine china and crystal glasses. A wine steward pours French claret while a chef, standing at a sideboard, carves the roast beef to each guest's taste. After the meal Cuban cigars are passed around the table. It is much more like dining in a private club in England than at a South African mining company.

I am especially indebted to a number of Anglo-American executives for explaining De Beers' diamond mining strategy. Peter J. R. Leyden, the manager of Diamond Services, provided me with an extremely helpful overview of how De Beers maintains equilibrium between world supply and demand. Dr L. G. Murray, the chief geologist for De Beers, gave me a useful account of the diamond prospecting activities. Barry R. Mortimer, the chief public relations consultant for De Beers, gave unstintingly of his time in arranging interviews and research material for me during this trip. And Ivor Sanders, the public affairs officer at Anglo-American, helped organize my trip to the various mines in South Africa and elsewhere.

The interview cited in the chapter with Harry Oppenheimer took place on 4 December 1978 in his office. It lasted for about an hour. Oppenheimer seemed to be remarkably candid and forthcoming. I was greatly impressed by the ease with which Oppenheimer could discuss the geopolitics of diamonds.

Chapter Two

One journalistic advantage I had in flying to the diamond mines on De Beers' airplanes was that I had the opportunity to meet en route a number of consulting engineers. Kenneth J. Trueman was, for example, seated next to me on the flight to Botswana, and his insights into the diamond mine there proved very helpful. In all, I flew on about a dozen of these mining flights.

I was shown around the Orapa mine by Jim Gibson, the chief geologist at the mine. As Mr Gibson had also discovered the mine and had helped develop diamond mining in Botswana, he was understandably enthusiastic about the subject.

Chapter Three

The section on the Lesotho mine is based entirely on interviews that I had on 6 December 1978, during my tour of the mine. I was especially impressed by Keith Whitelock, the general manager of the mine. He seemed to have genuine feelings for the country of Lesotho and the people, and mining seemed to be a means to an end, as opposed to an end in itself. I was also fortunate in meeting Rodney MacLean from the Diamond Trading Company in Lesotho. I later had drinks with MacLean in the Carpentells Hotel in Johannesburg and he explained a good deal to me about the sorting and evaluation of large diamonds.

Chapter Four

Because Namibia was in the throes of a political crisis, I arranged to have briefings with the South African General Staff on the guerrilla war with SWAPO in Namibia, and with a number of prominent businessmen in Windhoek, the capital of Namibia. Olga Levenson, who lives in Namibia and has written several books on politics there, was especially helpful in explaining the situation.

The internal reports by Anglo-American were also valuable in understanding the mining operation.

Chapter Five

In Kimberley I saw the entire history of the diamond cartel laid out before my eyes. There was the original open pit 'Big Hole' filled with water. On one side of it was the Mining Museum where De Beers had put together much of the original equipment and buildings used in the mining rush of the nineteenth century. Then there was the De Beers headquarters, which had originally been the headquarters of Barney Barnato, and the De Beers Club, where many of the big deals had been struck. 'De Beers is Kimberley – Kimberley is De Beers,' George Loew, the public relations man for De Beers in Kimberley, commented, as he showed me through the streets of Kimberley.

Chapter Six

De Beers generally controls the diamond trade through indirect levers. The most notable exception where a De Beers subsidiary, the Diamond Trading Company, directly exerts pressure on diamond wholesalers and manufacturers is at the London sights. I was in London for two of these occasions – in December 1978 and September 1980. Most of the information for this chapter comes from dealers and manufacturers who are regular customers of De Beers. For obvious reasons they requested anonymity, and since they risked losing a considerable portion of their business by talking to me, I decided against mentioning these dealers by name.

While the Diamond Trading Company was extremely cooperative in showing me through their headquarters in London and explaining the sorting and distribution procedures, I did not have an opportunity to interview a number of key executives there, including Monty Charles. The policy of De Beers, and the Diamond Trading Company, is to allow journalists access to their public relations department but not to the actual executives outside of that department. The description of Monty Charles comes from interviews with diamond dealers who attended sights regularly and knew him well for a long time. A number of major diamond brokers proved extremely helpful to me in articulating the rules of the game. I am especially indebted to Ben Bonas, Richard Hambro, I. Hennig, and Vivian Prins of I. Hennig. I also had interviews with a number of other dealers mentioned by name, including Ronald Winston of Harry Winston Inc., Albert Jolis of

Diamond Distributors Inc., Harris Baumgold of Baumgold Brothers and Saul Hershel of Star Diamonds.

Chapter Seven

The section on Cecil Rhodes is drawn from a number of biographies, including J. G. Macdonald, *Rhodes: A Life*, published by Chatto and Windus, London (1941); André Maurois, *Cecil Rhodes*, Collins, London (1953); Basil Williams, *Cecil Rhodes*, Constable, London (1921). An excellent economic overview of the period of Cecil Rhodes is provided by C. W. De Kiewiet in his *A History of South Africa: Social and Economic*, published by Oxford University Press, London (1941). Much of the detail of Rhodes' competition with the other diamond magnates in South Africa during this period is taken from Brian Roberts, *The Diamond Magnates*, Charles Scribners, New York (1972). The quote from Rhodes on page 61 comes from the book, *Old Kimberley*, by Anthony Hecking, published by the Kimberley Museum in South Africa.

The section on Barney Barnato is drawn from Thurley Jackson, *The Great Barnato*, published by Heinemann, London (1970), and Brian Roberts, *The Diamond Magnates*.

Chapter Eight

The primary source on the life of Sir Ernest Oppenheimer is the book by Theodore Gregory, *Ernest Oppenheimer and the Economic Development of Southern Africa*, Oxford University Press, Capetown (1962). This biography was commissioned by the Anglo-American Corporation, and the author had access to the letters of Sir Ernest and the records of De Beers and the Anglo-American Corporation. The letters quoted from Sir Ernest Oppenheimer in this chapter are taken from this book. Other sources include Anthony Hocking, *Oppenheimer and Son*, McGraw-Hill, New York (1973); Edward Jessup, *Ernest Oppenheimer: A Study in Power*, Rex Collings, London (1979); and Godeherd Lenzen, *The History of Diamond Production and the Diamond Trade*, London (1970).

The section about the Jews in the diamond trade comes from the *Jewish Encyclopedia*. The section about Oppenheimer's plan to jettison several tons of diamonds into the North Sea comes from documents I obtained under the Freedom of Information Act, which pertained to the United States government's antitrust suit against De Beers. The historical research was supplemented with interviews with a number of officials at De Beers, including Harry Oppenheimer, and also with interviews in the magazine *Indiaqua* with De Beers executives, pertaining to their memories of Sir Ernest Oppenheimer.

Chapter Nine

The question of how nations at war acquire the strategic materials they need from their enemies remains an especially difficult one to research. Throughout the Second World War, Germany was entirely dependent for its supply of industrial diamonds on its British enemy. There were no synthetic diamonds in those days, and the only source for many important types of diamonds were the mines and fields in the British Empire under the control of the diamond cartel. Despite embargoes and intensive policing by intelligence services, Hitler managed to acquire his diamonds.

The source of research for this chapter is a document I acquired under a Freedom of Information request. I had initially learned of the United States government's interest in the strategic smuggling of diamonds through a former attorney general named Bruno Schacter. When he had originally joined the Justice Department in 1939, he had been assigned to one of the least interesting tasks it had to offer: investigating private competition to the United States postal service. If such a case was brought against any offender, the maximum fine was $50. For months he labored in the legal doldrums, searching for an escape. Then, early in 1940, the Coast Guard arrested a German soldier whom they suspected of being a spy. The only grounds that could be found for detaining him was that he was carrying a letter, and this could be construed as violating the prohibition against competing with the Post Office.

Since Schacter was now the expert in the Justice Department on these arcane laws, he was brought into the case. He found that the letter the German sailor was carrying was encoded. Calling in a team of code-breakers from the Treasury Department, Schacter set about deciphering it. The message concerned a shipment of gem diamonds consigned to a firm in New York called the Pioneer Import Company. The diamonds, moreover, came from European areas that had been recently overrun in the Nazi blitzkrieg.

Schacter, himself a refugee from the Nazi pogroms in Austria, suspected that these diamonds had been seized from interned Jewish diamond cutters. For this reason he took 'a very personal interest in the case.' He began his investigation by visiting the various diamond-cutting factories in New York and learning the style, or 'signature,' of the different diamond cutters. It turned out that the diamonds that Pioneer was importing had the 'signature' of Dutch and Belgian cutters who had been shipped off to concentration camps by the Nazis. Schacter then began tracing the provenance of these diamonds through import licenses and records of money transfer. By 1941, he had established that they had all come from Germany. As a result of this investigation, the owner of Pioneer Importing, a man called Von Clemm, was prosecuted for trafficking in stolen diamonds and sent to prison.

Schacter had further learned during his interrogation of Von Clemm that the Nazis were involved in a triangular diamond trade whereby the records of the diamonds sold in New York were used to buy industrial diamonds in Brazil, which, in turn, were shipped to Germany through Switzerland. The category of industrial diamonds that the Germans seemed most interested in was bort (which is a form of powdered diamond dust used for diamond-grinding wheels). Even as early as 1941, Germany had a critical shortage of this bort.

Since Schacter recalled being consulted during this period about the status of the De Beers stockpile in London by the FBI and Justice Department officials, he suggested that somewhere in the Justice Department archives there existed a file on the diamond investigation.

I called an assistant attorney general at the Justice Department who told me, off the record, that most of the government's files on the diamond monopoly were in the antitrust dossier on De Beers, and suggested that I file a request under the Freedom of Information Act for the entire antitrust action against the diamond monopoly.

The Freedom of Information Act had been passed in 1967 during the Lyndon Johnson administration. President Johnson had at the time wanted to restrict, rather than expand, the flow of secret information to journalists, and the act in its original form was designed to channel information to appropriate officers at government agencies who could then deny requests on grounds of national security or violation of privacy. To ward off liberal and press criticism of the measure, Johnson decided to call it by the benign title of 'Freedom of Information.' During the 1970s, however, the courts decided that since Congress had called it by that name, the intent of the act was to make information freely available. Through these judicial interpretations, the act was gradually expanded to force the government to release files which it could not demonstrate a need to hold secret.

As it turned out, the antitrust division was far more cooperative than the CIA or FBI had ever been in facilitating requests I had made for other projects. Within a matter of weeks, batches of formerly classified files began arriving. They soon totaled more than 2000 pages of legal memoranda, FBI reports, embassy cablegrams, intelligence briefings, economic analyses, financial records, interviews with individuals in the diamond industry, and mail intercepts of correspondence between members of the diamond cartel, including Otto Oppenheimer (which were apparently read by military censors in Bermuda). The archive contained numerous gaps and unanswered questions, but gradually the main lines of the investigation emerged. Between 1940 and 1945 the United States government, with all the war powers at its disposal, had made every effort to gain control of the industrial diamonds it required for the war effort – but it failed.

The file obtained under the Freedom of Information Act contained only a few references to any actual investigation of the smuggling of diamonds by the cartel to the Nazis. There was, however, one reference to an OSS investigation. This led to the summer report, cited in the chapter, which strongly implied that De Beers was impeding Allied intelligence investigations. (The report can be found in *OSS: A Secret War*, edited by Anthony Cave Brown.) To find the field reports I went to the National Archives and consulted the military historian, John E. Taylor. Taylor, a quiet man with gray hair, has devoted a considerable part of his thirty-five-year career at the Archives to bringing some order to the military records deposited and, at times, literally dumped there by the various agencies of the government. In the case of the OSS, there were some 900,000 reference cards, divided by country and subject, cataloguing the tons of documents received from the CIA. Since much of this material was still classified, it was kept in a warren of locked rooms on the fifteenth floor of the stacks.

After Taylor had turned the dials of a combination lock on a door that had no handles, it creaked open, and I followed him to a row of green drawers that lined the walls of the room. In a moment, he found the index cards that referred to OSS operations in the Belgian Congo during 1943–4. One by one, I went through the orange cards he handed me, looking for some reference to Teton's field reports. There was, however, no trace of it in the index. Taylor, meanwhile, checked through another OSS index without any success. He finally concluded, months later, that the 'field reports' on diamond smuggling, if they had not been destroyed by the CIA, were in some kind of archival limbo.

Without access to these field reports, it was not possible to assess the quality of evidence on which the OSS predicated its suspicions about diamond smuggling, even though US Intelligence had traced most of these diamonds to mines in the Belgian Congo that were controlled by the De Beers syndicate. The question, however, of who, if anyone, in the mining operation cooperated with the smugglers in this massive transfer of diamonds has not been resolved – at least as far as the available records indicate.

In an attempt to find the agent Teton, I placed advertisements in the journal of the retired officers of the OSS and the *New York Times Book Review*, but I had no success.

The letters on the Belgian Congo cited in this chapter come from Sir Theodore Gregory's book on Oppenheimer, previously cited.

Chapter Ten

The description of the cartel's attempt to suppress the production of South American diamonds, cited in this chapter, comes from the fascinating autobiography of Sir Patrick Hastings, *Cases in Court*, Pan Books, London (1949), especially Part 3, 'A Case for the Diamond Syndicate.' Sir Patrick, one of the most distinguished of England's barristers, had the unusual opportunity to cross-examine Otto Oppenheimer and to take testimony in pre-trial motions.

The section on John Thornburn Williamson is drawn from a two-part series in *Indiaqua* magazine (9: 19–21 and 10: 15–17) which provides a biography. The material on the British Colonial Office comes from the Public Record, the *New York Times* and documents obtained under the Freedom of Information Act. Financial details are given in Edward Jessup's *Ernest Oppenheimer: A Study in Power*, previously cited. Ronald Winston, whose father Harry Winston dealt with Williamson, also provided in a series of interviews personal recollections of Williamson. At one point Harry Winston had contemplated taking over Williamson's mine, and negotiated with him, but decided against it as, according to Ronald Winston, he did not want to jeopardize his relations with De Beers.

The section on Harry Winston is taken from interviews with Ronald Winston, now president of Harry Winston Inc., and Nick Axelrod, the chief diamond buyer for Harry Winston Inc. A fascinating portrait of Harry Winston is also provided by Lillian Ross in her two-part piece in the *New Yorker*, 15 May 1954.

Chapter Eleven

The International Diamond Annual, a review of the world's diamond industry and trade, published by De Beers in two volumes in 1971 and 1972, furnishes a comprehensive picture of a diamond pipeline from the diamond mines to the cutting center to the retail business. They were published by De Beers as a service to the diamond industry. The quotation about keeping track of the market in this chapter comes from volume two of these books. Other trade publications, including *Indiaqua*, *Jewelers' Circular Keystone* and *Diamant*, illuminate different facets of the diamond trade and the diamond chain.

I was shown around Antwerp by Ivor Sanders, who flew over from London to take me to various diamond cutters. Most of the diamond dealers I visited, therefore, had a close relationship with De Beers. Raoul Delveaux, the director general of the Diamond High Council in Antwerp, was also helpful in arranging interviews in Antwerp. The history provided in this chapter is drawn in part from the 1978 Year Book of the Diamond High Council.

I interviewed Baron Barsamian in his office in Antwerp in January 1979.

In Israel, I was assisted in making contact with diamond dealers by James J. Angleton, the former CIA counterintelligence chief, who had served as a liaison between American and Israeli intelligence between 1960 and 1975. I met Angleton in the course of researching my book, *Legend: the Secret World of Lee Harvey Oswald* (Hutchinson, London, 1978), and when I told him that I was investigating the diamond cartel he offered to put me in touch with his contacts there. When I arrived in Israel in December 1978, I found that those in the diamond business were willing to discuss freely their relations with the De Beers cartel. In fact, almost every businessman seemed to be in the diamond business or have a close friend in it. During a week in Tel Aviv, I was able to see independent diamond dealers, diamond dealers with a sight at De Beers in London, former diamond smugglers, diamond bankers and even diamond speculators. They all shared a common view of De Beers – they held that De Beers was artificially restricting the flow of diamonds, both by stockpiling diamonds in their vault in London and by manipulating the open market so as to drive up the price. Most of these dealers and individuals in the diamond business also believed that the De Beers cartel was anti-Israel, in attempting to undercut Israel's preeminent position in the business of cutting small diamonds.

Chapter Twelve

Harry Oppenheimer has lived a very private life. An informative and anecdotal biography of him, written by Anthony Hocking, *Oppenheimer and Son,* McGraw-Hill, New York (1973), gives an especially good account of Oppenheimer's political career before his father's death in 1957. The letters cited in this chapter come from Sir Theodore Gregory's biography of Sir Ernest Oppenheimer. These biographies as well as newspaper accounts provide a basic outline of Oppenheimer's life. Oppenheimer filled in some of the gaps and motivations in an interview he gave me on 4 December 1978, in his office in Johannesburg. Before I was ushered into his office that morning, I had viewed a videotape of a special hour-long documentary about him that had been prepared by South African television to commemorate his seventieth birthday. Throughout this televised interview, Oppenheimer was treated with the sort of sober respect reserved for the most exalted royalty. In hushed tones he was asked about the economy, the nation and the state of the world. He answered with the supreme confidence of someone who is totally in control. This program was then followed on videotape by a second program, called 'A Family Affair,' that showed various aspects of Harry Oppenheimer's personal life. There were scenes of his arriving in Johannesburg in his own blue and white Gulf Stream jet, followed by his aide-de-camp and security police. Other scenes showed him at his palatial home, surrounded by his Goya paintings and greyhound dogs. There were also scenes of Oppenheimer at his stud farm outside Kimberley with his championship racehorses. On the program, he displayed an icy calm. He seemed to be a man who enjoyed the perquisites of power.

When I met Oppenheimer later that morning, I found that he was quite different from his television image. He was relaxed, though shy, and quite informal in the way he answered questions. He seemed genuinely proud of the empire he had built and frankly enjoyed discussing it. Even though he was undoubtedly the richest man in South Africa, and one of its most influential citizens, he showed little hesitation in expressing opinions or criticizing the government.

Aside from my interviews with Oppenheimer, I also gained some insight into how he operated from his executives, whom he treated as members of 'one big family,' as one of them put it. For example, Richard Wake-Walker, a young executive with the Diamond Trading Company in London, told me how he had been invited to Oppenheimer's game farm during weekends in South Africa. He recalled that Harry Oppenheimer would sit in his shirtsleeves on the terrace surrounded by various members of his family, executives of Anglo-American and De Beers and a few friends. Everyone would drink beer. When an elephant or a rhinoceros trudged up to the barrier in front of the terrace, a servant would throw a floodlight on it, and everyone would admire the wildlife.

In addition, I took some of the philosophy of Harry Oppenheimer and his business strategy from written questions he kindly answered for me, and from published statements, taken from annual reports, on the policy of Anglo-American that he made at stockholder and shareholder meetings of the Anglo-American and De Beers corporation.

I am indebted to Kees Schager of the investment firm of Arnhold and Bleichroeder for his assistance in unraveling the corporate labyrinth of the Anglo-American and De Beers complex. The annual reports of De Beers, Anglo-American and Charter companies provide some rough outline of the corporate relations in the Oppenheimer empire. The antitrust documents obtained by me under the Freedom of Information Act provided further clues to the interrelations. I also received some help from the Anglo-American corporation itself and its cooperative public relations office, including Ivor Sanders and Richard Dickson. There have also been numerous attempts in business magazines, including *Fortune*, *Forbes*, *Business Week* and the *Economist*, to diagram the holdings in this empire. I found, however, that almost all this information had been derived from the annual reports and press releases of the Anglo-American company itself.

Chapter Thirteen

I was fortunate in my Freedom of Information request to receive almost the entire files of the N. W. Ayer Company, which had designed the advertising campaign for De Beers. It seems that the prosecutors in the antitrust division were attempting to show that De Beers had an agent in the United States and that it was the N. W. Ayer Company. They therefore subpoenaed all its files and records. As it turned out, however, there was no real information in these files indicating that N. W. Ayer was a business agent for De Beers. The archives did contain an immense amount of material reviewing the strategy research and ambitions of De Beers.

A second source for this chapter was the N. W. Ayer Company itself. It provided me and my researcher with the volumes of campaign books. These included not only the advertisements used by N. W. Ayer in its campaign, but also the strategy it presented to De Beers. I also interviewed a number of executives at the advertising agency who preferred not to use their names.

Finally, I used the advertisements in trade magazines to check through the year-to-year advertising strategy of De Beers. The *Jewelers' Circular Keystone* was especially useful in this respect.

Chapter Fourteen

Ian Fleming, who invented James Bond, also wrote probably the best book on diamond smuggling – *The Diamond Smugglers*, Cape,

London (1957). He had extensive interviews with Percy Sillitoe's staff, who set up De Beers' intelligence system, and considerable access to De Beers itself. It is his only nonfiction book. Fred Kamil, the Lebanese mercenary who hijacked a South African aircraft in order to extort money from Harry Oppenheimer, has also written a book about smuggling called *The Diamond Underworld*, Allen Lane, London (1979), which is of great interest since Kamil was one of De Beers' diamond soldiers.

The section in this chapter on Percy Sillitoe and the organization of De Beers' intelligence is drawn mainly from Fleming's account. The section on Kamil is drawn mainly from his autobiographical book.

The section on Sierra Leone is based on interviews I conducted with a number of diamond dealers, including Maurice Tempelsman, Lazare Kaplan and Ronald Winston, who were involved in the importing of diamonds in Sierra Leone. I am also indebted to Michael Samuels, the former American ambassador to Sierra Leone, for briefing me on the political situation there.

The section on Zaire is based on personal interviews with a former CIA officer stationed in Zaire who prefers his name not be used. Other sources include New York diamond dealers who do business in Zaire. The account of the massacre of young Zaireans appeared in the *New York Times*, 13 November 1979. The section on Angola is based on interviews with Albert Jolis, a New York diamond dealer.

Chapter Fifteen

The story about Sir Ernest Oppenheimer rejecting the proposal to develop synthetic diamonds was told by Richard Hambro, an investment banker who worked in the industrial division of De Beers in South Africa. Eric Bruton, the former editor of the English magazine, *The Gemologist*, and *The Industrial Diamond Review* (which is owned by De Beers), has written a highly reliable and comprehensive book about diamonds in which he had the full cooperation of De Beers. His chapter on synthetic diamonds contains an excellent history of the early experiments in synthesis and notorious frauds. Emily Hahn has also investigated the Hannay diamond in the 21 May 1956 issue of the *New Yorker*. *The International Diamond Annual* (published by a De Beers subsidiary) provides an account of De Beers' entry into the synthetic diamond business.

The section on General Electric is partly based on documents I obtained under the Freedom of Information Act. In its 1973 lawsuit, the Department of Justice looked into the possibility that De

Beers had conspired with General Electric to fix the price of synthetic diamonds. The prosecutors found no substantive evidence of such collaboration, but the documents they turned up in their search provide a useful overview of the economic and political considerations involved in General Electric's development of synthetic diamonds. The section on the meeting between Harry Oppenheimer and William Courdier of General Electric comes from these documents, as does the section on Dr Bernard Senior.

Chapter Sixteen

The section on the origins of the Israeli diamond industry come from interviews I had with Ovi Ben Ami while I was in Israel in 1978. Vivian Prins, whose father had been the broker for Ben Ami in the Israeli diamond deals, gave a similar, though not coincidental, version of the story to me when I interviewed him in London in 1979.

The section on Goldfinger is based on my interview with Israeli dealers who had known his work, before his death. Vivian Prins, whose firm had brokered diamonds for Goldfinger, provided considerable details about the dealings between Goldfinger and De Beers.

Chapter Seventeen

The one subject that Harry Oppenheimer and other executives of De Beers seemed reluctant to discuss was the arrangement with the Soviet Union. When I was in Kimberley I was seated at lunch at the Kimberley Club next to Barry Hawthorne, a geologist who works for De Beers. He had recently returned from the Soviet Union, and casually mentioned the enigma of Soviet diamond production. However, when I addressed the question he raised about the Soviet production to executives of De Beers, they skirted the central issue of how the Soviet Union was producing such vast quantities of diamonds from a relatively small Arctic mine.

The section on the history of Soviet production is drawn from accounts in *The Industrial Diamond Annual* (1971, 1972). Another excellent source on Soviet production is the De Beers-sponsored magazine *Indiaqua* (especially no. 5, pp. 14–16; no. 6, p. 15; no. 11, p. 18; no. 14, p. 10; no. 15, pp. 8–11 and no. 16, p. 20).

In addition, John Massey Stewart wrote an extensive review of Siberian diamond mining in the magazine *Optima*, which is published by the Anglo-American Corporation and sent to stockholders (no. 2, 1976, p. 85). The section on Aikhal comes from the account in *The International Diamond Annual*, 1971 (pp. 79–90) entitled 'Red Diamonds from Siberia.' The quote from Victor Tikhonov also comes from the 1971 report in *The International Diamond Annual*. The data on the Finsch mine was provided for me by Dr L. G. Murray, another De Beers geologist in South Africa. The description of the diamond sorting was given to me by a former diamond sorter for the Diamond Trading Company in London who prefers to remain anonymous. The section describing Sir Philip's trip to the Siberian mines comes from Barry Hawthorne in 1978. Dr Henry Meyer provided the account of the Soviet synthetic diamonds in an interview I had with him in New York in 1980. Joseph Bonroy gave his account of Soviet synthetic diamonds in the Belgian trade magazine *Diamant* (November 1971).

The section on the silver bears is based on interviews I had with dealers in Antwerp and the report in *The International Diamond Annual*, 1971. The account of Goldfinger buying up the Soviet silver bears comes from interviews I had with his brokers, I. Hennig.

Chapter Eighteen

This chapter is drawn almost entirely from the documents I obtained under the Freedom of Information Act and interviews with prosecutors involved in the case. Biographical details about the life of Charles Engelhard are drawn from *Everybody's Business*, an almanac edited by Milton Moskowitz, Michael Katz and Robert Levering, Harper and Row (1980), p. 554. The biographical details on E. T. S. Brown are derived from an interview with him in *Indiaqua* (1980), pp. 55–60.

Chapter Nineteen

The section on Sam Collins is based on interviews I had with François Lamparetti, a geologist who worked briefly for the Marine Diamond Corporation. Background information concerning the attempt to smuggle diamonds from the forbidden zone comes from Ian Fleming's *The Diamond Smugglers* and *Indiaqua* magazine (nos. 12 and 13). The account of Collins' organization of his marine diamond venture appears in *Indiaqua* (no. 6 in *The International Diamond Annual*, 1972). Fred Kamil provides in his biography, *The Diamond Underground*, the description of an encounter he had with Collins.

The section on Albert Jolis is drawn mainly from a long series of interviews I had with him in New York. Jolis proved to be extremely friendly, intelligent, and enlightening about the diamond business. He appeared before the grand jury investigating the diamond cartel in 1975, and the reference to his dealings in the Central African Empire and Yubangi come from documents I obtained under the Freedom of Information Act. I also discussed the story about the Angolan concession with Chipanda, the former Minister of Natural Resources for Angola, who confirmed Jolis's story. I met Chipanda and Sevimbe at a lunch at Freedom House in New York in 1980.

The section on Harry Winston is based mainly on interviews with his son Ronald Winston and Nick Axelrod, the chief diamond buyer for Harry Winston Inc. The biographical background comes in part from Lillian Ross' profile of Harry Winston in the *New Yorker* (1954). The meeting with Dr Williamson was described to me by Ronald Winston.

The best analysis of De Beers' strategy to take over other aspects of the diamond business can be found in David Federman's 'Checkmate – De Beers' Move to Protect the Cartel,' *Jewelers' Circular Keystone*, 1979. The article was coauthored by Mitchel Gilbert, the executive editor of the *Jewelers' Circular Keystone*. Diamond dealers I spoke to in Antwerp, Tel Aviv and New York confirmed the basic thesis of this article. Richard Dickson from the Diamond Trading Company in London took me to see the De Beers facilities in Brussels.

Chapter Twenty

The section on Stanley Mark Rifkin is based on interviews with executives of the Security Pacific National Bank in Los Angeles in 1980 and reports in the *New York Times* and *Los Angeles Times* in December and January 1977–8.

The investigations of the Dutch Consumer Association and the London magazine, *Money Which?* were reported in the gemstone section of the *Jewelers' Circular Keystone* magazine in January 1977. The magazine's editor, David Watt, supplied details.

The attempt to trade diamonds as a commodity proved a dismal failure and was later studied by the New York Commodity Exchange. Susan Rosenberg, who was commissioned by the exchange to study diamond trading in the summer of 1980, provided me with the data and documents involved in the earlier failure. William Goldberg, the president of the New York Diamond Club, was kind enough to allow me to witness a diamond transaction in his office in April 1979. The woman who told me the story of attempting to sell her diamond ring prefers to remain anonymous.

In examining the price of diamonds I relied on the table provided by the *Jewelers' Circular Keystone*, and on data published by the *Economist* intelligence unit in 1978, 1979 and 1980.

The section on Empire Diamonds comes from my observations in 1980 at Empire Diamonds with Jack Braud, its president, and some of his diamond buyers. Diana Rossant, then an assistant district attorney in New York City, was helpful in providing me with information about fencing diamonds.

The section on Elizabeth Taylor's diamond is based in part on the article by Kenneth Schwartz and F. Peter Model, 'Diamonds Are a Girl's Best Friend,' which appeared in the *Washingtonian* magazine, January 1980. Ronald Winston of Harry Winston, Inc., also gave me his perspective on the Taylor diamond.

The section on the Bokassa diamond comes entirely from interviews I had with Albert Jolis in New York in 1979.

Chapter Twenty-one

There were literally hundreds of cases of individuals reporting that they had been swindled by being sold diamonds over the telephone. Diana Rossant of the New York district attorney's office was again helpful in bringing some of these cases to my attention, also numerous reports in trade magazines and business magazines about these swindles. For example, John Train's 'The Diamond Hustle,' *Forbes*, 18 September 1978, p. 194; 'Investing in Gems,' *Business Week,* 2 October 1978, pp. 128–30; Al Jaffe's 'Synthetic Sparkle Fakes,' *New York Post*, 8 June 1978; 'Diamonds seem speculator's best friend despite strong warnings by major firms,' *Wall Street Journal,* 27 March 1979; 'Would Donald Nixon apparently link three dots to a diamond ford,' by Charles Kaiser, *New York Times*, 19 December 1978; Jay Maidenberg, 'Swindlers invade the diamond markets,' *New York Times*, 11 February 1979; 'Now the Diamond Bugs,' *Forbes*, 15 April 1977. On the subject of investment diamonds, David Birnbaum, a New York diamond dealer who writes on investment diamonds for the magazine *Diamant*, was especially helpful in providing me with a picture of the investment diamond business in 1980. Diana Motmans, perhaps the leading diamond journalist in Antwerp, provided information on the international diamond investment business.

Chapter Twenty-two

The quote from N. W. Ayer comes from the material provided to me under the Freedom of Information Act and referred to in ch. 13. The quote from Harry Oppenheimer is taken from a statement Oppenheimer made to Anglo-American shareholders.

The section on the Israeli overhang is drawn from David Meadows' report in the *Jewelers' Circular Keystone*, 'Checkmate' (see September 1979) and from interviews with Israeli diamond dealers and bankers. The quote about retailers comes from the above-cited article.

Chapter Twenty-three

The data on the Israeli banks comes from reports in the *New York Times* on 4 September and 16 September 1981. The Australian projections were reported in a highly informative story, 'Diamonds in the Rough,' by Daniel D. Nossiter, in *Barron's*, September 1981. I am indebted to Xan Smiley, the editor of *Africa Confidential*, for his insights on Zaire.

Index

THE LEAN YEARS

BY RICHARD BARNET

THE LEAN YEARS is the first book to take an overall look at the world's resources – how much we have got, where they are, and who controls them. Richard Barnet, the distinguished economic and political analyst, unravels the scarcity puzzle, exploring the politics of the 'petroleum economy', revealing the role of the giant oil companies and evaluating the energy alternatives to OPEC oil. He examines the changing face of global power and the struggle for food, water and mineral resources which we can expect in the coming lean years, and reports on the role of the multinational corporations in the world employment crisis. In addition, he discusses the politics of a world in transition, the consequences of the growing industrialisation of labour worldwide, and the absurdities of scarcity in a world of plenty. And, finally, he offers positive proposals for reorganising global resource systems to meet the needs of Earth's burgeoning population.

CONSERVATION/ECONOMICS 0 349 10238 4 £2.50

A selection of bestsellers from **SPHERE**

FICTION

A PERFECT STRANGER	Danielle Steel	£1.75	☐
MISSING PERSONS	C. Terry Cline Jr	£1.95	☐
A GREEN DESIRE	Anton Myrer	£2.50	☐
FLOODTIDE	Suzanne Goodwin	£1.95	☐
JADE TIGER	Craig Thomas	£2.25	☐

FILM & TV TIE-INS

STAR WARS	George Lucas	£1.75	☐
THE YEAR OF LIVING DANGEROUSLY	C. J. Koch	£1.75	☐
FAME	Leonore Fleischer	£1.75	☐
WIDOWS	Lynda La Plante	£1.50	☐
UPSTAIRS, DOWNSTAIRS	John Hawkesworth	£1.50	☐

NON-FICTION

A QUESTION OF BALANCE	H.R.H. The Duke of Edinburgh	£1.50	☐
SUSAN'S STORY	Susan Hampshire	£1.75	☐
THE INCREDIBLE TESTS	Ian Botham	£1.50	☐
SECOND LIFE	Stephani Cook	£1.95	☐
SIOP	P. Pringle & W. Arkin	£2.95	☐

All Sphere books are available at your local bookshop or newsagent, or can be ordered direct from the publisher. Just tick the titles you want and fill in the form below.

Name ____________________

Address ____________________

____

Write to Sphere Books, Cash Sales Department, P.O. Box 11, Falmouth, Cornwall TR10 9EN

Please enclose cheque or postal order to the value of the cover price plus:

UK: 45p for the first book, 20p for the second and 14p per copy for each additional book ordered to a maximum charge of £1.63.

OVERSEAS: 75p for the first book and 21p for each additional book.

BFPO & EIRE: 45p for the first book, 20p for the second book plus 14p per copy for the next 7 books, thereafter 8p per book.

Sphere Books reserve the right to show new retail prices on covers which may differ from those previously advertised in the text or elsewhere, and to increase postal rates in accordance with the PO.